THE ART OF SOUTHWEST LANDSCAPING

A Desert Gardener's Guide to Landscape Plant Selections

Dawn Fried

Landscape Designer, Photographer and Arizona Horticulturist

PAGE PUBLISHING, INC.
New York, NY

First originally published by Page Publishing, Inc. 2018

ISBN 978-1-64027-421-1 (Paperback)
ISBN 978-1-64027-422-8 (Digital)

Printed in the United States of America

Contents

Introduction

A garden is friend you can visit anytime.
—Cora Lee Bell

**Early summer color with Crape Myrtle,
Red Bird of Paradise and Yellow Lantana**

I am very passionate about creating beautiful outdoor living spaces using a variety of color and greenery. I have spent years designing and installing award-winning landscapes for my company Horticulture Unlimited in Tucson, Arizona. Each of the plant species listed in this book has been used many times in my practice to create beautiful Southwest gardens. I hope that my second book in this series will provide you with some creative and inspiring planting ideas and interesting plant materials to utilize in your landscape. It is so much fun helping people in Southern Arizona beautify their homes and gardens and expressing creativity and style through landscape design. From the bougainvillea to the variety of agave species, the plant options are as broad and beautiful as your imagination!

This book is dedicated to the wide variety of trees, palms, shrubs, groundcovers, vines, desert accents, cacti, and succulents to grow and enjoy in your Southwest gardens. I have included a broad selection of plant material that I have used for the past thirty-five years in my practice. Some of these plant choices may be toxic or invasive in some situations or may not be as popular as others but nevertheless should be considered for use in the right conditions.

All of these plant choices are wonderful selections for the Southwest. I hope you enjoy the amazing variety of plant material suggested for all the different areas of your landscape along with photographs to give you an idea of the wonderful characteristics of varying textures, colors, fragrances and uses of landscape plants for the Southwest.

Enjoy!

Each of the landscape plants in this section are listed alphabetically beginning with the genus and species followed by the common name. Some plants have more than one scientific name and names change frequently. I have tried to use the most accurate and recent scientific names in this book. All of these plant materials are native to warm climates and will work well in our Southwestern deserts. *My favorite picks are listed with an asterisk.*

1 Trees
for Southwest Landscapes

All trees are categorized by small, medium and large-sized plant material. Small trees will grow ten to twenty feet tall. They can be used in small spaces or patios. Medium trees will grow fifteen to twenty-five feet tall. Large trees will grow over thirty feet and reach up to fifty or sixty feet tall or more.

*Acacia aneura
Mulga
Medium-sized tree

Mulga is a striking evergreen that grows to a moderate fifteen to twenty feet with a ten- to twelve-foot spread. It is an upright, broad-leaved tree with dense, needlelike, silvery gray foliage that gives it an interesting visual, pyramidal appearance. The dark red branches become a darker grayish brown at maturity. This slow to moderately growing plant can develop a single or multiple trunk. It produces golden yellow, puffy blooms that appear heaviest in the spring or summer but continue blooming three or four more times during the year. After flowering, flat, brownish tan, oblong pods appear and then drop from the tree. It is hardy to fifteen to twenty degrees Fahrenheit. The mulga prefers full sun and reflected heat. It is drought resistant but likes regular water to increase its growth rate. The tree tolerates any soil as long as it is well draining. It is mostly disease free, but sometimes, it develops an iron deficiency and should be treated with an iron chelate fertilizer in the spring. Use it as a freestanding, street tree or in medians. The mulga also makes a great screen or windbreak specimen or a background tree that is a good choice around pools or water features since it does not produce messy leaves. The tree is native to Western Australia, South Australia, New South Wales, and Queensland, where it grows in clay soils. The Aboriginal word for mulga is "dream seed."

Acacia aneura
Mulga

*Acacia cultriformis
Knifeleaf Acacia
Small- to medium-sized tree

This drought-resistant, multitrunk evergreen grows twelve to fifteen feet tall and wide. It has an open growth habit with interesting twisted or drooping branches that support small, grayish green, leathery, triangular leaves. In spring, the tree produces fragrant, creamy yellow blossoms that form into dense clusters. The blossoms are edible, and a yellow dye can be extracted from them. After flowering, it produces linear seedpods that are covered in fine, fuzzy hairs. Knifeleaf acacia is hardy to about twenty-five degrees Fahrenheit and likes full sun to light shade and well-draining soil. Its flowers and branches look nice mixed into flower arrangements. This is an interesting plant because of its unique leaf shape

Acacia cultriformis
Knifeleaf Acacia

Acacia cultriformis
Knifeleaf Acacia

*Acacia pendula

Weeping Myall
Medium- to large-sized tree

The graceful medium-sized evergreen grows twenty feet tall and fifteen feet wide with pendulous, weeping branches and multiple trunks. It has striking shiny, silvery, grayish blue foliage that is long and thin, along with inconspicuous, pale yellow, ball-like flowers that appear in spring and winter. In Australia, Aboriginal hunters used its dark, grainy wood to make boomerangs. The heartwood of the tree produces a deep chocolate to dark toffee color that has been used by craftsmen to make furniture. The oil

and color. It can be used as a small specimen or accent tree planted with other drought-tolerant vegetation, a large hedge, screen or installed to protect hillsides. It is fast growing, low maintenance and should be used more frequently in our Southwest landscapes. This tree is native to Queensland and New South Wales where it grows on rocky ridges. It is widely cultivated and has naturalized in many parts of the world.

Acacia pendula
Weeping Myall

Acacia pendula
Weeping Myall

produced after cutting into the wood of the tree has a violet fragrance. This interesting specimen tree should be utilized in the landscape more often because it tolerates a wide range of soils from acidic to alkaline, is drought tolerant, low maintenance, and does not produce litter. Additionally, it is frost tolerant to about fifteen degrees Fahrenheit and likes full sun and reflected heat. It should be irrigated deeply to encourage a good root system. This tree looks interesting in front of a tall, white wall or large structure with its shiny, blue foliage. It can also be used in groupings of two or three for an interesting look. Use it as a windbreak or in the background of ponds and water features or as a focal point at the entrance to a building or home with it willowy appearance. The tree is a native to the river floodplains and dry outback areas of central and Western Australia.

Acacia salicina

Willow Acacia
Large-sized tree

This exquisite, skyline evergreen forms single or multiple trunks with grayish green leaves and has a graceful, weeping growth habit. It reaches heights of forty feet with a ten- to twenty-foot span. Its long, willowy branches droop and flow toward the ground. When young, the tree has smooth, grayish bark that becomes darker and rougher with age. The leaves of this tree are long, narrow, and grayish green in color. It produces slightly fragrant, creamy white, puffy blooms during the year, but they are most abundant in spring. After flowering, it develops grayish green seedpods that can be straight or curved. The acacia is drought resistant but likes deep, infrequent irrigation to develop a strong root system. Plant it in full sun and well-draining soil. This fast grower

Acacia salicina
Willow Acacia

is hardy to twenty degrees Fahrenheit. It can blow over or break major limbs in summer monsoons; therefore, prune regularly to thin out the tree to protect it against strong winds. The willow acacia develops suckers and may resprout in other parts of the landscape. Use it in parks, along streets and roadways, as a large screen, shade tree or in large open areas and along tall buildings. Also, consider using around ponds, water features and in narrow spaces along walls, where its amazing silhouette graces the landscape. It produces minimum litter from leaf drop, and is easy to grow. This is another Australian evergreen native tree that is found growing in central Queensland, the western region of New South Wales, in addition to South Australia and Victoria.

Acacia stenophylla
Shoestring Acacia
Large-sized tree

The large evergreen tree has a main, upright trunk that supports spreading, weeping branches. It can reach heights of twenty to thirty feet with a spread of fifteen to twenty feet. Shoestring acacia has long, thin, needlelike leaves that look like shoestrings hanging down from its branches. The tree produces inconspicuous, creamy white blooms that appear throughout spring and fall, followed by interesting greenish tan seedpods that resemble a sting of pearls and hang downward from the tree. It produces leaf droppings and litter from time to time. The specimen is hardy to about fifteen degrees Fahrenheit and tolerates many different soil types as long as they are well draining. Since it is found naturally growing along streams

Acacia stenophylla
Shoestring Acacia

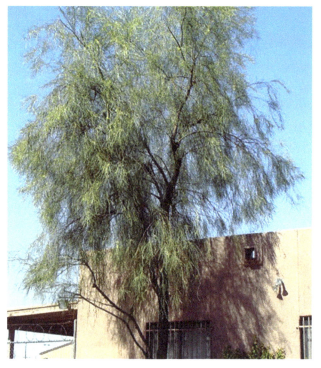

Acacia stenophylla
Shoestring Acacia

and riverbeds, it will tolerate flooding and heavy clay soils. This tree is heat tolerant, easy to grow and can be used in a wide range of landscape situations. It is a moderate- to fast-growing tree that likes full sun and reflected heat. It is drought resistant and prefers deep, infrequent irrigation. This acacia has a long lifespan if it is not overwatered. Use it in parking lots, medians or along tall buildings in smaller, narrow growing spaces, and against large walls or structures. Also use this tree as a specimen or grouped together in masses to produce a grove effect. Since it produces filtered shade with its fine shoestring like leaves, "understory" plants that require some filtered sun can be planted beneath its canopy. This is an excellent choice if you are looking for an upright, erect tree with a narrow form. It is native to arid regions of Northeastern Australia in the northern territory of Queensland, New South Wales, South Australia, and Victoria, where it is grown for lumber and has been used as a food source for the Aborigines.

Albizia julibrissin
Mimosa, Silk Tree

partial shade and can be planted in a wide range of soils as long as they are well draining. This plant is very hardy to twenty degrees Fahrenheit. It is drought resistant but prefers additional irrigation during the hot summer months. Its open growth habit makes it prone to high wind damage since it has brittle wood. At certain times of the year, it creates litter and requires maintenance. For best results, fertilize with ammonium phosphate in the spring. Use this sculptural tree for oriental and tropical effects around a pond or other water feature, up near a house, or in patios and courtyards. It is native to Asia, Australia, and Africa and has been cultivated as an ornamental plant throughout the United States and parts of Europe.

Albizia julibrissin
Mimosa, Silk Tree
Medium-sized tree

This medium- to fast-growing, deciduous tree has a multiple trunk and an open, growth habit, reaching thirty feet tall and ten to twelve feet wide. It has a smooth, grayish brown trunk and an umbrella-shaped canopy producing filtered shade. Its dark green, long, lacy foliage gives it a feathery effect. In spring, this tree has an amazing show of distinctive, tiny pink clusters that resemble a powder puff. The flowers are highly fragrant and attract bees, hummingbirds, and butterflies. After blooming, it produces a large, green, flat seedpod that hangs dramatically from the tree. The mimosa grows best in full sun but tolerates

Araucaria bidwillii,
Bunya-Bunya,
False Monkey Puzzle Tree
Large-sized tree

This magnificent evergreen has evenly spaced, graceful, horizontal branches that are arranged in even tiers around a central trunk. When young, the tree looks very symmetrical and grows from

Araucaria bidwillii
Bunya-Bunya, False Monkey Puzzle Tree

fifty feet to over one hundred feet in its native environment and produces a twenty- to forty-foot spread. When mature, the lower branches drop off, and it develops a dome-shaped crown. The juvenile leaves of this magnificent tree are distinctive, glossy, and narrow with stiff and sharp pointed edges. It produces male and female cones instead of flowers, and after about fifteen years develops twelve-inch-long, pineapple-shaped cones. The cones are heavy and may cause damage if they fall on a car or person. The seeds inside the cone are edible and were considered a delicacy by Aborigines. It likes full sun to partial shade, well-draining soil, and regular but not frequent irrigation. It is hardy to twenty degrees Fahrenheit. Plant it in wide-open areas away from walkways and parking lots, in city parks, or as a windbreak for its woodsy effect and elegance. The tree is native to the mountains and subtropical rainforests near the coast of Southeast and Northern Queensland, Australia.

Brachychiton populneus
Bottle Tree
Medium- to large-sized tree

The bottle tree is a fast-growing evergreen with poplar-like, dark green, dense, pointed foliage. It has a broad trunk that tapers into a pyramidal shape when young. As it matures, the trunk wid-

Araucaria bidwillii
Bunya-Bunya, False Monkey Puzzle Tree

Brachychiton populneus
leaf up close

Brachychiton populneus
Bottle Tree

Cascabela thevetia
Yellow Oleander, Lucky Nut
Small- to medium-sized tree

Cascabela thevetia
Yellow Oleander, Lucky Nut

ens and has the ability to store water. The tree grows from thirty-five to sixty feet and spreads thirty feet wide. In late spring, it produces creamy white, bell-shaped blooms streaked with purple. After flowering, dark brown, woody seedpods appear that contain yellow seeds. Hairs on the seedpod may cause an allergic itching reaction in some people. Aborigines roasted seeds from the pods, used the soft, spongy wood to make shields and used the bark as a fiber. The species prefers full sun, withstands reflected heat, and grows best in well-draining soils that are not rocky. This tree is drought resistant but needs occasional, deep irrigation during the warmer weather. It is hardy to twenty to twenty-five degrees Fahrenheit and may suffer frost damage in colder, low-lying locations. The bottle tree is highly susceptible to Texas root rot fungus. It requires an annual application of fertilizer in the spring. Use it as a street tree in medians, along roadways, in parking lots or wide-open spaces like parks, or residential settings. This is a great tree choice to use around large buildings or as a screen. It is native to dry forests, wet coastal areas, and interior semi-arid areas of Victoria, New South Wales, and Queensland in Australia.

The tropical evergreen grows ten to twenty feet tall and six to twelve feet wide. It produces single or multiple trunks and can be grown as a tree or large shrub. Its bark is light brown and turns darker and more furrowed with age. The foliage is long and dark green with veins along the leaf. Yellow oleander produces fragrant, yellow, cream, apricot, or orange trumpet-shaped flowers in clusters. They bloom for a long period of time during the warm weather and attract bees, butterflies, and birds. After flowering, a greenish, two-inch long, lantern-shaped seedpod appears. The foliage of this plant can be damaged at twenty-eight degrees Fahrenheit, but it will recover quickly in the spring. Use the yellow oleander in protected areas in colder locations. It likes partial shade or full sun with plenty of reflected heat and prefers regular irrigation. The yellow oleander also likes to be planted in rich, well-draining soils. This will help prevent problems with iron chlorosis. All parts of the plant are poisonous if

Cascabela thevetia
Yellow Oleander, Lucky Nut

ingested. Keep away young children and animals. This plant contains a milky sap compound that can be an eye and skin irritant. Use it in gardens for tropical effects, against walls, as a screen, in protected patios, and around pools for its lush, striking appearance. It can also be used in entry courtyards as a color and accent plant. The plant is a native to Peru, Central America, the Southern United States, and the Galapagos Islands.

Cedrus deodara

Deodar Cedar
Large-sized tree

This stately evergreen grows to heights of more than one hundred feet in its native habitat. In the Southwest desert, it reaches heights of forty to fifty feet or more with a spread of thirty to forty feet. The moderate- to fast-growing tree has a tall, conical shape with long, horizontal, graceful branches that bend downward as they grow. The bright green to greenish blue, needlelike foliage has stiff, sharply pointed edges and is very dense. The female cones are purplish brown, erect, and shaped like small barrels. They appear on the

Cedrus deodara
Deodar Cedar

upper portion of the tree. The male cones are longer, appear on the lower portion of the tree, and shed pollen in the fall. The bark on this tree is smooth when young and develops short furrows along the trunk at maturity. This tree is an important source of timber in India, where it is a native. Deodar cedar prefers full sun and reflected heat, along with well-draining, slightly acidic soil. It is hardy into the low teens and needs additional water when young. It is drought tolerant at maturity and should not be overwatered. Plant this handsome specimen tree in wide-open spaces such as a park or large commercial or residential landscape where it has plenty of room to grow, mature, and spread as a screen plant, windbreak, or massive, picturesque tree with beautiful coloring and graceful branches. This cedar is native to the Himalayas, India, and Pakistan, where it grows in mountainous regions at high elevations on north-facing slopes.

Celtis ehrenbergiana
Desert Hackberry
Small tree

This gnarly, thorny tree or large shrub with semi-evergreen foliage grows to twelve feet and spreads to eight to ten feet. It has smooth, grayish brown stems and a trunk armed with spines. This tree produces small, oval, bright grayish green foliage with slightly serrated edges. The leaves drop when the temperature falls below twenty degrees Fahrenheit. Inconspicuous, greenish white flowers form in the spring and again during summer monsoons. Pea-sized, bright orange, edible berries appear later, attracting cactus wrens, green jays, coyotes, jackrabbits, and other wildlife. Quail especially like to forage for fruits that have fallen to the ground, and they use this plant to nest. The desert hackberry likes full sun to partial shade and prefers some irrigation, especially during the hot, summer months. It grows natively

Celtis ehrenbergiana
Desert Hackberry

in dry, rocky soils and tolerates most soil conditions that are well draining. Be careful of its thorns when pruning or shaping. This tree is a tough-as-nails plant that can survive rugged conditions. Use it as a barrier plant, screen, or wildlife attractor, or for revegetation and erosion control. The desert native is a host to a few species of butterfly larvae that feed on its new leaves in the spring. This tree can also be found in southern Texas, Arizona, and in the Chihuahuan and Sonoran deserts of Baja California and east to Chihuahua and south to Oaxaca, Mexico, where it grows naturally in washes at elevations of 3,000 to 8,000 feet.

Celtis ehrenbergiana
Desert Hackberry

Celtis laevigata var. reticulata

Netleaf Hackberry
Large-sized tree

Celtis laevigata var. reticulata
Netleaf Hackberry

This deciduous or sometimes semideciduous tree grows twenty-five to forty-five feet tall and twenty to thirty feet wide with pendulous, twisting branches and stems that form an irregular shape when young. With proper pruning, it grows upright into a wonderful shade tree. The bark has interesting, corky ridges along its trunk and grayish green, saw-toothed foliage that feels like sandpaper. The top part of the leaf is bright green, and the underneath is a much lighter green. Inconspicuous, greenish white flowers appear in the spring. After flowering, green, pea-size berries develop and turn orange-red in the fall. The berries are a major source of food for desert wildlife and birds. The plant is hardy, surviving well below zero degrees. Netleaf hackberry likes well-draining soil and supplemental water during the summer but is extremely drought resistant. This desert native likes full sun and reflected heat. Trees require yearly pruning to maintain their size and appearance. These plants are susceptible to the parasite mistletoe—therefore, watch for infestations. Prune infected areas as needed. It is a great choice for open areas and natural wildlife habitats in desert landscapes as a shade tree or for restoration. The wood from the tree has been used to make furniture and other products. It grows natively in Northern Mexico on dry, rocky hillsides, in canyons, and along dry stream beds at elevations of 2,500 to 6,000 feet.

Celtis laevigata var. reticulata
Netleaf Hackberry

Ceratonia siliqua

Carob, St. John's Bread
Large-sized tree

Carob is a large evergreen reaching thirty to fifty feet tall and forty feet wide with a dense branching habit. This tree has smooth, grayish bark and large, round, leathery, dark green leaflets that create a dense canopy of shade. Inconspicuous male or female flowers appear together on the same tree, but it is the female flowers that produce dark green beans that ripen into large brown, edible pods. These sugar-rich pods take almost a year to fully develop and are used as a cocoa substitute. Animals also forage on the pods. The species enjoys full sun and reflected heat and is drought

Ceratonia siliqua
Carob Tree in bloom

tolerant, but it likes occasional irrigation, especially for pod production. This tree is hardy to twenty-five degrees Fahrenheit; foliage is damaged into the low twenties. Avoid planting in low-lying areas. The tree grows anywhere that is warm enough for citrus. It requires dry, warmer climates for seed production. Carob trees are susceptible to Texas root rot, therefore, plant them in well-draining soil and fertilize annually. Use it as a large, handsome, ornamental tree for dense shade in courtyards and on the south side of a property. It is native to arid regions of Southern Europe, Western Asia, and the Middle East.

Ceratonia siliqua
Carob, St John Bread

*Chilopsis linearis

Desert Willow
Medium- to large-sized tree

Desert willow is a deciduous, multitrunk tree that grows fifteen to twenty-five feet tall. It has long, narrow, green leaves with prominent veins and both its foliage and growth habit create a weeping appearance. In late spring, it produces fragrant,

Chilopsis linearis
Desert Willow in bloom

Chilopsis linearis
Desert Willow

trumpet-shaped, showy blossoms in pink, lavender, white, or fuchsia. After flowering, a thin capsulelike pod appears. Inside the pod are papery seeds. Native Americans used the blossoms, leaves, and bark of the desert willow for medicinal purposes, bows, and baskets. There are many varieties available that differ in flower color, leaf color, and leaf size. Two favorites include "Lucretia Hamilton," which produces intense pink to lavender flowers and is smaller in size, and "Warren Jones," which has amazing spring and summer flowers that attract hummingbirds. Desert willow is drought resistant and grows in full sun with reflected heat but can also take partial shade. Although it is endemic to streams and low-lying areas, growing in rocky or gravel-like situations, it performs best in well-draining soils. Desert willow is hardy to ten degrees Fahrenheit. It grows quickly at first and slows down as it matures. Prune any suckers from the base in the spring and summer to keep the tree in it best form. It makes an exquisite landscape specimen, focal point, or shade tree. This tree is native to parts of Southern California and Southern Utah and Nevada, Southern Arizona, New Mexico, and

Texas. In Mexico, it grows naturally throughout the states of Sonora, Baja California, Chihuahua, Coahuila, Nuevo Leon, Zacatecas, and into San Luis Potosi, along washes and riverbanks at around 5,000 feet.

*Cordia boissieri

Texas Olive
Medium-sized tree

Texas olive is an evergreen to semideciduous tree reaching fifteen to twenty feet tall and about twenty-five feet wide. It has multiple trunks with a dark gray bark and deep green, oval leaves that are large and leathery in texture. The undersides of the leaves are covered in fuzz with deep, yellowish white veins. From spring to fall, it

Cordia boissieri
Texas Olive

produces beautiful clusters of creamy white blossoms with yellow throats that attract hummingbirds. After flowering, a small, nonedible fruit forms that resembles an olive and is eaten by birds. The fruit has also been used to make jellies in Mexico. Plant this tree in full sun with plenty of reflected heat. It is hardy to about twenty-five degrees Fahrenheit. If frosted, it recovers quickly in spring. The Texas olive likes supplemental irrigation but can handle low to moderate water conditions with tolerance to salty soils, but prefers soil that is well-draining. Water newly planted trees once a week until established and fertilize in the spring with ammonium phosphate. This is an excellent specimen and patio tree and can also be used as a screen, windbreak, or background planting in courtyards or medians and along roadsides. It is a great substitute plant

for the white oleander tree. This tree is native to Southern Texas at the tip of the Rio Grande and also grows natively in Mexico in Coahuila, San Luis Potosi, Nuevo Leon, and Tamaulipas.

Cupressus arizonica

Arizona Cypress
Large-sized tree

This fast-growing evergreen reaches heights of thirty to forty feet and spreads twenty feet with a pyramid shape and horizontal spreading branches. Its striking leaf colors range from silvery blue to bluish green with a reddish brown bark. The cypress has inconspicuous flowers that are followed by brownish gray, small, smooth-looking cones. It is tolerant of many soils and likes full sun with reflected heat. The tree is extremely cold

Cordia boissieri
Texas Olive Flower

Cupressus arizonica
Arizona Cypress

hardy to zero degrees or lower, and encounters few diseases or insect problems. Plant it in loamy or sandy well-draining soils and provide supplemental irrigation to encourage faster growth. It needs minimal pruning to develop a strong structure. The variety "Blue Ice" has foliage with a distinctive blue color and makes a great accent color plant for large settings. There are many other varieties with different leaf forms, denser foliage, and different colors as well as distinctive conical shapes. This single trunk tree adds woodsy drama to the landscape and its foliage produces a wonderful aroma. Use it as a large specimen for a screen or windbreak in parks, in large, open spaces, along roadsides, or as a visual barrier or background plant. It is native to Arizona, Texas, New Mexico, and Mexico growing from 3,000 to 8,000 feet on dry, rocky mountain slopes and canyon walls.

Cupressus glabra
Smooth-Barked Arizona Cypress

ally by irrigating monthly for the first few years. Afterwards, provide supplemental water during the hot, dry season. Use it in large, open spaces as an ornamental in parks, schoolyards, roadways, or medians, or as a screen, large hedge, or windbreak tree. This tree grows naturally in rocky or gravelly canyon soils in Central to Western Arizona at elevations of 3,500 to 8,500 feet. Some botanists list Cupressus glabra into the same genus and species as Cupressus arizonica.

Cupressus glabra
Smooth-Barked Arizona Cypress
Large-sized tree

The smooth-barked cypress is an impressive evergreen with a symmetrical canopy and pyramidal shape that reaches thirty to fifty feet with a twenty-foot or greater spread. Its beautiful, blue-green, scalelike foliage is similar to Cupressus arizonica. It produces a turpentine fragrance from resin glands on the leaves. This tree gets its name from its peeling outer bark that reveals a glossy, cherry red, attractive inner bark. The cypress produces spherical, reddish brown, inconspicuous cones that remain on the tree for two years or more. It is cold hardy to zero degrees, prefers full sun, reflected heat, and well-draining soils with some acidity. The tree is moderate- to fast-growing, requiring proper staking when young to prevent toppling over. While it is drought resistant, provide at least ten inches of water annu-

Cupressus sempervirens
Italian Cypress
Large-sized tree

Italian cypress is a stately, evergreen reaching skyline heights of forty to sixty feet or greater. It is a slender, vertical, single-trunk tree with needlelike, dark green, dense foliage and horizontal growing branches. There are many cultivars available that look slightly different, and the

Cupressus sempervirens
Italian Cypress

foliage color varies. The tree has inconspicuous flowers, and cones may develop in cool temperatures. This cypress grows best with sun, reflected heat, and in rich, fertile soils that are well draining and allowed to dry out between irrigations. It is hardy to ten degrees Fahrenheit. Once established, the plant is drought tolerant but irrigate younger plants regularly and deeply. The Italian cypress is susceptible to spider mite damage. Treat it with proper systemic insecticide or hose it down with a strong blast of water if insects are present. Sometimes, older trees require pruning to keep their columnar shape. Do not overfertilize or overwater this plant. Italian cypress needs a lot of space and does not usually work well in a residential setting where it can outgrow the area. Use it as a strong, vertical accent against tall buildings or in wide-open spaces for architectural quality. Install this plant for its dramatic, dark foliage and interesting, tall silhouette in the landscape. The variety "Stricta," which remains shorter with a narrow growth habit, is an excellent vertical windbreak or screen. "Glauca" has bluish green foliage and a tight, columnar form. The variety "Horizontalis" has a horizontal branching pattern. The Italian cypress is native to Northeast Libya, Southeast Greece, Southern Turkey, Cyprus, Western Syria, Lebanon, Israel, Western Jordan, and Iran.

*Dalbergia sissoo
Indian Rosewood
Medium- to large-sized tree

The handsome semi-evergreen tree grows thirty to fifty feet tall and thirty feet wide with lush, glossy green, oval leaflets that are lighter green on the undersides of the leaves. It develops inconspicuous, fragrant, white flower clusters that appear in spring. After the flowers have died, slender, elongated, brown seedpods form. It has an irregular silhouette and produces a great splash of lush green that provides shade in the landscape. The bark is shaggy and reddish brown, becoming darker as the tree ages. Its trunk and beautiful wood is used for fine furniture, cabinetry, flooring, instruments, and timber. This tree is hardy to twenty-five to thirty degrees Fahrenheit. When temperatures drop well below freezing, the foliage may show significant frost damage. However, new growth appears quickly in spring. Mature trees are hardier to frost conditions than younger trees. It tolerates a wide variety of soils, likes full sun and reflected heat, and is a moderate to fast grower. The size of this tree can be controlled by pruning, and it should be correctively pruned during the dormant months to develop a strong structure. Keep young trees well

Dalbergia sissoo
Indian Rosewood

Dalbergia sissoo
Indian Rosewood

watered until established and then provide supplemental irrigation during the hot, dry season. Surface roots of this tree can become a maintenance problem and possibly lift sidewalks. Use it in parking lots, lawns, parks, medians, or roadsides, or as a residential or commercial shade tree. The Indian rosewood is also a great choice for oriental effects. It is native to India, Pakistan, and Afghanistan and widely grown in warmer climates around the world.

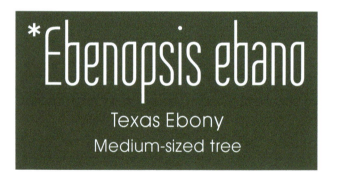

*Ebenopsis ebano

Texas Ebony
Medium-sized tree

The Texas ebony is a multi- or single-trunk evergreen growing fifteen to thirty feet tall with equal spread. Its gnarly, zigzagging, gray stems make this an interesting accent tree. The wood is a rich, dark brown and has been used for making furniture, cabinetry and other products. This exquisite tree produces thin, green, round leaflets on curved, thorny branches. In late spring, small, creamy white, fragrant, puffy, spiked blossoms appear that cover the tree in significant clusters. Leathery, dark brown bean pods about four inches long with fine hairs hang down from the

Ebenopsis ebano
Texas Ebony

tree and last for a long time. The pods eventually open and display small, brownish black seeds. The seeds can be used as a coffee substitute. This slow- to medium grower adapts to harsh conditions, including drought, but grows quicker with supplemental irrigation. It is hardy to about fifteen degrees Fahrenheit and survives in areas that are extremely hot and dry. In some extreme summers, it may slightly defoliate if not given any water but will recover during the summer monsoons. Plant it in full sun with lots of reflected heat and provide yearly pruning, especially when young, to shape and train it. The species provides

Ebenopsis ebano
Texas Ebony in bloom

Ebenopsis ebano
Texas Ebony up close

Eriobotrya japonica
Loquat

valuable shelter and food for wildlife including deer, javelina, and various birds. Use the Texas ebony as a specimen tree, barrier plant, or privacy screen in a patio or courtyard, or along highways, medians, or parking lots. The tree can be trained as a bonsai with its interesting shape and form. It is extremely thorny, so keep it away from pedestrian traffic. Texas ebony is a native to Southern Texas along the plains of the Rio Grande, in deserts and scrubland area of Nuevo Leon, San Luis Potosi, and Tamaulipas, Mexico, and into Baja California.

ters of scented, wooly looking, white blossoms in late fall, which attract hummingbirds, bees, and butterflies. In the spring, edible yellowish orange, pearlike, oval fruit appears in clusters. The fruit can be used for jams and preserves and is sweetest when it becomes soft and yellow in color. The tree requires good drainage and full sun to produce flowers and fruit, and it can handle some filtered sun. It also needs regular irrigation when

Eriobotrya japonica

Loquat, Japanese Plum
Medium-sized tree

Eriobotrya japonica
Loquat Fruit

This evergreen grows in an upright, rounded form to twenty feet with lush, tropical, leathery, grayish green, textured leaves that turn a bronzy red color. The bottom surface of the leaf is light green and slightly fuzzy. The tree produces clus-

Eriobotrya japonica
Loquat

Eucalyptus erythrocorys
Red-Cap Gum
Medium-sized tree

This evergreen with its graceful form and open crown grows to heights of fifteen to thirty feet and fifteen to twenty feet wide. Its name comes from the gummy, aromatic sap it produces and the bright red, colored caps that cover the flower buds. The Latin word *erythrocorys* means red helmet. It is a moderate- to fast-growing tree with emerging foliage and branches that are reddish bronze when young, turning a dark and thick

young but becomes more drought tolerant as it matures. This tree is very hardy to about twelve degrees Fahrenheit. The Japanese plum is very susceptible to fire blight, a bacterial disease that causes the leaves to look scorched and then die. Remove damaged leaves and stems, and afterwards, sterilize pruning tools. The tree produces some leaf drop and does require light raking and sweeping of plant litter and debris. Use it as an ornamental tree in the Southwest desert, and plant it in frost-free areas for fruit production. It is a great choice for an accent in patios and courtyards, or for tropical, oriental, or ornamental effects; it boasts lush, bold foliage and an attractive form that adds a nice contrast with other plants. This tree is native to Southeastern China and was introduced and naturalized in Japan and India. This moderate growing tree has also been naturalized in Cyprus, Egypt, and France.

Eucalyptus erythrocorys
Red-Cap Gum

glossy green with age. The leaves are long with a pointed tip and highly aromatic. Like many other eucalyptus trees, it sheds its bark, exposing a whitish gray color with a few patches of brown. In late summer, it produces spectacular blooms in clusters of yellow tufts with red-capped buds. When in bloom, its flowers are so abundant that they tend to weigh it down. Its leaves will drop when the flowers appear, making it quite messy. The tree develops either a single or multiple trunks and requires pruning and staking in order to achieve an ideal shape. It likes rich, well-draining soil and is less drought tolerant than other varieties of eucalyptus. However, it can get by on a once-per-month watering schedule after it is established in the soil. It is hardy to twenty-five degrees Fahrenheit and should be planted in a sunny, protected area. Like most eucalyptus species, it attracts few pests or diseases but is sometimes affected by iron chlorosis if grown in alkaline or heavy clay soil or overwatered. Treatments of iron chelate fertilizer can be used to control iron deficiency. Use it as an ornamental in commercial and residential landscapes or in groupings for its dramatic and bold presentation. Red-cap gum is native to Western Australia, north of Perth.

Eucalyptus microtheca
Coolibah

Eucalyptus microtheca
Coolibah

Eucalyptus microtheca

Coolibah
Tiny Capsule Eucalyptus
Large-sized tree

This multitrunk evergreen is a great choice for Southwest desert landscapes. It is a fast-growing, upright tree that reaches heights of thirty-five to forty feet with an equal spread. Coolibah produces long, slender, silvery gray or gray-green aromatic leaves. Small, insignificant, creamy white blossoms appear in terminal clusters in late spring. After blooming, tiny seed capsules develop—they are what give the tree its name. It has smooth, whitish gray bark that is smooth when young and peels to reveal a dark gray, mottled bark. This plant is hardy to ten degrees Fahrenheit or slightly lower. It grows in any soil condition as long as it is well draining. Coolibah takes ample water if planted in a lawn and will also survive in drought situations. This tree is not as susceptible to iron chlorosis as other eucalyptus species. Use it in large areas against tall buildings or in groves, as a barrier, windbreak or mass planting. Its silvery leaves and weeping form make it a showy tree in parks and other wide-open spaces. This tree is native to rivers and floodplains, growing in heavy soils in Northern Australia and New South Wales.

Eucalyptus polyanthemos

Silver Dollar Gum
Large-sized tree

Eucalyptus polyanthemos
Silver Dollar Gum

The fast-growing evergreen with a single or multiple trunk reaches heights of twenty to sixty feet with a twenty to forty-foot spread. It has whitish gray, peeling bark and strong, aromatic foliage that is round like a silver dollar and bluish green to silvery green. The silvery round leaves are commonly used in floral arrangements. As the tree matures, its foliage becomes more elongated. Small, creamy white, inconspicuous flowers appear in clusters in spring. Cylindrical, cup-shaped, small seed capsules develop after the tree finishes blooming. It grows in full sun with reflected heat and well-draining soils. Irrigate it fre-

Eucalyptus polyanthemos
Silver Dollar Gum

quently when young and then provide deep irrigations every month or two. It is hardy to fourteen to eighteen degrees Fahrenheit and is extremely drought resistant when established. This eucalyptus needs proper pruning when young to train and shape it, and it may need some additional pruning as the tree matures. It drops its leaves from time to time, requiring cleanup on patios, walkways, and hard surfaces. Use this majestic skyline tree to provide shade or as a specimen in parks or other large landscapes. Its cascading branches sway back and forth in the wind, creating a soft rustling sound. Silver dollar gum can be used in groves, around parking lots, along roadways, or as a tall silhouette against a building or wall. It is native to Victoria and New South Wales, Australia.

*Ficus benjamina
Weeping Fig, Weeping Chinese Banyan
Medium- to large-sized tree

Weeping fig grows at a moderate to fast rate reaching heights of thirty to sixty feet and spreads fifteen to twenty feet wide at maturity. The evergreen has bright green, glossy, tropical-looking, oval leaves with pointed tips. The foliage is dense and provides shade in warmer areas. It produces an inconspicuous flower in the spring. The tree does well in either full sun or shade; requires deep, infrequent irrigation and well-draining, acidic soils; and tolerates the desert heat. It is hardy to twenty-eight to thirty degrees Fahrenheit. If it is damaged by frost, it recovers

Ficus benjamina
Weeping Fig

slowly in the spring. Hot, summer sun may also cause the leaves to sunburn. Plant the weeping fig in a protected area of the landscape, preferably in a warm microclimate. Leafy parts of this plant may be poisonous if ingested. When the stems and branches are pruned or broken, the tree emits a white, sappy liquid that may be a skin irritant. Its roots can be very invasive when planted in warmer climates. Use it as a shade tree, hedge, screening plant, or specimen in courtyards, under covered patios, or on porches in large, attractive containers. The variety "Exotic" has a weeping habit and the trunk is often braided or twisted together in an interesting pattern. There are many other varieties available in local garden centers, including a variegated form. The weeping fig is native to Southeast Asia, the Southwest Pacific, Northern Australia, and India.

*Ficus carica
Common Fig, Edible Fig
Medium-sized tree

The common fig tree is a deciduous, spreading, multitrunk tree with smooth, gray bark that grows to heights of fifteen to thirty feet and has a wide but low, open canopy. It has large multi-lobed, showy, dark green foliage and produces small, inconspicuous flowers. The fig tree usually sets two crops of fruit during the warm season. The first crop appears in spring when the leaves first emerge. The second crop produces fruit into late summer to early fall. The edible, brownish purple fruit is pollinated by a small wasp that enters the flower through a small opening. The fruit has high sugar content and can be eaten fresh, dried, or canned and is used in a number of recipes. It does not last long on the tree after ripening. In the winter, the foliage drops from the tree, and when bare of leaves, it creates a distinctive and inter-

Ficus carica
Common Fig, Edible Fig

Ficus carica
Common Fig, Edible Fig

Ficus carica
Common Fig, Edible Fig

esting silhouette in the landscape. The common fig is drought resistant once established, but likes regular, deep irrigations for the first few years after planting. It prefers well-draining soil high in organic matter and tolerates full sun or filtered shade. If planting more than one tree, space each one about twenty to thirty feet apart to allow a natural sprawl. Apply ammonium phosphate fertilizer in spring and early fall during the growing season. This tree is hardy to fifteen to twenty degrees Fahrenheit. There are many different varieties of the fig tree. Two of the most common in the Southwest desert are "Black Mission" and "Brown Turkey." It is native to Southeast Asia and the Eastern Mediterranean areas from Greece to Turkey where it is found growing in rocks or in shrubby areas. The fig is grown commercially in Texas, California, Oregon, and Washington.

*Ficus elastica

Rubber Plant
Large-sized shrub or tree

In tropical climates, the rubber plant is a vigorously growing evergreen tree reaching heights of forty feet or more, forming large aerial roots and bearing figlike, inedible, green fruit. In colder climates, it is grown indoors as a houseplant. However, in the Southwest desert, this plant reaches about fifteen to twenty feet when grown in protected areas. It is used as a landscape accent for its bold foliage and tropical accent. The rubber plant has large, thick, glossy green leaves that grow a foot long. The newly emerging foliage is pink in color at first, then turning a deep green. The rubber plant is a great choice for a shady, well-lit area and is easy to grow and care for. To avoid leaf burn, plant it in filtered sun or shade in well-draining, fertile soil. Provide ample water during the warm months, but do not overwater.

Ficus elastica
Rubber Plant

Reduce irrigation during the winter months. A well-established rubber tree is hardy to about thirty degrees Fahrenheit. Younger plants freeze at thirty-two degrees. This shrub can be lightly pruned at anytime to shape. Avoid contact with the milky, latex sap in its stem, which may cause skin irrigations or allergic reactions. Use it as a specimen in large containers in a shady area, in an atrium, in entries, or under covered patios. It also works well as an understory plant in the shade of tall palms in protected locations. Rubber plant is native to the tropical zones of Northeastern India, the Eastern Himalayas, and throughout Malaysia and Indonesia, growing at elevations of 3,000 to 5,000 feet.

Ficus microcarpa

Indian Laurel Fig, Cuban Laurel
Medium- to large-sized tree

This moderate- to fast-growing, tropical evergreen reaches forty to fifty feet in the wild, with an equal spread. In Southwest desert landscapes, it grows to thirty-five feet with an upright, compact growth habit and dense, smooth, glossy,

Ficus microcarpa
Indian Laurel

bright green foliage. It develops a grayish white, smooth bark with inconspicuous greenish white flowers that attract hummingbirds, butterflies, and birds. After blooming, small, inedible fruits appear with tiny seeds inside. The seeds are ingested and dispersed by birds and pollinator wasps to germinate elsewhere. The Indian laurel fig likes full sun or partial shade, ample irrigation, and well-draining soil. This tree will freeze into the mid to low twenties and needs to be planted in warm microclimates. The species is susceptible to the laurel mite, which feeds on the foliage, distorting it. The compact-growing variety "Green Gem" has some immunity to mites. The tree can be sheared and shaped to fit into most landscape situations. Use it as a specimen, bonsai, screen, large container plant, in a courtyard or as an interior mall plant. It also works well as a street, median, or parking lot tree, in a lawn setting or around ponds and water features. The Indian laurel fig is native to Malaysia and India.

Fraxinus greggii
Little Leaf Ash
Small-sized tree

The hardy evergreen is a multitrunk tree that grows quickly to eighteen feet with a spread of twelve to fifteen feet. Its smooth, brownish gray bark darkens as the tree matures. This tree produces bright green leaves that are small, thick, and leathery. Older foliage suddenly drops from the tree in late spring to make way for new, green leaves. Small, inconspicuous flowers appear in early spring, with male and female parts on sep-

Fraxinus greggii
Little Leaf Ash

arate flowers, but together on the same plant. After flowering, a small, winged fruit appears with dark, flat seeds. The pod clings to the tree for a long period of time. This tree likes well-draining soil and full sun or partial shade. It is drought tolerant but prefers supplemental irrigation during the hottest months of the summer. It is hardy to about twelve to fifteen degrees Fahrenheit. Little leaf ash is a low-maintenance plant but requires some pruning and shaping to keep its multitrunk form. Use it as a patio tree, around pools, or in large containers or planters. It is also a great shade tree and privacy screen, and adds a nice touch of deep green color and a delicate, airy feel into the garden. Little leaf ash is native to Western Texas, Southern New Mexico, Southern Arizona, and in Coahuila, Nuevo Leon, Zacatecas, and Tamaulipas, Mexico, growing along washes and rocky slopes at elevations of 2,500 to 7,000 feet.

Fraxinus greggii
Little Leaf Ash

*Fraxinus velutina

Arizona Ash, Velvet Ash
Large-sized tree

This fast-growing, deciduous tree reaches thirty to forty-five feet and spreads twenty-five to forty-five feet or more, depending on conditions. It produces dark green, three- to six-inch-long leaves that are divided into multiple leaflets to form a dense, rounded canopy. The leaves turn a brilliant yellow in the fall just before falling off the tree. Its flowers are dioecious with male and female blooms forming on separate trees. Male trees produce inconspicuous flowers in the spring that can cause a mess. Female trees drop a winged fruit that resembles a maple seed. It is drought resistant but grows best with occasional, deep irrigation during the hot, dry season. This tree is hardy to about ten degrees Fahrenheit. Plant it in full sun and well-draining soil. Careful pruning and branch selection ensures a strong trunk and stable branch development. Treat the tree with iron chelate fertilizer yearly or as needed to prevent iron chlorosis. This plant is also susceptible to Texas root rot. The variety "Modesto" is symmetrical, compact and a little smaller in size but a vigorous grower. "Fantex" produces dark green, leathery foliage and is the best variety for residential landscapes. Use this magnificent tree for dense shade, as a street tree or in parks. It can also be used in large residential settings in combination with other evergreen plants. The Arizona ash

Fraxinus velutina
Arizona Ash

Fraxinus velutina
Arizona Ash

is native to California, Texas, and Arizona. It is also endemic to Mexico, ranging from Northern Baja California east to Coahuila and Nuevo Leon, where it grows along canyons and water sources at 2,000 to 6,000 feet in elevation.

Gleditsia triacanthos var. inermis

Thornless Honey Locust
Large-sized tree

Gleditsia triacanthos var. inermis
Thornless Honey Locust

The deciduous tree has a spreading growth habit and vase-shaped crown. It will grow to thirty feet wide and reaches thirty to forty feet tall with a beautiful, rounded canopy. The bark is grayish brown and becomes furrowed as it matures. When it leafs out in the spring, the lacy foliage is a light greenish yellow. This tree produces inconspicuous, fragrant, greenish yellow flowers in spring. Large, attractive seedpods hang onto the tree in the fall. As the weather cools in autumn, the leaves turn a golden yellow and drop to the ground. The tree is hardy to about ten degrees Fahrenheit. It grows best in full sun or partial shade and has no particular soil preferences. The thornless honey locust is relatively free of pests or diseases. Provide supplemental irrigation every week during the hot, dry season. Stake this tree when young and prune as needed to help it develop a strong structure. This fast-growing tree is a great choice along a roadway, in parking lots, in parks, or as a residential shade or street tree. It can also tolerate small planting spaces. Some varieties to consider include "Sunburst," "Imperial" and "Shademaster." The thornless honey locust is native to the Midwest, where it grows along streambeds.

Gleditsia triacanthos var. inermis
Thornless Honey Locust

Grevillea robusta

Silk Oak Tree
Large-sized tree

This fast-growing evergreen tree will reach heights of forty feet or more with a twenty-thirty foot spread. It creates a tall silhouette with a mass of thick green fernlike foliage. The underside of the leaves is grayish white in color. Golden orange, bottlebrush-type blooms form on the top of the tree in spring. Flowering occurs on mature trees after eight to ten years. A podlike fruit appears that opens to produce dark brown, winged seeds in late winter to early spring. If conditions are right, the seeds will germinate very easily. The flowers and seeds can be very toxic. The silk oak prefers full sun and can take reflected heat. Younger trees will do fine with filtered shade. This tree is drought resistant but prefers deep irrigation during the hot summer season. It does not like to be overwatered.

Grevillea robusta
Silk Oak Tree in bloom

The silk oak is hardy to twenty-four degrees Fahrenheit. It does well in our sandy, desert soils, but prefers them to be well draining and slightly acidic. This tree is very disease resistant, but the branches are somewhat brittle and may break during high winds. It will produce some leaf litter in the spring when older foliage drops from the tree. Use the silk oak tree as a windbreak, shade tree, in parking lots, along roadways, or as an ornamental against a wall. This tree is native to the eastern coastal regions of Australia where it grows in subtropical rainforests. Its wood was valued for timber and used in furniture making. The silk oak has also been naturalized in Hawaii and Southern Florida.

Grevillia robusta
Silk Oak Tree

*Jacaranda mimosifolia

Jacaranda
Large-sized tree

This magnificent, tropical beauty grows twenty-five to forty feet with an equal spread. Its tall canopy has an open, irregular shape and usually develops multiple trunks. Jacaranda produces soft, delicate, velvety, fernlike foliage and arching branches. In late spring, clusters of two-inch, showy, lavender, tubular blossoms appear. The blossoms sometimes appear before the flush of foliage, and the tree blooms heavily after mild winters. Its extravagant blooms completely cover the tree, and when they fall, they carpet the ground in color. There are some varieties available with white blossoms. After blooming, the tree produces a distinctive, brownish, two-inch-long, flattened capsule that contains winged seeds. The seedpod remains on the tree for a long time. This showy specimen has brownish gray bark that darkens with age. It is a fast-growing

Jacaranda mimosifolia
in bloom

tree that needs full sun and reflected heat. This tree is resistant to most pests and diseases and tolerates hot, dry conditions. Plant it in well-draining soil and provide infrequent, deep irrigation

Jacaranda mimosifolia
in bloom

Jacaranda mimosifolia
Jacaranda

during, hot, dry summers. The tree is hardy to about twenty-six degrees Fahrenheit. Colder temperatures and frost can cause some damage; however, this specimen beauty quickly recovers in the spring. Prune frozen limbs and branches in the spring. As the tree matures, it is less susceptible to frost damage. It develops large surface roots that can lift sidewalks and walls. Use it in landscapes for tropical effects as a tall specimen on the south or west side of a building or around water features and larger ponds. It can also be used as a shade tree in warmer climates, a tall silhouette against a large building or wall or a color accent. It is native to Brazil, Argentina, and Peru where it grows in Amazon regions.

Juniperus chinensis 'Torulosa'

Hollywood Juniper, Twisted Juniper
Medium-sized tree

Hollywood juniper is a distinctive, evergreen tree that has bright green, finely textured, scale-like foliage and grows at a moderate rate from fifteen to twenty feet tall to six to ten feet wide. Its exquisite branches grow in a twisted, distorted, irregular growth habit. Each plant seems to take on its own unique, freeform shape -- no two plants are alike. The conifer produces inconspicuous flowers and greenish, blueberry-like cones. Hollywood juniper likes full sun, tolerates light shade, but does best in wide-open locations in well-draining, acidic to alkaline soils. It likes ample, regular irrigation but also withstands some drought conditions when established. This plant is heat-, wind- and salt-tolerant and hardy

to the low teens. The Hollywood juniper is very easy to grow but can be susceptible to spider mites and aphids. Treat it with insecticides to fight infestations. Do not overprune, and let this interesting plant maintain its natural and artistic growth habit. Use it as a thick privacy screen. Since this juniper has a nice pine aroma, it can be used for woodsy effects in the landscape or as a background tree, as a focal point, or as a single-specimen planting. It looks interesting when planted against a large wall with its twisting habit, and works well in Japanese gardens. It is often planted in coastal areas where the winds tend to sculpt and shape the plant into interesting, dramatic, and twisted forms. Hollywood juniper is native to Japan, Mongolia, and China and was

Juniperus chinensis 'Torulosa'
Hollywood Juniper

brought to the United States in the early 1700s. This plant is a popular tree in Southern California, and is widely cultivated in Los Angeles.

Juniperus scopulorum 'Tolleson's Blue Weeping'

Tolleson's Blue Weeping Juniper
Large-sized tree

**Juniperus scopulorum
'Tolleson's Blue Weeping'**
Tolleson's Blue Weeping Juniper

This tall, weeping evergreen has silvery, bluish gray, fine textured, scalelike foliage that dangles from its pendulous branches. The needles are opposite and pressed very close to the stem with vertical branches and twigs. It grows twenty to twenty-five feet tall with long, graceful, arching branches stretching ten to twelve feet. The moderate to slow grower produces a bluish, fleshy, berrylike cone that takes about two years

to mature. This juniper is tolerant of most soils but prefers them to be well draining. The plant likes full sun or some reflected heat and shuns areas high in humidity. It is drought resistant when established but likes supplemental, deep, infrequent watering. Feed with a general fertilizer before new growth appears in the spring. Watch for infestations of aphids or spider mites on its branches during the warm weather. This is a relatively low-maintenance plant that looks best without pruning. It is also deer resistant and hardy to zero degrees and below. Use it as a single specimen tree or focal point for woodsy effects as a privacy screen or in mass plantings. Plant this juniper against a tall building or wall to dramatize its silhouette or to soften the corner of a wall. It can add beauty around large ponds or water features. It can also be used in containers in an entryway or patio. It is very tolerant of salty air and soils and works well in coastal situations. "Tolleson's Green Weeping Juniper" is a similar landscape plant available in nurseries that has been grafted from a rootstock of another plant. The blue version is native to the eastern foothills of the Rocky Mountains where it grows in dry soil on rocky ridges.

Koelreuteria paniculata

Golden Rain Tree
Large-sized tree

Golden rain tree is a deciduous, single-trunk specimen with a multiple spreading branch pattern up to thirty or forty feet tall and wide. It produces a rounded canopy with dense foliage and grayish brown bark that becomes furrowed and ridged

36

Koelreuteria paniculata
Golden Rain Tree

*Lagerstroemia indica

Crape Myrtle
Small- to medium-sized tree

with age. When the leaves bud out in the spring, they are reddish pink and turn a deep green color, providing a delicate feathery or lacy appearance. In spring, large, airy clusters of yellow blossoms cover the entire tree. In summer, papery, greenish yellow seedpods appear that contain small, round, blackish brown soft seeds. The seedpods are extremely ornamental and resemble small Chinese lanterns over the entire tree. The leaves turn a golden yellow in winter before dropping to the ground. The golden rain tree needs full sun and reflected heat to produce flowers and seedpods. It grows best in fertile, well-draining soil, is heat- and drought-tolerant, and hardy to twenty degrees Fahrenheit. Provide deep, supplemental irrigation during the hot, dry season. This tree can reseed in other parts of the landscape and in some areas can be invasive. Its leaves and seed drop require some cleanup throughout the year. Use this exciting specimen tree in groupings to create deep shade and as a single, free-standing accent in parks, as a street tree, in medians, or around parking lots. It is native to China and Korea.

This deciduous tree grows quickly to heights of fifteen to twenty feet and six to fifteen feet wide, with single or multiple trunks and a rounded crown. The leaves are small, rounded and deep green and turn beautiful colors of orange and red in the fall. The tree drops its foliage in winter, exposing an exfoliating bark that is whitish tan with a smooth, attractive trunk. It produces prolific blooms in colors of watermelon red, pink, lavender, and white. In the Southwest desert, crape myrtle blooms June through September with extremely showy flowers borne in clus-

Lagerstroemia indica
in bloom

Lagerstroemia indica
Crape Myrtle

Laurus nobilis
Bay Laurel, Sweet Bay
Medium- to large-sized tree

Bay laurel is a pyramid-shaped evergreen that grows ten to twenty feet with smooth, greenish brown bark. It has aromatic thick, long, leathery, dark green, glossy foliage and clusters of small yellow blossoms on the female trees in spring, followed by black or purple berries. The leaves and berries of this plant contain essential oils and have a distinctive aroma. The dried leaves are used as a popular seasoning in soups, stews,

ters that add a dramatic accent to the landscape. After blooming, brown or black fruit appears and then dries out to release small, rounded seeds. The small, capsulelike seedpod with upright spikes hangs on the tree throughout the winter. Plant it in full sun or reflected heat and provide plenty of supplemental irrigation. It is hardy to ten degrees Fahrenheit, prefers well-draining soils with added amendments. Fertilize it in the spring with ammonium phosphate and iron chelate as needed. While long-lived, it is susceptible to powdery mildew in cooler, summer climates and may suffer from iron chlorosis. In late winter, prune off old seedpods, dried blooms, and any suckers growing from the base of the tree. Crape myrtle is an excellent color plant for the summer but needs the heat to bloom. Use it as a patio tree, in groupings, or as a smaller specimen tree at the entry of a house. Dwarf varieties are available that grow from five to seven feet tall. It originated in China and has been naturalized in the United States, where it was first introduced in the eighteenth century.

Laurus nobilis
Bay Laurel, Sweet Bay

Laurus nobilis
Bay Laurel

sauces, and other culinary dishes as well as massage oils, perfumes, and when dried, in potpourri. In ancient Greece, wreaths were constructed from bay laurel as symbols of prosperity, victory, accomplishment, and wealth. The tree likes partial shade to full shade and thrives in rich, amended, well-draining soil. This slow to moderate grower prefers weekly irrigation and additional water during the hot, dry seasons. It is hardy in the high-twenty-degree-Fahrenheit range and should be protected from frost conditions. Plant it in an area safe from high winds. Treat it in spring with ammonium phosphate fertilizer. Use this tree for woodsy effects, as a screen, or as a tall vertical on the north side of a building, or train it as a topiary or bonsai plant in a garden or large container in an area that receives shade during the hot, dry summer months. This easy-to-grow plant is native to the Southern Mediterranean, and is grown commercially in Turkey, Algeria, Morocco, Portugal, Spain, Italy, France, and Mexico.

Leucaena retusa

Golden Lead Ball Tree
Small- to medium-sized tree

This slow to medium growing deciduous tree offers a beautiful silhouette, brown bark, and reaches heights of twenty to twenty-four feet with a spread of fifteen to twenty feet. It is a striking, thornless ornamental that develops multiple trunks and has an irregular, upright growth habit and moderately spreading crown. The plant has bright green, feathery leaves that shed in the fall. In spring and again in the fall, it produces showy, golden yellow, ball-like, one-and-a-half-inch flowers that are fragrant. Following the bloom cycle, six-inch-long woody seedpods appear with shiny seeds inside. The tree is frost tolerant to about thirteen to fifteen degrees Fahrenheit, grows in full sun, and prefers well-draining soil. It is also somewhat drought resistant, requiring

Leucaena retusa
Golden Lead Ball

Leucaena retusa
Golden Lead Ball

Lysiloma watsonii
Desert Fern, Feather Bush

deep, infrequent irrigation. The tree reseeds itself in the landscape if water is available, particularly after a monsoon. It has striking features and should be used more as an ornamental specimen in the landscape. This tree is susceptible to wind damage because of its brittle branches, so prune it as needed to develop a strong structure. Use it as an accent plant or screen on a patio or deck or in smaller planting beds. It is also a great tree choice for median strips in parking lots or smaller spaces as a specimen tree. This plant can be left to grow naturally as well. The golden lead ball tree is native to the dry, rocky slopes of Western Texas and Chihuahua, Mexico, where it grows at elevations of 1,500 to 5,500 feet.

appear, brown, flat, leguminous seedpods hang from the branches. They contain reddish brown, flat seeds that last on the tree for a long time. The bark is grayish brown and turns darker when mature. The feather bush requires minimal water to survive but grows faster with additional irrigation, especially during the hot, dry season. Plant

*Lysiloma watsonii

Desert Fern, Feather Bush
Small-sized tree

Feather bush is a graceful, single or multitrunk evergreen or semideciduous tree with a wide, spreading growth habit to heights of fifteen to twenty feet and widths of about fifteen feet. It has lacy, bright green to grayish green leaves and produces clusters of creamy white, fragrant, puffball blooms in early spring. After the blooms dis-

Lysiloma watsonii
Desert Fern, Feather Bush

it in a protected area—it is susceptible to frost damage at temperatures of twenty-five degrees Fahrenheit. If it suffers frost damage, prune back the frozen branches, fertilize the tree, and give it supplemental irrigation. It likes full sun and will take alkaline soils as long as they are well draining. The tree requires corrective pruning to remove suckers and to help develop good structure. It produces some leaf and seedpod litter that requires light maintenance. Feather bush is a good selection for the landscape when light shade is needed for smaller, understory plants. Use it around pools or ponds for a desert oasis theme, tropical effect, or background screen. Its feathery, semi-deciduous foliage also makes for a nice patio tree or specimen for small spaces. Feather bush grows natively in Southern Arizona and northern parts of Sonora and Sinaloa, Mexico.

Magnolia grandiflora
Southern Magnolia

Magnolia grandiflora
Southern Magnolia
Large-sized tree

The large, striking, broad-leaved evergreen reaches heights of forty feet with a spread of thirty feet. It has an erect trunk with spreading branches that form a dense, upright crown. The foliage is five to eight inches long, dark green, thick, and leathery. The underside of each leaf is cinnamon brown. Magnolia produces twelve-inch, fragrant, showy, white blossoms in springtime. After blooming, the tree develops a reddish brown conelike fruit that attracts birds. The bark is smooth and darkish gray. Many varieties are available with slightly different characteristics. This plant likes enriched, well-draining, acidic garden soil; grows in full sun or partial shade; and does not like reflected heat. Plant it on the east side of a house or building to protect from the afternoon sun. It takes moderate to ample irrigation but withstands some drought conditions at maturity. This tree is hardy to ten to fifteen degrees Fahrenheit and requires minimal care except an occasional raking of leaves and flowers

Magnolia grandiflora
Southern Magnolia

41

Magnolia grandiflora
in bloom

that drop to the ground. Apply ammonium phosphate fertilizer in the spring. Use magnolia for its bold form, foliage, and tropical effects as a shade, screen, specimen, or street tree, or for large, open spaces or to frame a building or house. It is native to the coastal plains of North Carolina, south to Central Florida, and west to Eastern Texas. It grows natively along streams, swamps, and on rich, loamy, moist soils. The magnolia is most prevalent in Louisiana, Mississippi, and Texas and is the state tree of Mississippi.

Mariosousa willardiana

Palo Blanco
Small- to medium-sized tree

The slender, weeping tree with distinctive, silvery white, peeling bark and multiple trunks reaches heights of twenty to twenty-five feet with a ten-foot spread. It is deciduous with long, grayish

Mariosousa willardiana
Palo Blanco

green, lacy foliage that produces tiny leaflets. In spring, this thornless specimen produces small, creamy white, puffed flower balls, followed by dark brown, three- to eight-inch seedpods in the summer. This moderate-growing, delicate accent tree likes full sun and reflected heat. The palo blanco is extremely drought resistant but requires periodic irrigation during the hot, dry season. It

Mariosousa willardiana
Palo Blanco

prefers a well-draining soil but also tolerates dry, rocky soils. This tree is hardy to temperatures in the mid-twenties and suffers major foliage and branch damage when temperatures drop below that. Protect from frosty conditions in low-lying areas. Use the palo blanco in entryways, patios, as an accent tree against a tall wall or building. It can also be used along medians and roadways as a nice silhouette or background tree in tight spaces. Use the palo blanco in masses or groupings. This tree is a great choice in low-water-use landscapes or xeriscape situations. It is native to the rocky hillsides of Sonora, Mexico, Northwest Sinaloa, and along coastal locations growing at 3,000 feet.

Melaleuca citrina
Lemon Bottlebrush

Melaleuca citrina

Lemon Bottlebrush, Crimson Bottlebrush
Small- to medium-sized tree

The lemon bottlebrush is a good choice for smaller areas since it grows to twelve feet with a six- to nine-foot spread. Its evergreen leaves are narrow, leathery, and produce a citrus aroma. Bright red fuzzy, fragrant blossoms arranged on the stems in clusters appear in early spring and sporadically throughout the summer. Its distinctive blooms attract hummingbirds, birds, and bees. The plant is hardier than the weeping bottlebrush, withstanding temperatures down to twenty to twenty-five degrees Fahrenheit. It grows best in full sun and in well-draining, sandy, or loam soils, and it prefers to have its roots dry out between irrigations. Once established, it can tolerate drought and does not like to be overwatered. This tree is also susceptible to iron chlorosis and requires chelated iron fertilizer as needed, and an application of ammonium phosphate in the spring. Heavy, unnecessary pruning or hedg-

Melaleuca citrina
Lemon Bottlebrush

ing will reduce flowering. It is a relatively easy plant to grow as a specimen tree in a tropical setting, around a pool, as a patio tree, or against a pale wall. Plant it in an area that is somewhat protected but where it can be admired. This plant is native to Australia and New Zealand.

Melaleuca viminalis

Weeping Bottlebrush
Medium- to large-sized tree

This beautiful, tropical evergreen with long weeping stems grows quickly to a height of thirty feet with a fifteen-foot spread. It forms a wide crown when the lower branches are pruned off. Its foliage is narrow and bronzy green in color, especially when new growth emerges in the spring. The leaves turn dark green as the spring foliage matures. In spring, the tree produces magnificent scarlet blossoms that contain brilliant red sta-

Melalecua viminalis
Weeping Bottlebrush

mens resembling brushes. After the bloom cycle, it develops cuplike seed capsules that are distinctive to this genus. The weeping bottlebrush likes full sun, reflected heat, and well-draining soil. It prefers frequent irrigation but tolerates periods of drought once it is established. Young trees benefit from corrective staking to protect them from the wind. This plant is susceptible to frost at around twenty degrees Fahrenheit and does not like windy locations. Plant the weeping bottlebrush in lower desert locations to protect it from frost damage. Also, regularly treat it with chelated iron fertilizer to prevent iron chlorosis. Bottlebrush can be grown as a specimen tree along a wall or building. Its weeping appearance creates a nice silhouette against any background. Also consider using as a strong, vertical accent plant or screen, or plant it in masses at the edge of a pond or lake, creating a tropical effect. The bottlebrush is native to waterways in New South Wales, Australia.

Melalecua viminalis
Weeping Bottlebrush

Oleo europaea 'Fruitless'

Fruitless Olive
Medium-sized tree

Oleo europaea 'Fruitless'
Fruitless Olive Tree

The fruitless olive is a distinctive evergreen that grows at a slow to medium rate to twenty-five to thirty feet tall and wide and has an airy appearance. It is either a single or multiple trunk, has narrow, gray-green foliage with a light silvery green on the undersides of the leaves. This fruitless variety does not produce fruit, eliminating any messy fruit drop, maintenance, and possible allergic reactions to pollen produced by the flowers. The tree has a dark gray, rough bark, and it grows with a twisted open canopy. Mature olive trees often develop contorted, massive trunks, and are quite interesting in appearance. In the spring, this tree produces insignificant yellowish white, tubular blooms that grow in clusters at the end of the leaves. However, the flowers are sterile, and the tree will not produce olive fruit.

Several municipalities in the Southwest desert have banned the planting of the fruiting olive tree from residential and commercial landscapes due to allergy-producing pollen and the mess created by the fruit. Olive trees are hardy to fifteen to twenty degrees Fahrenheit, enjoy full sun and reflected heat, and require little water. However, an occasional irrigation during the hot, dry summer provides a boost. The plant species is generally long-lived; olive trees have been known to live for several hundred years. However, it is susceptible to Texas root rot. It also produces tree suckers and needs yearly pruning to maintain its interesting form. Fertilize it with a high-nitrogen fertilizer once a year before growth begins in the spring. Use the olive as a specimen tree or shade tree or mixed with deep green or evergreen plants in the foreground. The species provides a Mediterranean feel and presentation in the landscape. The popular fruitless varieties "Swan Hill," "Majestic Beauty," and "Wilsonii" are available in local garden centers. The tree is a native of the Mediterranean region near Crete and Syria and is commonly grown throughout the Southwest desert.

Oleo europaea 'Fruitless'
Fruitless Olive foliage

*Olneya tesota
Desert Ironwood
Medium- to large-sized tree

Desert ironwood is a member of the pea family, and its leaves and flowers resemble the sweet pea. This single or multitrunk tree reaches heights of twenty-five feet with a nearly equal spread and is slow growing. Ironwood is one of the oldest living tree species and provides desert plants and animals with nutrients and shelter, providing shade for quail, doves and small rodents. It produces a bluish gray, leathery, oval leaf with fine hairs and develops an attractive wide-spreading crown at maturity. The bark on young trees is smooth and gray, becoming wrinkled as the tree ages. The young trees have branches with thorns that disappear as they age. In early spring through late spring, clusters of pealike flowers appear which range from pale rose to pink or white. The blossoms grow in arches at the end of the branches in a beautiful color display. After the flowers fade, edible, brown seedpods develop, which become a major food supply for wildlife. When given supplemental irrigation, the tree remains an evergreen. In its natural hab-

Olneya tesota
Ironwood Tree in bloom

itat, it sheds its leaves during dry periods to conserve water. The wood of the ironwood is hard and dense and is used for woodworking, charcoal, and firewood. Its heartwood is dark brown and takes a beautiful polish. The tree is drought resistant, prefers well-draining soil, full sun, and reflected heat. It is hardy to about twenty degrees Fahrenheit and needs some protection from frosts when young. Do not overwater this tree or plant it with other vegetation that requires a lot of irrigation. Overwatering of the ironwood can cause its demise. This dramatic plant produces very little litter and is relatively easy to grow and maintain. Use it as a screen, background, buffer tree, or as a transitional plant to separate the desert from more tropical and high water use plantings. Ironwood is also a good choice for shading a patio or an informal sitting area. The tree is native to the Sonoran Desert in Arizona, where it grows below 2,500 feet in sandy washes, rocky slopes, and valleys. It also grows natively in the Southeastern California deserts, Baja California, and Sonora, Mexico.

Olneya tesota
Desert Ironwood

Parkinsonia florida
Blue Palo Verde
Large-sized tree

The beautiful, deciduous tree grows to heights of twenty to twenty-five feet and spreads to twenty-five feet with blue-green bark and leaves, a graceful trunk, and multibranched stems. When properly pruned, the tree takes on a sculptural appearance that exemplifies its name, which translates into "green stick" in Spanish. As the tree matures, the bark darkens and becomes very woody with pits and deep ruts. This is the first of the palo verde species to bloom in the spring. There is nothing more striking than looking out into the desert at its intense, bright yellow flowers in April or May. After blooming, numerous, flat, greenish tan, three-inch seedpods appear on the tree. The tree also has some thorns. It provides a home for wildlife and birds that feed on the flowers and seeds. It is hardy to fifteen degrees Fahrenheit, likes well-draining, sandy soil, and

Parkinsonia florida
Blue Palo Verde in bloom

full sun with plenty of reflected heat. The blue palo verde is drought tolerant but prefers supplemental irrigation a few times per month during the hot, dry season. While it can survive in a lawn area, it tends to have a shorter lifespan. Prune annually to remove dead branches and possible mistletoe infestations. This stately tree also needs pod and flower cleanup after blooming. It is susceptible to an insect called the palo verde root borer (Derobrachus geminatus) which feeds on the roots of distressed trees. After a few years of feeding on one tree, the insect departs, leaving exit holes visible around the roots of the tree. Use it in the hottest, driest situations as a single specimen, in large groupings and groves, or as a shade tree on an open patio or backyard play area. It can be planted in parking lots, along fairways in golf courses, throughout subdivisions, or as a transitional tree from landscaped areas into the natural desert. It is native to the Sonoran Desert in Arizona and also grows naturally in Baja California and into Northern Sinaloa, Mexico, from sea level up to 4,000 feet in dry washes and on dry, hot floodplains.

Parkinsonia florida
Blue Palo Verde

47

Parkinsonia microphylla

Foothills or Little Leaf Palo Verde
Medium-sized tree

Parkinsonia microphylla
Foothills Palo Verde in bloom

The deciduous palo verde is the smallest of all the Parkinsonias and one of the slowest growing, reaching twelve to twenty feet tall and wide. It has many crossing branches that create a gnarled appearance and produces small leaflets that are yellowish green and have a sharp, rigid spine at their ends. Its Latin name, *microphylla*, means tiny leaf. The tree blossoms in April or May with bright yellow blooms that last a long time. After blooming, one-and-a-half- to three-inch long, green seedpods appear and turn dark tan as they mature. The pods are edible and wildlife feed on the seeds contained inside as well as the flowers. Its trunk is brownish green and darkens with age. If exposed to severe frost or drought, the plant immediately responds by dropping its leaflets. It is hardy to fifteen to seventeen degrees Fahrenheit, is drought resistant, and survives on very little water. However, like most other desert natives, it grows faster with supplemental irrigation. The tree is susceptible to mistletoe infestations and the palo verde root borer. It grows in extremely hot locations with full sun and reflected heat. Allow this palo verde species to take on a natural rugged appearance. Prune only to shape the canopy, remove mistletoe, and keep the multiple trunk structure. While the flowers and seedpods may create seasonal litter, this tree is a great choice to use as a specimen or perimeter plant in desert landscape situations. Use this species in entry courtyards, on small patios, or in areas where limited space and irrigation is available. It lives a long time in its native habitat, growing along rocky slopes, mesas, washes, and foothills throughout Southeastern Arizona, Southeastern California, Baja California, Sinaloa, and Sonora, Mexico, where it grows at elevations below 4,000 feet. This tree is found growing naturally along rocky slopes, mesas, and washes, and in the desert foothills.

Parkinsonia microphylla
Foothills or Little Leaf Palo Verde

*Parkinsonia praecox

Palo Brea
Medium- to large-sized tree

Parkinsonia praecox
Palo Brea

The semideciduous tree grows twenty to thirty feet tall with a spread of twenty to forty feet, producing an umbrella-like canopy. It adds sculptural beauty with its greenish blue leaves and smooth, structural green trunk. Palo brea produces brilliant yellow blossoms in abundance in spring and then intermittently throughout the summer and fall. After blooming, long, flat, papery, tan seedpods hang from the tree. While hardy to fifteen to twenty degrees Fahrenheit, the species could suffer some tip damage in a cold winter. It is more sensitive to frost than the other palo verdes; however, it is a fast grower and recovers quickly in the spring. It grows with moderate to light irrigation and prefers well-draining soils, full sun, and reflected heat. Palo brea needs some pruning to maintain its form and character but be cautious of its spiny branches when pruning. Avoid planting it near walkways or pedestrian traffic. The branching habit and silhouette of this tree makes it a good accent, streetscape, or median tree. It can also be used as a landscape specimen tree or focal point at the entry of a residential or commercial setting. Its distinctive quality with its smooth green trunk and interwoven branches makes this an attractive tree and great landscape plant. It grows natively on desert plains and mesas at elevations up to 2,500 feet in Central Sonora, Mexico and Baja California. It is also found growing in Peru, Venezuela, and Ecuador.

Parkinsonia praecox
Palo Brea

*Parkinsonia x 'Desert Museum'

Desert Museum Palo Verde
Medium- to large-sized tree

This semideciduous, "thornless" tree has characteristics of the foothills, blue, and Mexican palo verde. It is quite similar to the other Parkinsonia species, growing rapidly to heights of twenty to twenty-five feet with an equal spread. This tree has small, bright green foliage and an attractive,

Parkinsonia x 'Desert Museum'
Desert Museum Palo Verde

Parkinsonia x 'Desert Museum'
Desert Museum Palo Verde

Parkinsonia x 'Desert Museum'
Desert Museum Palo Verde

smooth, green bark. Brilliant masses of yellow blossoms appear in the spring and again intermittently into the summer, if given extra water. The flower blossoms on this species of palo verde are larger than those of the parent trees. This hybrid produces all of the excellent traits of the other palo verde trees. It is hardy to about fifteen degrees Fahrenheit or lower, produces lightly filtered shade and is a great tree for attracting birds and butterflies. This species likes full sun and plenty of reflected heat, is drought resistant, but needs regular irrigation, particularly through the first few years of growth. Do not overwater because it could grow too fast, become top-heavy, and the roots may not be able to support the tree. Protect the lower young bark from javelina, rabbits, or deer. This fast-growing tree produces some litter and debris. Prune to enhance its form and keep its upright appearance as a magnificent shade or specimen tree in parking lots, on school playgrounds, in commercial and home landscapes. Use this tree to cast light shade on patios and porches. It was hybridized at the Arizona Sonora Desert Museum in Tucson and is a genetic cross between Parkinsonia microphylla, Parkinsonia florida, and Parkinsonia aculeata.

Phanera purpurea and Phanera variegata

Purple and White Orchid Trees
medium-sized tree

Phanera purpurea
Purple Orchid Tree

The orchid tree is deciduous to semideciduous, depending on the climate. It reaches heights of twenty to thirty feet and spreads twelve to fifteen feet, depending on the species. This exotic tree develops single or multiple trunks and green, butterfly-shaped, papery foliage. In late winter through early spring, an abundance of two- to three-inch, orchid-shaped, fragrant blossoms appear in purple, pink, magenta, or white and attract butterflies and hummingbirds. It blooms over a long period. The flower variations are visible on the inside of the flower petals. This tree produces brown seedpods of six to eight inches. The seeds and plant parts are poisonous if ingested, and handling of the plant may cause skin irritation. The orchid tree grows best in full sun to partial shade in well-draining, acidic soil. It has average water needs and does not like to be overwatered, especially during the winter months. This tree is cold hardy to the mid-twenties Fahrenheit but defoliates when temperatures drop in the low thirties. It is not uncommon for the species to drop leaves in Tucson and other

Phanera variegata
White Orchid Tree

Phanera variegata foliage
White Orchid Tree

lower elevations after a frost. While the foliage will regenerate, it is best to plant it in protected microclimates of the landscape. Fertilize this plant at least once a year with a slow-release fertilizer. Since the species is susceptible to iron deficiency, also treat with iron chelate fertilizer as needed to prevent iron chlorosis. Use this exceptional tree for oriental, tropical and sub-tropical effects in mediums, on patios, porches and smaller protected areas for its amazing flower show. The tree is native to the tropics and subtropics in India and China.

Pinus canariensis
Canary Island Pine
Large-sized tree

Pinus canariensis
Canary Island Pine

This vertical pine with a pyramidal shape grows fast to heights of fifty to eighty feet and thirty feet wide in moist climates. It has silky, ten- to twelve-inch, weeping needles in bundles of three that are bluish green when young, turning a deeper green when mature. The bark is grayish brown with a reddish tint and very scaly. After taking a year to mature, it produces a brown, glossy, six- to nine-inch cone in the spring. This aromatic pine likes full sun with plenty of reflected heat and is hardy to twenty degrees Fahrenheit. It is drought resistant but needs supplemental irrigation during the hot, dry summer. Young trees require even more frequent irrigation. While it prefers sandy soils, the tree is tolerant of most soil conditions if they are well draining. It is low maintenance, but needles drop in the spring and need raking. Use this attractive pine as a tall skyline tree in large, open areas like parks. It can also be used for its strong visual and vertical effects up against a tall building. Canary island pine works well in some tropical areas around large lakes or ponds as a background plant. Use this plant as an ornamental, large screen, or windbreak tree. The tree is native to the western, outer Canary Islands in the Atlantic Ocean, where it grows in rocky and sandy soils. This pine is also the tallest tree growing in the Canary Islands. The wood is very durable and strong and the heartwood of this tree is very aromatic.

Pinus eldarica

Mondell Pine, Afghan Pine
Large-sized tree

Mondell pine is a tall, thin evergreen that grows thirty to fifty feet tall with a spread of fifteen to twenty feet and has become popularized as a Christmas tree. It has many dense branches that grow in an upright pattern producing a tall, central leader without thorns. It grows quickly, producing aromatic, irregularly twisted needles that are five to six inches long in bundles of two or three, along with inconspicuous yellow flowers in spring. Blooms are followed by oval cones about one to three inches that attract squirrels and other small rodents. Male cones are yellow, and female cones are green when young, turning brown at maturity. The twigs and foliage drop often and branches may break since the wood is weak. The bark is silvery gray, turning darker and more deeply furrowed with age. It grows in full sun with reflected heat, preferring most soils as long as they are well draining. This pine is also drought resistant but grows faster with supplemental, deep irrigation since it has a deep, invading root system. It prefers extra irrigation during the hot, dry season. As the plant matures, it becomes more cold tolerant and is hardy to five degrees Fahrenheit. Mondell pine is also mildly susceptible to Texas root rot. Use it in groups as a screen or windbreak or as a single specimen for shade for a woodsy effect to hide an unsightly area or up against a wall or building. This pine is native to Afghanistan, Pakistan, and Southern Russia.

Pinus eldarica
Mondell Pine, Afghan Pine

Pinus halepensis

Aleppo Pine
Large-sized tree

The fast-growing evergreen reaches thirty to fifty feet tall and thirty feet wide. It is a lush, massive pine able to can grow ten feet in five years. It appears billowy with slender, light green needles that are two to four inches long and appear in pairs. After maturity, in the fall, the tree produces an abundance of three-inch long, oval cones. Its bark is brownish gray with small scales. The Aleppo pine can grow in full sun with plenty of reflected heat. It will take our hot dry summers and extreme heat. This pine is also quite drought resistant and hardy to fifteen degrees or less. It is highly susceptible to a condition known as Aleppo pine blight. This is a serious disease that attacks the tree in wintertime when there are extreme temperature changes from daytime to nighttime. The blight is more severe in drought

Pinus halepensis
Aleppo Pine

*Pistacia chinensis

Chinese Pistache
Large-sized tree

The deciduous shade tree grows at a moderate rate of thirty-five to forty feet tall and twenty-five to thirty-five feet wide, producing a rounded canopy and attractive branching pattern. Lower branches droop toward the ground at maturity, creating a beautiful, dense crown. In poorly draining soils with bad growing conditions, the tree may only reach about twenty-five feet in height. It produces two-inch, dark green, pointed leaves that turn a brilliant orange and then scarlet before shedding. The flowers are red and attractive, and both the seeds and young shoots of the pistache are also edible. This tree is susceptible to Texas root rot and should not be used in areas where the fungus is present. Double-stake newly planted trees to help them develop a thick trunk. Chinese pistache requires pruning to develop a strong growth

conditions, causing the needles to turn gray and dry up and twigs and branches to die. To reduce blight conditions, irrigate deeply and infrequently during the dry months and fertilize with a nitrogen fertilizer in the spring. Use this skyline plant in wide-open spaces like a park or large yard. It can also be used as a screen, windbreak, or shade tree. Aleppo pine is a great choice to use in areas for its large silhouette and skyline appearance. It is native to the Mediterranean, growing at lower elevations from Morocco and Spain and in parts of France, Croatia, and Italy, and east to Greece and Libya.

Pistacia chinensis
Chinese Pistache in fall color

Pistacia chinensis
Chinese Pistache

structure. This tree will tolerate most soils but prefers sandy, clay, or rich loamy soils that are well draining. It will grow well in full sun with plenty of reflected heat and does not do well in the shade. The Chinese pistache is very hardy to below freezing temperatures and needs periodic irrigation during its growing season. Once it is established, it is very drought resistant. This tree is very low maintenance except for leaf drop in the winter. Use the Chinese pistache for its amazing dense shade or as a freestanding ornamental. It is a great choice to use for its showy fall color. This specimen can be used as a street, park, or lawn tree. It also works well in parking lots and large commercial locations. The Chinese pistache is a good choice for large spaces where it has ample room to grow. It is native to East Asia in the Philippines and Southern China, where it grows along riversides and in cultivated areas in the Himalayas. In the United States, it has been naturalized in Texas.

*Pistacia lentiscus

Evergreen Pistache, Mastic
Medium-sized tree

This dense evergreen makes an excellent screen, growing twenty to twenty-five feet high and wide. It can be trained as a single or multistem tree or a large hedge. Its small, leathery leaves are olive green and have three to five pairs of leaflets. It produces inconspicuous flowers in the spring followed by black or red seeds. Its attractive stems are reddish in color when young, turning gray as they mature. The mastic is hardy into the mid teens with leaf and stem damage at lower temperatures. This plant loves full sun but can take some partial shade. It is drought resistant, but weekly irrigation accelerates its growth rate. It prefers well-draining soil, is low maintenance and requires little pruning. It is also a disease- and insect-resistant tree. The evergreen pistache was given its name because it produces a sweet-flavored resin called mastic, which comes from the bark of the trunk and softens when chewed. The resin is used as a breath freshener and to flavor puddings and cakes. Use it in the landscape as a hedge, windbreak, screen, or patio tree, or around pools and water features. It can also be used in

Pistacia lentiscus
Evergreen Pistache, Mastic

Pistacia lentiscus
Evergreen Pistache, Mastic

areas as a lush transitional plant between low-water-use and oasis-type landscapes. The tree is native to Mediterranean regions such as Spain, France, Portugal, Greece, Turkey, and Africa, growing on dry hillsides usually by the coast.

Platanus wrightii
Fall Color on Trees

Platanus wrightii

Arizona Sycamore
Large-sized tree

Arizona sycamore is a stately deciduous tree that grows to heights of fifty to sixty feet or more with an equal spread. This majestic specimen has an open and spreading crown with beautiful, arching, white limbs. In its natural habitat, one limb is often extended over the water, and it is valuable for erosion control along streams and banks. The foliage is glossy green and lobed with deep margins and turns a brilliant yellow in late fall before dropping all of its leaves. This tree produces large, glossy green foliage with fuzzy undersides and deep margins. Its inconspicuous, balled flowers with male and female blossoms are borne on the same tree. In the fall, large, round, tan seed balls appear and the individual

seeds disperse with the wind. The Arizona sycamore has distinctive, whitish brown bark that peels, revealing interesting colors on the trunk. Once the tree matures, the bark becomes thicker and grayish brown with deep furrows. This tree likes full sun, reflected heat, and well-draining soil. It needs a good amount of irrigation, especially during the hot, dry season. Arizona

Platanus wrightii
Arizona Sycamore

Platanus wrightii
Arizona Sycamore

Populus fremontii
Fremont Cottonwood
Large-sized tree

sycamore is susceptible to iron chlorosis and should be deeply fertilized in spring. It is hardy to below freezing temperatures. Even though the Arizona sycamore is deciduous, it holds on to its dry leaves for a long time in the winter before the foliage finally drops to the ground. This tree requires some maintenance when the leaves fall as well as corrective pruning to develop it into a statuesque giant. Woodpeckers and other birds make their homes in hollow trunks of old, decaying trees. Use it for dense shade in large, open areas such as parks and large commercial settings. This moderate- to slow-growing riparian plant grows natively along streams and riverbeds in Arizona and New Mexico and into Mexico. It is also a native of Southern Europe, Northern Africa, and Western Asia at elevations up to 5,000 feet.

Cottonwood is a fast-growing, riparian, deciduous tree that grows to seventy-five feet tall with a spread of thirty feet or more. It derives its name from the female trees, which produce a cottony seed in spring that can be very messy. In nature, it grows faster with an underground water source. This stately tree is known for its wide, open crown and massive trunk that reaches four feet in diameter at its base. In spring, it produces rich, dark green, glossy foliage that is two to four inches long with triangular, serrated edges and a long, flattened leaf stalk. The twigs are yellowish brown in color and turn a deep golden yellow before dropping to the ground in late fall or early winter. Its bark is a light, grayish brown and becomes deeply furrowed with age. The trees are dioecious with male and female catkins forming on different plants. The cottonwood likes full sun, reflected heat, and any soil type. It prefers a well-draining, sandy to clay loam with a good amount of organic matter and a great deal of moisture. This tree is hardy to ten degrees

Populus fremontii
Fremont Cottonwood

Populus fremontii
Fremont Cottonwood

Fahrenheit. Native Americans used the bark and leaves of the cottonwood to relieve swelling, treat wounds and broken limbs, and cure headaches. The twigs were used for basket weaving and the wood was used for tools and bowls. Today, the cottonwood is planted for stream bank protection, wildlife shelter, and food. It is also used as shade for livestock and to build recreation facilities. In Southwest desert landscapes, use this massive specimen as a large shade tree, striking ornamental, or windbreak. It can also be used in large areas such as parks and wide-open spaces. Do not plant it in a residential situation, since its large roots can invade septic systems and grow into power lines. The tree is native to streams, rivers, creeks, washes, and canyons in the Western United States up to 6,000 feet. It is endemic to parts of Arizona, New Mexico, California, Texas, Colorado, and Utah.

*Prosopis chilensis
Chilean Mesquite
Large-sized tree

The semideciduous tree has become popularized over the years and is one of the most widely used trees in Southwest landscapes. It grows thirty feet tall and wide with dark, rich bark that is rough and turns blacker with age. Chilean mesquite is a semideciduous tree with lush green, narrow leaflets. In late spring, the tree will produce pale yellow catkinlike flowers in spikes. In

Populus fremontii
Fremont Cottonwood

Prosopis chilensis
Chilean Mesquite

Prosopis chilensis
Chilean Mesquite

*Prosopis glandulosa

Honey Mesquite, Texas Mesquite
Large-sized tree

early summer, brown seedpods mature and shed to the ground. Some varieties are thornless. Most of these trees are hybrids and may have a wide variation of thorns and growth characteristics. The tree can have single or multiple trunks and is a wonderful shade specimen. It is hardy to about fifteen degrees Fahrenheit. This fast-growing tree requires full sun and reflected heat and will tolerate any soil type. It is drought tolerant but grows at a quicker rate with supplemental irrigation. After trees have matured, taper off their irrigation to encourage the development of a deep root system. Prune at least once per year to encourage a strong canopy, prevent breakage of limbs, and establish the strong root system needed for young trees to properly mature. Mature trees will usually need to have mistletoe pruned from their branches as least every six months. Proper staking is also helpful on young trees, and an annual feeding of ammonium sulfate helps induce new growth. Use it in areas for revegetation, as a street or shade tree, or in a park setting. This tree can also be used as a large screen, windbreak, or barrier planting that can be easily incorporated into formal and traditional situations. The tree is a native to Bolivia, Central Chile, Peru, and Northwestern Argentina.

Honey mesquite is a willowlike, deciduous tree with an open, spreading crown and low growing, twisted branches. It reaches heights of thirty-five feet with a thirty- to forty-foot spread. The tree has a delicate leaf canopy and gray, sculptural, single or multiple trunks, and produces a weeping structure with willowy, deep green foliage. It likes full sun and reflected heat and is hardy to ten degrees Fahrenheit or lower. The honey mesquite grows in a variety of soils but prefers them to be well draining. It loses all its leaves in winter and new foliage sprouts in early spring. Creamy white, slightly fragrant blossoms appear in the spring followed by long, thin, tan seedpods in summer. The blossoms contain a great deal of nectar and are pollinated by bees. When the tree is about three years old, it begins to produce seeds, which are encased within a fruit that is eaten and then dispersed by deer, antelopes,

Prosopis glandulosa
Honey Mesquite

Prosopis glandulosa
Honey Mesquite Leaflets

*Prosopis velutina
Velvet Mesquite
Large-sized tree

javelina, squirrels, quail, and turkeys. Seedpods from the honey mesquite are still used today in Mexico for food and to make a beverage. This tree is considered an important food source since it bears fruit even during extreme drought situations. The structural branches of the mesquite produce tiny thorns, but there are some thornless varieties available. It is drought tolerant, but grows quicker with supplemental irrigation. Prune during the dormant season and stake young trees as needed to develop a sturdy trunk. Use it as a shade or specimen tree in residential areas, commercial locations, or park settings where it can spread out since it has a natural, irregular growth pattern. It can also be used as a shrub or low growing tree for screening or as a windbreak. Also, consider creating a grove of three or more trees to attract wildlife. The tree grows natively along stream banks, plains, and foothills and in areas where groundwater is available in Southwestern Arizona, Southern California, and Northern Mexico, east to Central Texas, and north to Kansas and Oklahoma.

This mesquite is a magnificent, deciduous, multitrunk tree with a wide, spreading crown that grows twenty to forty feet tall with a spread of fifteen to twenty-five feet. Mature trees have brownish black, shaggy bark, and in spring through fall, produce feathery, green foliage that creates filtered shade. In mild winters, the tree may hold some of its foliage, producing year-round shade. This native mesquite can be distinguished from the other species by the short, dense hairs that cover the entire tree, including its seedpods and leaves. This is the trait that has helped to give this plant the common name of velvet mesquite. In late spring through early summer, this species produces cream-colored catkins that are long and hang from the tree. In late summer, dark tan seedpods form. The seedpods are very sweet and were

Prosopis velutina
Velvet Mesquite

60

used by Native Americans for food and other resources. Today, these trees still serve as a home to wildlife and to provide shade to understory plants and creatures living in the Southwest desert. The native mesquite likes full sun, reflected heat, and well-draining soils and is hardy to five degrees Fahrenheit. It is also drought resistant and survives in nature on natural rainfall. In the landscape, it benefits from deep, monthly soakings to form a solid root system and ensure longevity. Periodically prune this tree to reinforce its structure and form. Watch out for infestations of the mesquite girdler in late summer through early fall. Treat as necessary for control of this insect. Use it as an individual specimen, shade, or desert accent on golf courses, in large landscapes, or in groupings. It is native to washes, valleys, and desert plains throughout Central and Southern Arizona, Southern California, and Southern New Mexico at elevations of 1,000 to 4,000 feet. It is also found growing in Mexico along Baja California and into North and Central Sonora.

Prunus caroliniana
Carolina Cherry Tree

Prunus caroliniana

Carolina Cherry Laurel
Medium- to large-sized tree

The hardy evergreen grows in a columnar pattern to heights of twenty to forty feet with a twenty-five-foot spread. It has glossy leaves that are rich, textured, dark green. The upper surface of the leaf is dark green and shiny, and the lower surface is duller and lighter in color. Fragrant, creamy white blooms appear in early spring and are followed by fleshy, black fruits that are toxic to humans but a great treat for birds. The flowers attract birds, bees, and butterflies. This tree requires pruning to enable its development into an upright form with a central trunk. Carolina cherry laurel has been a longtime garden specimen in European gardens. This fast-growing tree likes full sun exposure but tolerates some shade. It prefers an acidic, well-draining, loamy soil and can become chlorotic in alkaline soils. While somewhat drought resistant, it prefers supplemental irrigation. Carolina cherry laurel is hardy to about ten degrees Fahrenheit. If it develops chlorotic leaves, treat with an iron chelate fertilizer. Plant it in the landscape as a specimen tree or use it to create a bird or butterfly habitat. Use it in parking lots, near decks and patios, or as a screen or large hedge or ornamental shrub, or as a small tree. Its rich green foliage makes it a nice contrast next to other vegetation or against a pale house or building. It grows natively in rich, moist soils found in woody areas, open fields, and thickets from North Carolina to Florida and into Louisiana and Texas.

*Prunus cerasifera

Purple Leaf Plum
Small- to medium-sized tree

Prunus cerasifera
Purple Leaf Plum

The attractive, deciduous tree has an upright, spreading habit with a rounded crown and is a moderate- to fast-grower reaching fifteen to twenty-five feet tall and about fifteen to twenty feet wide. In spring, beautiful cranberry-burgundy foliage emerges with a medium textured, oval leaf arrangement. By fall, the foliage matures to greenish bronze. It produces pinkish white springtime blossoms that make a showy appearance before the leaves emerge. After blooming, one-inch purple fruits appear and attract birds and squirrels. The fruit can be used to make an edible jam preserve. The tree enjoys full sun and well-draining soils that are slightly alkaline and does not do well with compacted soils. It also prefers regular irrigation and is hardy to zero degrees. Purple leaf plum requires little pruning to develop a strong structure. Apply applications of ammonium phosphate fertilizer in early spring to encourage flowering and fruiting. The tree is highly susceptible to Texas root rot and is usually short-lived. Two popular varieties are "Thundercloud" and "Atropurpurea." Use it as a specimen or small shade tree near a deck or patio or in oriental gardens where its showy foliage, attractive, dark bark and spring flowers provide great contrast against other landscape plants. The species originated in Central and Eastern Europe, Southeast Asia, and Central Asia.

Prunus cerasifera
Purple Leaf Plum in spring bloom.

Prunus persica 'Bonanza'

Dwarf Bonanza Peach
Small-sized tree

The dwarf peach is a deciduous tree that is adaptable to small, residential gardens, growing seven feet tall with a three- to four-foot spread. It offers a mounded form with multiple trunks and showy, pinkish white blossoms in early spring followed by sweet, edible fruit. About three or four years after planting, the tree produces fruit. The peaches have orangey red skin and a sweet yellow flesh. The tree takes another eight years before it reaches peak fruit productivity. Bonanza peach needs full sun, well-draining, acidic soils,

Prunus persica 'Bonanza'
Bonanza Peach

Prunus persica 'Bonanza'
Bonanza Fruit

Prunus persica 'Bonanza'
Dwarf Bonanza Peach

and regular irrigation. This plant also prefers lots of heat and some humidity and is hardy to fifteen degrees Fahrenheit. To boost fruit and flower production, apply ammonium phosphate fertilizer in early spring. The tree also benefits from corrective pruning for fruit production to maintain its size and encourage new growth. Cover trees with a bird netting to protect newly emerging fruit from birds. It is easy to grow and care for because of its dwarf size. Plant it on the south or west side of your property directly in the landscape or in a container or whiskey barrel for a whimsical look. Use it as a single specimen planting in oriental gardens or with low-growing shrubbery and perennial winter color plants. Check local nurseries for the best varieties available. The plant originated in East Asia and China.

*Pyrus kawakamii
Evergreen Pear
Medium-sized tree

This semi-evergreen has an upright, rounded appearance and produces single or multiple trunks with drooping branches. It grows moderately from fifteen to thirty feet with a ten- to fifteen-foot spread. This tree has dark green, glossy, oval-shaped leaves with pointed tips and

Pyrus kawakamii
Evergreen Pear

63

Pyrus kawakamii
Evergreen Pear

*Quercus buckleyi

Texas Red Oak
Medium- to large-sized tree

Texas red oak is a deciduous, single or multitrunk tree with dense, spreading branches. It grows moderately from thirty to fifty feet in height and has interesting dark grayish black bark with furrowed ridges on the lower trunk and older branches. The twigs are slender and grayish brown, and the leaves are dark green and divided into several lobes that end in bristlelike, sharp teeth. The leaf is shiny green above and a paler green below. The foliage turns brilliant shades of red and orange in the fall. The male plant produces one- to three-inch, reddish catkin blooms, and the female plant produces flowers at the end the stem in the spring.

a smooth texture. In late December and January, the foliage turns a beautiful orange-red. The leaves drop off the tree and it becomes deciduous for a short time. It is one of the first trees to bloom in the early spring—a reminder that spring has arrived in the desert. In mid-February, the tree produces an amazing display of brilliant white, fragrant blossoms in one-inch clusters that attract birds, butterflies, and bees. After flowering, a small, round, tan, inedible fruit forms. This showy tree prefers regular irrigation but does not like to be overwatered. It also likes full sun and sandy or clay well-draining soil and is hardy to about fifteen to twenty degrees Fahrenheit. Apply ammonium phosphate fertilizer in the spring and iron chelate if the tree shows signs of iron deficiency. It is susceptible to Texas root rot and fire blight, which can disfigure and kill the tree. Stake and shape it until the tree is self-supporting. Overpruning may inhibit flower production. Use it as an ornamental tree against a house foundation, in patios, in courtyards, or as a single specimen for oriental, ornamental, or tropical effects. The evergreen pear is native to China, Japan, and Taiwan.

Quercus buckleyi
Texas Red Oak

Quercus buckleyi
Texas Red Oak

Quercus ilex
Holly Oak

The fruit is an egg-shaped acorn that appears in fall, is a valuable food source for wildlife, though they take about two years to mature. The leaves and acorns can be toxic to humans. The tree does well in low-lying, colder areas of the Southwest desert and is quite hardy. It likes full sun with reflected heat and is drought resistant. Irrigate it infrequently during the cooler months and give it supplemental irrigation during the hot weather. It needs light pruning when young and requires some raking of fallen leaves in late fall. Use for woodsy effects and crimson red fall color for parks, city streets, parking lot islands, and road-sides. In its native habitat, the tree grows in alka-line limestone, sand, or gravelly soils of North central to Central Texas, and along the Pecos River. It was named after Samuel B. Buckley, a Texas botanist and geologist.

is dense, leathery, and green with serrated or smooth edges. Its bark is blackish gray and can be smooth or scaly. The undersides of the leaves are yellow and have a dense covering of fine hairs. The tree produces an edible acorn fruit that is enclosed in a cap. This oak prefers sun with reflected heat but also does well in partial shade. It is extremely drought resistant but likes deep, supplemental irrigation and matures faster with

Quercus ilex

Holly Oak, Holm Oak
Large-sized tree

Quercus ilex
Holly Oak

Holly oak is a slow-growing evergreen tree that reaches heights of thirty feet tall and wide, pro-ducing a dense canopy, pyramidal shape, and rounded crown with age. The hollylike foliage

water. Holly oak is hardy to twenty-five degrees Fahrenheit and does not like to be exposed to cold temperatures for a long time. Use along a street or median or as a windbreak or specimen tree. This plant can also be used in seaside gardens and will withstand salty air and soil. Use this attractive tree in parking lots, parks, and golf courses, and against a tall building. The holly oak can be heavily sheared and trained as a hedge or used as a screening plant. This long-lived specimen is native to mixed forests or grows in solitary stands at low to medium elevations throughout Southern Europe and Northwest Africa and has been naturalized in the Mediterranean.

Quercus polymorpha
Mexican White Oak
Medium- to large-sized tree

Quercus polymorpha
Mexican White Oak

The showy, semi-evergreen Mexican white oak grows quickly in an upright pattern when young to thirty to forty feet and spreads twenty to thirty feet. It has a broad crown and is usually a single-trunked tree. Mexican white oak also has dense branches, brown, scaly bark, and leathery leaves that range from light green to blue green. This tree produces two different types of acorns on the same tree. One is brown and narrow, the other is brilliant purple and larger. It is a hardy tree to ten degrees Fahrenheit but also thrives in hundred-degree temperatures. The foliage drops when temperatures hit the mid teens. New foliage emerges in the spring with pinkish red leaves and an inconspicuous flower. The tree is drought tolerant but likes supplemental irrigation and is a fast grower. It handles alkaline soils as long as they are well draining and prefers sun. It also offers resistance to pests and diseases that affect other oak species. Use with a mix of pine trees for an interesting woodsy effect or as a screen to block freeway noise, views, or the wind. This tree is native to the canyons of Western Texas and is widespread in parts of Mexico and Guatemala.

Quercus polymorpha
Mexican White Oak

Quercus virginiana

Southern Live Oak
Medium- to large-sized tree

This majestic evergreen grows forty to fifty feet tall and almost as wide with a broad, rounded canopy, horizontal branches, and thick, leathery, green leaves. During cold winters, the tree defoliates and new green leaves emerge in the spring. Its bark is dark and deeply furrowed at maturity. Southern live oak produces inconspicuous, tan, catkinlike flowers in the spring that are typical of most oak trees. After flowering, brownish black acorns appear in abundance, which are sweet and edible, and are eaten by birds and other animals. It takes full to partial shade, likes moist, well-draining, sandy soil, and tolerates drought conditions when established. It needs supplemental irrigation during the hot, dry season. This fast grower is long-lived and hardy to fifteen degrees. It is excellent to use for fuel or firewood. The tree needs minor maintenance and some pruning to remove occasional suckers at the base of the tree. Use it as a shade or specimen tree on golf courses, in front of large-scale buildings,

Quercus virginiana
Southern Live Oak

along streets, around parking lots, and in parks as a screen, or planted in masses in wide-open spaces. Southern live oak is the designated state tree of Georgia. It is native to scrub lands and coastal and inland wetlands throughout Virginia. This tree also grows natively in parts of Florida, Texas, and southeastern portions of the United States. It can also be found in isolated mountain areas of Northeastern Mexico.

Quercus virginiana
Southern Live Oak

Rhus lancea

African Sumac
Large-sized tree

The African sumac is an evergreen shade tree with a dense canopy and grows between fifteen and thirty feet tall with an equal spread. The foliage is long, willowy, and shiny green on the outside leaf with a pale green underneath. This tree is dioecious with male and female parts on separate plants. There are inconspicuous greenish white flower clusters that produce a light fragrance in late winter or early spring. On the female tree, tiny, round fruit appears and attracts birds and wildlife. The tree has an attractive gray-black trunk that provides beautiful contrast to its green foliage. It grows best in full sun with reflected heat and also tolerates some shade. African sumac is drought tolerant when established but likes additional irrigation during the hot, dry season. It prefers well-draining soils and may become chlorotic if planted in poorly draining soils. This tree is hardy into the low twenties and the foliage can be damaged when temperatures drop to nineteen degrees Fahrenheit or lower. Prune it to keep the basal suckers from growing during the summer monsoon season and anticipate some seed and leaf debris. This tree is susceptible to Texas root rot and the flower pollen can be an allergen. Use the African sumac as a shade or large screening tree in residential or commercial landscapes. This is a good tree choice for parks, golf courses, and hot locations in the landscape. The African sumac is native to South Africa, growing in temperate regions.

Schinus molle

California Pepper Tree
Large-sized tree

The California pepper tree is a tall, fast-growing evergreen that reaches heights of forty feet or more with an equal spread. It can be a single or multitrunk tree, has a magnificent pendulous, weeping habit and produces a great deal of shade. Its trunk is gray when young but sheds with age to reveal interesting, reddish bark. The California

Rhus lancea
African Sumac

Schinus molle
California Pepper Tree, up close

Schinus molle

California Pepper

pepper tree likes full sun with reflected heat and prefers well-draining soils. It is drought resistant when established but does well with regular irrigation to keep its ornamental appearance. Do not overwater this tree. It is hardy to twenty to twenty-five degrees Fahrenheit. In spring, it produces attractive, round, red seeds that drop to the ground and are toxic and can be a skin irritant to some people. Some maintenance is involved with this species. It needs to be properly pruned to maintain its form when young and produces leaf and twig drop in strong winds, requiring debris to be raked from the ground. Inspect trees for damaged branches after a high wind. The tree is also susceptible to Texas root rot. Do not plant it too close to sidewalks, patios, or driveways, as its shallow root system may lift pavement. Even with its issues, this majestic tree is a great choice to use in the landscape. Use it as a large specimen or shade tree to create a lush, tropical appearance in wide-open areas like parks. It is a native of the Andean Desert in Peru as well as northern areas of South America but has become naturalized in Mexico and Southern California.

Senegalia berlandieri

Guajillo
Medium-sized tree

The guajillo reaches heights of nine to fifteen feet and at maturity is almost as wide. It forms multiple trunks with a shrublike appearance, or it can be trained into a small patio tree. This semi-evergreen produces lush, lacy, green, fernlike foliage with a few scattered thorns along its stems and bark. White or creamy, ball-like, fragrant flowers appear in spring and attract birds, butterflies, and bees. In Phoenix, Yuma, and other warm microclimates, it may retain its wispy foliage and stays somewhat semi-evergreen. After the tree flowers, long, broad, brown seedpods appear which split and drop seed. These pods give the tree an attractive appearance. The guajillo looks similar to Lysiloma watsonii but tolerates lower temperatures to about twelve degrees Fahrenheit. It is a slow- to medium-speed grower that prefers well-draining soil, sunny locations, reflected heat, and low to moderate water. This tree is a good

Senegalia berlandieri

Guajillo

Senegalia berlandieri
Guajillo

choice when combined with other natives such as mesquite, palo brea, or California rosewood as a lush accent at the entrance of a property or in a native plant garden. Its delicate foliage creates a beautiful, tropical appearance, making it perfect for screenings or planted as a backdrop to a smaller plant. The species contains alkaloids that can cause toxic reactions in animals. *Guajillo* means foolish or funny in Spanish. The plant was given this name because in nature, it grows in funny or unusual places. The tree is native to the Rio Grande plains in Texas, New Mexico, Queretaro, Hidalgo, and Veracruz, Mexico.

*Ulmus parvifolia

Chinese Elm
Large-sized tree

This fast-growing shade tree grows thirty to forty feet tall with an equal spread and develops a broad, vaselike shape with a pendulous, weeping branch habit. It is semideciduous, losing its leaves in late December in the Southwest desert, but retaining its foliage in milder climates. The leaves are glossy, delicate, and dark green with

Ulmus parvifolia
Chinese Elm

an alternating leaf arrangement. The foliage turns a yellowish brown before falling from the tree in cold weather. It has inconspicuous flowers in late summer followed by decorative green fruit. The Chinese elm has beautiful grayish green, mottled bark that sheds with age, displaying varying colors. It likes full sun and is adaptable to most soil types as long as they are well draining. This tree is drought tolerant but likes deep irrigation during our hot, dry weather. Chinese elm is hardy to about twenty degrees Fahrenheit. The tree requires minor pruning for clearance beneath its canopy and to develop a strong structure. It also needs light maintenance to rake up leaf drop in the winter. Prune and remove suckers that may resprout in other parts of the landscape. Use it as a single or multiple-trunk tree and give it plenty of water for fast growth. It has many traits that make it a great landscape tree, producing a dense canopy of foliage that creates a graceful appearance. Use it as a specimen, residential shade, or street tree, in parking lots, or in a large patio

Ulmus parvifolia
Chinese Elm

area. It is a great reclamation plant or transition plant between the lush landscape and the desert. Chinese elm is native to China, Korea, and Japan.

Vachellia farnesiana

Sweet Acacia
Large-sized tree

Sweet acacia grows twenty to thirty feet tall as an evergreen or semideciduous tree, depending upon winter temperatures. This adaptable tree develops single or multiple trunks with its symmetrical and large, open canopy. Its dark brown trunk is smooth when young, becoming more furrowed at maturity. The limbs and slender twigs have sharp thorns toward the base of each leaf. It produces deep green leaflets. This tree gets its name from the highly fragrant, yellow, puffball flowers that bloom in the spring. After flowering, elongated, woody, brown seedpods appear

Vachellia farnesiana
Sweet Acacia

that attract birds and other animals. While attractive, the flowers and seedpods pose a seasonal maintenance problem. Sweet acacia is drought resistant but prefers regular irrigation, especially during the summer months. It is hardy to fifteen to twenty degrees Fahrenheit. Trees planted in low-lying areas suffered frost damage during the Southern Arizona freeze of 2007 and again in 2011, but recovered quickly in the spring. Plant this moderate- to fast-growing tree in full sun with plenty of reflected heat and well-draining, fertile soil. It has brittle limbs and branches and is highly prone to wind damage, especially

Vachellia farnesiana
Sweet Acacia in bloom

during summer monsoons or intense windstorms. It does require pruning at least once a year and could produce suckers at the base that need to be maintained from time to time. Prune to open up its canopy and reinforce its structure. Avoid planting in smaller patios or pool areas since it needs a good amount of space to grow. Use it as a median or roadway plant, on golf courses, or in a park setting. The plant is native to warmer regions in Western Florida, and Northern Mexico and is frequently grown throughout Southwestern Texas, Southern Arizona, and California.

*Vitex agnus-castus
Monk's Pepper Tree, Caste Tree
Small- to medium-sized tree

Vitex agnus-castus
Monk's Pepper Tree

The monk's pepper is a deciduous tree reaching twenty to twenty-five feet tall and wide. It has green, aromatic leaflets that are grayish green on top and a lighter green on the leaf's underside. The foliage also resembles the leaf of a marijuana or hemp plant. In late spring, attrac-

tive spikes of lavender, purple, or white blooms appear in abundance and attract bees, butterflies, and hummingbirds. The exotic blooms are followed by a dark purple, fleshy fruit that contains dry, seedlike capsules that have a peppery smell. The leaves, stems, and fruits have been used as a food and medicinal source in some parts of the world. The berries have been used as an herb to treat reproductive problems. This tree prefers full sun, reflected heat, and well-draining soil, tolerates drought conditions but will grow more rapidly with supplemental irrigation. It is hardy to twenty degrees Fahrenheit and can also handle the summer heat. The tree is messy when its leaves and flowers shed. It is still an exceptional choice for desert landscapes and showy from the early spring through late fall. Use for light shade on patios, as a focal point for early spring color, or as a background plant. Monk's pepper makes a nice addition in mixed border beds with nondeciduous shrubbery. The tree is native to Southern Europe, Asia, and the Mediterranean,

Vitex agnus-castus
Monk's Pepper Tree

where it grows in woodlands and drier habitats. It has become naturalized in parts of Texas and the Southwest.

Ziziphus jujuba
Chinese Date
Medium-sized tree

Ziziphus jujube
Jujube

The jujube is a deciduous, single or multitrunk tree that grows fifteen to thirty feet tall with a ten to thirty-foot spread. It is a slow to moderate grower that produces rounded, spiny, pendulous branches and an open, irregular silhouette. As this plant ages, it develops a mottled, grayish black, shaggy bark. The leaves are shiny green with a slight oval shape and have noticeable spines at the base of each leaf. The foliage turns a beau-tiful, yellow fall color. In the spring, it develops inconspicuous, yellowish white, fragrant blossoms. After flowering, edible, shiny red, sweet fruit appears. Trees produce fruit every two years. The fruits have been used in traditional Chinese and Korean medicine to treat stress and sore throats. Freshly harvested fruit can be eaten or dried for tea. The fruit may also be a litter problem and can lightly stain a sidewalk or patio. Therefore, locate this plant in an area away from concrete. It needs some pruning to help it develop a strong structure. It grows in partial shade or full sun with reflected heat and is hardy to zero degrees. Jujube prefers well-draining soil that is either acidic or alkaline but does not contain heavy clay. It is tolerant of drought conditions when established but prefers supplemental irrigation for fruit production. The tree is susceptible to Texas root rot and requires a biannual application of ammonium phosphate. Use it as an accent, background, patio, lawn, or shade tree for its distinctive branching pattern and fruit. It is native to dry, gravelly, or rocky slopes, hillsides, and mountains in Southern and Central China, Southern Asia, Northern India, and Southeastern Europe. This tree has been cultivated in China for more than 4,000 years.

Ziziphus jujube
Chinese Date, Jujube

2 Palms

for Southwest Landscapes

Palm trees are evergreen plants that are heat-loving and drought resistant. They can add beauty and ambiance to our desert landscapes. Palm trees are a great addition to use for tropical and dramatic effects. They can be planted around water features, used in patios, courtyards, entryways, as a background plant, in containers, or as a strong vertical accent plant. They come in many shapes and sizes, and add great drama to our desert landscapes.

*Brahea armata

Mexican Blue Palm,
Blue Hesper Palm
Medium-sized palm

Brahea armata
Blue Hesper Palm, Mexican Blue Palm

Brahea armata
Blue Hesper Palm, Mexican Blue Palm

This outstanding palm with distinctive, pastel blue or waxy, aquamarine, fanlike fronds grows twenty to forty feet and spreads to sixteen feet. It offers the bluest leaves of any of the palms. The Mexican blue palm may produce thirty or more fan-shaped, circular palm fronds at maturity. In summer, showy, creamy white flower clusters appear on fifteen-inch-long stems that hang down from this magnificent specimen. After flowering, it produces a shiny, brownish black, edible fruit that contains a single seed. It is a slow-growing palm that becomes more tolerant to frosts as it matures. It needs some protection when young and is hardy to eighteen degrees Fahrenheit. Major leaf damage will occur at ten degrees. The Mexican blue palm likes well-draining, alkaline soils and full sun. It is somewhat drought resistant and prefers supplemental irrigation during the hot, dry summer. This palm can also withstand extreme heat. When transplanting or planting, protect its sensitive roots from damage. Use near water features such as ponds for a focal point or tropical accent, or wherever its distinctive color can be maximized. It looks nice when combined with the Mediterranean fan palm and Mexican fan palm.

Brahea armata
Blue Hesper Palm, Mexican Blue Palm

Its leafy branches are armed with thorns, so be careful when handling this plant and do not install it near pedestrian traffic areas. It is native to lower altitudes in rocky limestone soils, cliffs, and desert canyons of Baja California and Sonora, Mexico.

*Butia capitata,

Pindo Palm
Medium-sized palm

Butia capitata
Pindo Palm

Butia capitata
Pindo Palm

Pindo palm is a beautiful, feathery plant with long, arching fronds that curve toward the ground from a stout trunk. It reaches ten to twenty feet in height with a twelve- to fifteen-foot trunk but generally grows only to ten feet in desert climates. Its stems have spines along the edges and its large leaves range in color from light green to blue-gray. In late spring through summer, it produces small, magenta blossoms. The flowers are in groups of three with male and female parts on the same plant. This palm produces a bright orange, edible fruit referred to as the pindo date in the Deep South. The fruit has a tart but sweet flavor and is used to make jelly. Pindo palms that are grown in the Southwest desert tend to be smaller than those cultivated in Florida and similar climates. This unique specimen is very easy to grow. It is drought tolerant and is also hardy to fifteen degrees Fahrenheit. The pindo palm takes full sun with reflected heat but also grows in filtered to moderate shade. It prefers well-draining, sandy soil. Use it as a container plant or exotic accent in courtyards, patios, and entries. Pindo palm works well around pools, fountains, and water features. This palm is native to grasslands and woodland areas in Southern Brazil, Argentina, Paraguay, and Uruguay.

*Chamaerops humilis

Mediterranean Fan Palm
Medium-sized palm

Chamaerops humilis
Mediterranean Fan Palm

Chamaerops humilis
Mediterranean Fan Palm

This attractive, low-maintenance palm grows to heights of five to fifteen feet with an equal spread. It has up to eight shaggy trunks at maturity and triangular, fan-shaped, deep green leaves that grow twenty to twenty-four-inches wide. This palm has sharp thorny nubs along its stem, which makes it a little difficult to prune. By pruning some of the lower fronts, its multiple trunks are exposed. The palm produces many suckers as well as small bright yellow flowers that are held in bundles close to the plant's trunk. The blossoms appear in spring and are not very attractive. After blooming, orangey brown fruits appear that are about a half-inch to one inch in diameter. This palm prefers well-draining soil and is adaptable to many soil types. It likes full sun or partial shade and is hardy to fifteen degrees Fahrenheit. The Mediterranean fan palm is fast growing and drought resistant and likes regular, deep irrigation once per week during the summer season. Use it as an accent in an entryway or patio, either planted alone or in groups. The palm is a great addition to any bare corner of the landscape where you need a tropical looking plant. It works well as an understory plant beneath larger palms as an accent. This plant is native to the hot, dry hills and mountains of the Mediterranean Sea basin. The Mediterranean fan palm is also native to the mountains of Africa, Spain, France, and Turkey.

Cycas revoluta

Sago Palm
Medium-sized palm

The sago palm is actually not a real palm but is a cycad growing ten to twelve feet tall. It belongs to a primitive group of unusual ornamental plants. Cycads produce cones instead of flowers and have an upright trunk. They have a whorl of shiny, dark green, feathery, palmlike leaves that grow three to five inches long. The leaves have a very sharp point, and the plant should not be used near walkways or pedestrian traffic. In the spring or summer, it develops a flush of new leaves from the center core that grow in a circular pattern, looking like light green spikes. As the plant matures, it produces suckers that branch from the core plant and add to its interest. Sago plants are dioecious, which mean that each plant is either male or female. In late spring, the male plant produces a large, showy, creamy white pine cone that is two feet long. The female plant produces a fluffy, ivory, non-showy bloom that opens if the plant was fertilized. This long-lived plant does not bloom or produce seed until it is well established in the landscape. It can take up to fifteen years or more for the plant to produce seed or flowers. The sago palm likes organic, well-draining soil and is hardy to about seventeen degrees Fahrenheit. The plant benefits from applications of a slow-release fertilizer in the spring. Plant it in full sun to shade, avoiding reflected heat, since the leaves can sunburn. This palm is somewhat drought resistant but prefers irrigation once per week during the warmer growing season. If the older leaves turn yellow, then reduce the water and let the plant dry out. The seeds are the most poisonous part of the plant and can be extremely toxic to humans and pets. Use this palm in containers, as an understory plant, or as an accent in courtyards, entryways, and patios

Cycas revoluta
Sago Palm

for tropical or oriental effects. It is native to Japan and grows in the subtropics.

Phoenix canariensis
Canary Island Date Palm
Large-sized palm

Phoenix canariensis
Canary Island Date Palm

This evergreen reaches heights of forty to sixty feet with a spread of twenty to forty feet. It is a slow-growing palm with feathery fronds that are fifteen to twenty feet long. The leaves arch at the top of the plant and are dark green and armed with sharp spines. The Canary Island palm has a stout trunk that resembles a pineapple and is covered with diamond-shaped leaf scars. The flowers are small and creamy white and appear on six-foot-long stalks. After flowering, the female tree forms a round mass of orange fruit in the fall. The fruit, while inedible, is showy but can create a litter problem. This palm likes full sun, lots of heat, and deep, infrequent, watering. It also prefers well-draining, fertile soil. It is hardy to about twenty degrees Fahrenheit and does not recover quickly after a frost. Use it as a backdrop around pools or with other tropical plants and as a skyline tree along roadsides. It can also be used in large campuses and wide-open spaces for an oasis or Mediterranean effect. Also use in parks or as a specimen against tall buildings. This palm will make a dramatic statement in any large space that can accommodate it and looks interesting when planted in groupings. It is a native of the Canary Islands, located in the Atlantic Ocean off the coast of Northeast Africa.

Phoenix dactylifera
Date Palm
Large-sized palm

Phoenix dactylifera
Date Palm

The date palm reaches heights of forty to eighty feet or more with a large, single trunk. It produces green to grayish blue, erect leaves that grow to twenty feet long. The featherlike leaves are rough and have sharp tips on the ends. The gray trunk is patterned with diamond-shaped, interesting leaf scars. It has nondistinctive white clusters of blossoms in the spring and produces edible fruit that is orange or yellow and grows in pendulous clusters from the tree. The dates are oblong and surrounded by a sweet, sugary flesh. Male and female flowers grow on separate trees, but the female palm only produces dates if a male palm tree is nearby. Dates also only form on trees in warm climates with lower humidity. This slow-growing palm likes full sun with reflected heat and is somewhat drought resistant. It has deep roots that will seek out underground water sources, but it prefers regular irrigation for faster growth. This palm likes sandy, well-draining soil. The Phoenix dactylifera is hardier than Phoenix canariensis, tolerating temperatures into the low twenties. Remove the suckers that develop at the base of the tree while the palm is young to train it into a single trunk. Also, remove any sharp spines at its base. Plant it when the weather warms up in the spring. The palm requires some degree of maintenance, especially cleanup of the fruit on female trees, which can be quite messy. Use it as a skyline, street, or specimen tree in wide-open spaces for an oasis effect, against a large-scale building, in parks and parking lot islands, or on a golf course. The date palm is native to North Africa and has been used as a food source for thousands of years in the Middle East and North Africa. Commercial date groves are also found in Southern California and Arizona.

Phoenix roebelenii
Pygmy Date Palm
Small-sized palm

Pygmy date palm grows slowly, reaching eight to ten feet tall and five feet wide with a graceful

Phoenix roebelenii
Pygmy Date Palm

*Sabal uresana

Sonoran Palmetto
Medium- to large-sized palm

Sabal uresana
Sonoran Palmetto

straight or curving trunk. It has delicate, dense, bright green fronds that are three to four feet long and very spiny with sharp thorns at their base. The fronds are very graceful as they gently arch from the center of the plant. This plant is dioecious, with cream-colored flowers followed by small, black dates on female plants. Male flowers are borne on separate plants. It is adaptable to most soils but prefers those that are light and fast draining with applications of fertilizer once or twice per year. This plant likes regular irrigation but does not like to be overwatered. It tolerates drought and full sun to partial shade. The pygmy date palm is very tender and freezes when temperatures dip below thirty degrees Fahrenheit, so plant it in a protected area. When frosted back, it recovers quickly when the weather warms up. This palm requires minimal maintenance except for pruning spent fronds and removal of old blooms and fruit. Be careful when working with this palm because of the sharp thorns along its fronds. Use this attractive plant in entryways, raised planters, or containers, on a south-facing site in a patio, under a tree, or as a specimen plant. It can also be planted in groups for tropical effects around pools and water features. Its delicate, lacy appearance makes this a great understory palm in warm, frost-free locations. Do not plant near high-traffic or pedestrian areas. It is native to the tropical forests of Southeast Asia in Southern China, Vietnam, and Laos.

This large, robust, solitary-growing palm reaches heights of thirty feet or more with a fifteen- to twenty-foot spread. It has a dense crown and large, fan-shaped, split leaves that are silvery green to greenish blue with fibers hanging in between unarmed leaflets. The leaves become a deeper green as the tree matures. Its large, dramatic fronds emerge directly from the trunk of the plant and arch downward as they mature, with many hanging threads. Each leaf can grow five to eight feet, and a mature palm may have twenty to thirty-five fronds. In late spring, a long flower stalk appears with small, white blossoms that hang downward from the palm. A one-inch, blackish brown fruit develops from the flower stalk. The palm is hardy to eighteen degrees

Sabal uresana
Sonoran Palmetto

Syagrus romanzoffiana
Queen Palm

Fahrenheit, is extremely drought tolerant when mature, and grows best in full sun with reflected heat. Young plants require more frequent irrigation. This low-maintenance palm has deep roots and takes a variety of soils as long as they are fertile. Use it as a specimen plant for tropical effects, in pool areas, around water features, in larger courtyards, or in combination with other palms. Also, consider planting against a dark wall or brick building to expose its bold foliage and interesting silhouette. The palm is native to wet, riparian areas and riverbeds in Mexico from Sonora to Northern Sinaloa and down into Chihuahua at elevations up to 4,000 feet.

fronds. The foliage is a dark glossy green with fronds that grow in a downward appearance to ten feet. In the spring, it produces a flower stalk that is creamy white. After the queen palm flowers, a bright orange, round fruit appears in late spring, creating a colorful show. When the fruit drops, it can be messy and requires frequent cleanup. The queen palm is tolerant of most soils but prefers sandy, well-draining, enriched soils. The plant may suffer from salt damage and show signs on the end of the foliage. Fertilize the queen palm twice a year with a complete fertilizer that contains micronutri-

Syagrus romanzoffiana

Queen Palm
Large-sized palm

Syagrus romanzoffiana
Queen Palm

This tall, fast-growing regal palm grows to heights of forty to fifty feet with its ringed, straight, gray trunk and canopy of feathery, lacy

ents, especially manganese. This palm likes full sun and reflected heat. It prefers supplemental irrigation but can take some drought and grows faster with irrigation. The queen palm is hardy to twenty-five degrees Fahrenheit and freezes in the low teens but recovers in the spring. Use this palm as a specimen or street tree for topical effects. It works well against tall buildings as a strong vertical accent. Use it in pool areas, around ponds, near water features, in patios, or as a background planting. When used in masses, the queen palm casts shade or filtered sunlight to understory plants. It is easy to grow, but in the lower deserts, it needs protection from frost and winds. This palm likes to be planted along a southern or western exposure. It is native to Brazil, Paraguay, and Northern Argentina.

Trachycarpus fortunei
Windmill Palm

Trachycarpus fortunei

Windmill Palm
Small- to medium-sized palm

Trachycarpus fortunei
Windmill Palm

Windmill palm has a slender, hairy-looking trunk that grows fifteen to twenty feet tall and eight to ten inches in diameter. It is narrower at the base than the top. This palm has light to dark green palmate leaves that are arranged in a symmetrical crown. It is a dioecious plant where male and female blossoms are borne on separate plants. Flowers are white and inconspicuous with panicles of fragrant blooms that appear in the summer. The male plant will have a yellow inflorescence and the female flower will be white. This fanlike palm is hardy to ten degrees Fahrenheit. It likes full sun, tolerates filtered shade and does best with supplemental irrigation, becoming more drought tolerant with age. Its fronds may become damaged or tattered by the wind. The windmill palm is susceptible to sunburn, so avoid planting it in an area with reflected heat. It makes a great accent plant to use in tropical or oriental landscapes. This palm works well in courtyards and pool areas, around water features, or as a container plant. Use it in groupings as an interesting accent. It is native to the subtropics and mountains of Asia, Southeastern China, Taiwan, and Northern Burma.

Washingtonia filifera

California Fan Palm
Large-sized palm

Washingtonia filifera
California Fan Palm

Washingtonia filifera
California Fan Palm

This stately, skyline tree is one of the most popular palms grown in the Southwest desert. It reaches heights of fifty to sixty feet with a spread of fifteen feet. This palm has a massive trunk shaped with rings from old leaf scars. It has grayish green, glossy leaves with white, thread-like fibers between the leaf segments. The leaves blow freely in the wind, and if left unpruned, they form a petticoat around the crown of the plant and down its trunk. The dried-out fronds will remain on the tree for a long time and create a habitat and shelter for birds, insects, rodents, and other small creatures. In spring through summer, the palm produces numerous, long flowers stalks that branch out from the crown to produce small, creamy white blooms. After blooming, black berries about a half inch in diameter develop. The berries produce a dried seed that is surrounded by a sweet pulp. Birds and other animals eat the fruit and disperse it, sometimes re-propagating the fan palm to other areas of the landscape. Historically, Native Americans used the fruit produced by this palm in foods and beverages. It was cooked and eaten raw while its leaves were used to make baskets, huts and roofs, and the stems were used to make cooking utensils. Today, the dried fronds of this palm are still used to construct palapas,

Washingtonia filifera
California Fan Palm

streams, canyons, and open areas in arid regions of California, in the desert oases of Western Arizona, and in Baja, California.

Washingtonia robusta
Mexican Fan Palm
Large-sized palm

Washingtonia robusta
Mexican Fan Palm

grass huts, and covered ramadas in Mexico and other hot, dry regions. The palm grows in a wide variety of soils and responds well to slow-release fertilizers during the warm season along with deep, infrequent irrigation. It is disease- and pest-resistant as well as drought- and salt-tolerant. It also prefers full sun and reflected heat. Established California fan palms are hardy to fifteen to twenty degrees Fahrenheit. The foliage freezes when subjected to lower temperatures, but the palm recovers quickly in the spring. Plant it in wide-open areas to accommodate its wide crown. Also, plant or transplant during warm seasons to avoid root sensitivity to cooler soils and frosts. It requires some maintenance, including the removal of dried fronds and the clearing of fruit from walkways and pool areas. Use it in natural or formal settings and in large, open areas as a street tree, along roadsides, and in parklike settings, or for a vertical effect to line an entry or long driveway. The tree grows naturally in

The fast-growing palm grows eighty to one hundred feet with a slender, gray trunk that has ringed scars covered with a heavy leaf thatch. It

Washingtonia robusta
Mexican Fan Palm

Washingtonia robusta
Mexican Fan Palm

is thicker at the base and thins out toward the top. The Mexican fan palm can be distinguished from the California palm because it grows taller, leans slightly as it matures, and its fronds are a richer color. The California palm is denser, more compact, and has a thicker trunk. This palm produces large, glossy green fronds that are five feet long and four feet wide and have thorns along the stems. A distinguishable reddish streak runs along the underside of the leaf stalk. The older leaves form a skirt along the trunk of the palm as the plant matures. The thatch can be removed or left on the tree. Creamy white blooms about eight to twelve-inches long extend out from the leaves in early summer. After flowering in the fall, round, black, pea-sized berries appear and are eaten by birds, rodents, and other small animals. In its natural environment, many species of desert animals are dependent on this species for food and shelter. The Mexican fan palm prefers rich, well-draining soil but will survive in poor, sandy soils. It tolerates some shady conditions when young, but as it grows, it needs full sun to survive. It is drought resistant when established but grows faster with supplemental irrigation, especially during the hot summer season. The Mexican fan palm is hardy to twenty degrees Fahrenheit. The foliage can be damaged in lower temperatures, but the plant recovers quickly in the spring. Plant or transplant it during the warm season. Hire an arborist or professional to prune dead fronds and flower stalks as needed. Seed drop can also be somewhat messy and requires cleanup. The palm generally has a long lifespan and is resistant to most fungus and bacterial infections, as well as salty air and soil, making it a good specimen in hot areas and in coastal situations. Use this stately plant in masses, as a street planting, in groves and large open areas as a silhouette or skyline tree, or against tall buildings for dramatic effects. This plant is not a good choice for residences with small yards, but it looks very regal when lining an entry or long driveway. The Mexican fan palm is native to the canyons, valleys, and dry waterways of the Southern Sonora and Central to Western Baja, Mexico, where it grows at elevations of up to 3,000 feet. Native Mexican fan palm groves can be found in Clark County, Nevada and La Paz and Yavapai Counties in Arizona.

3 Shrubs and Herbaceous Perennials

for Southwest Landscapes

A shrub is a woody plant and is distinguished from a tree by its multiple stems and shorter height with several main stems arising at or near the ground. A large number of plants can be either shrubs or trees, depending on the growing conditions they experience. An herbaceous perennial is a plant that has leaves and stems that are soft or succulent; they have no persistent woody stems above ground. Their soft, green herbaceous growth will die back to the ground in cold winter climates. The roots of the perennial plants are alive and will have new growth that emerges in the spring.

Acacia craspedocarpa

Leather Leaf Acacia
Large-sized shrub

Acacia craspedocarpa
Leather Leaf Acacia

Acacia craspedocarpa
Leather Leaf Acacia

The dense evergreen resembles the boxwood, except that it can reach heights of ten feet or more with a spread of six to eight feet. It is more rounded when young with grayish green leaflets that are brittle to the touch and have distinctive veins. Stems and new growth are brownish red, turning darker as the plant matures. Attractive, bright yellow blooms appear in spring through summer followed by dark, flat seedpods con-

taining two to three large seeds. The pods hang onto the plant before falling to the ground. The medium- to slow-growing shrub prefers full sun with reflected heat and likes well-draining, slightly rocky soil. Established plants are drought tolerant but grow faster with supplemental irrigation. This shrub is hardy to fifteen to twenty degrees Fahrenheit. Established plants are very adaptive to our hot summers and do well in drought situations. This low-maintenance shrub can be used as a background planting, screen, windbreak shrub, smaller patio tree, foundation plant, or individual specimen with proper pruning. It can also be used as a background or transitional planting and works well in low-water-use

Acacia craspedocarpa
Leather Leaf Acacia

or xeriscape situations. In its natural habitat in Western Australia, the shrub grows along water and in thick groves as an understory plant with other acacia species.

Acanthus mollis

Bear's Breech
Medium-sized perennial shrub

Acanthus mollis
Bear's Breech

The lush, herbaceous evergreen grows six feet tall and three feet wide with deep green, deeply lobed, shiny leaves, a clumping growth form, and underground rhizomes that spread as the plant matures. Stunning flower spikes reaching three feet tall are white with purple and can be used in fresh or dried flower arrangements. The dramatic blooms last for a very long time, but the plant does not produce flowers every year. In the Southwest desert, bears breech becomes dormant in summer after it blooms, and the leaves die to the ground. It leafs out again in the cooler weather. The foliage can be damaged at twenty-five degrees Fahrenheit, so plant it in a protected location in rich, moist, acidic, well-draining soil. It prefers shade or partial shade and light

applications of fertilizer during the warm season. It is slow growing when young and grows quickly when established. Use for bold accents in atriums, entryways, shady courtyards, and planters to provide a lush addition with its bold, tropical appearance. It can also be used as an understory plant for woodsy effects in shady corners. The plant is native to Southwestern Europe and Northwestern Africa. It is a common plant in Mediterranean regions, particularly in Greece, where it is adored for its blooms.

Acca sellowiana

Pineapple Guava
Medium- to large-sized shrub

Pineapple guava is a slow-growing, subtropical evergreen with silvery, grayish green, leathery foliage that can reach heights up to ten or fifteen feet with an equal spread. The bark is pale gray, and the wood is very hard, dense, and brittle. In the spring, the plant produces a showy blossom that is borne in clusters, with pinkish white petals that surround red stamens. The edible flower petals have a soft texture and taste sweet. When

Acca sellowiana
Pineapple Guava

Acca sellowiana
Pineapple Guava

shade. It plant thrives with minimal care but needs supplemental irrigation to look good. Fertilize pineapple guava with ammonium phosphate in the spring to encourage flower and fruit production. Use it as a hedge, trained espalier, screen, or container plant, or as a single accent plant. It can also be trained as a small patio, entry, or foundation shrub in tropical landscapes, in pool areas, or around water features. Pineapple guava is grown commercially in California and New Zealand, and many varieties are available in local nurseries. The plant is native to Paraguay, Northern Argentina, Southern Brazil, and Uruguay.

birds and bees feed on the flowers, they help pollinate the plant. The flowers are used in salads or to accent food. After flowering, edible fruits form that have a pineapple, mint flavor. The fruits are about a half inch long and round with waxy green skins. They are sweet and juicy with a gritty pulp and are used in jellies, preserves, fruit drinks, wines, and other food products, especially in New Zealand. The plant is hardy to about ten degrees Fahrenheit and likes most soils as long as they are well draining. Plant this shrub in full sun or partial

Agapanthus africanus

African Lily, Lily of the Nile
Small-sized shrub

This tropical evergreen reaches heights of eighteen inches to two feet and grows two feet wide with fleshy rhizomes that spread and reproduce.

Acca sellowiana
Pineapple Guava

Agapanthus africanus
African Lily, Lily of the Nile

Agapanthus africanus
African Lily, Lily of the Nile

Agapanthus africanus
African Lily, Lily of the Nile

to grow but requires regular irrigation and partial shade. There are about ten different varieties available that produce varied flower color. Use caution and wear gardening gloves when handling this plant because it is a skin and eye irritant. It can be easily divided for propagation and transplanting. Use it in containers, borders, small courtyards, and atriums, as accents mixed with other plants in tropical settings, or in shady conditions around ponds and water features. The flowers can be cut for indoor use and last up to a week in a vase. The dried seed part of the plant looks interesting in arrangements as well. This plant is a native of South Africa in the Cape Peninsula, where it grows from sea level up into mountainous terrain in acidic, sandy soils between large boulders and rocks and on sheets of sandstone rock.

Alyogyne huegelii
Blue Hibiscus
Medium- to large-sized shrub

From spring to late fall, clumps of long, shiny leaves grow upright into a whorl and then start to arch in a downward appearance. The showy, pendulous flowers grow upright out of the plant and are topped with large, funnel-shaped clusters of white, violet, or blue flowers resembling lilies. The plant is hardy to about twenty degrees Fahrenheit and does not tolerate freezing temperatures for long periods of time. It likes rich, well-draining soil that is amended with organic materials and light applications of ammonium phosphate fertilizer in spring. The plant is easy

Alyogyne huegelii,
Blue Hibiscus

Blue hibiscus is a tropical evergreen that grows four to six feet high and wide. It has an open, bushy shape and lobed, hairy, dark

Alyogyne huegelii
Blue Hibiscus

Anigozanthos flavidus

Kangaroo Paw
Medium-sized, perennial shrub

Anigozanthos flavidus
Kangaroo Paw

green foliage. This fast-growing shrub produces prolific, showy, bluish purple, four- to six-inch blossoms. The blooms last one to two days and continue to flower profusely throughout the warm weather, starting in late spring and extending through early fall. Blue hibiscus likes full sun to partial shade but prefers afternoon shade. It has average water needs, requiring deep, weekly irrigation or sometimes more during the hot, dry season. The plant does not like to be overwatered and needs little water in the winter. Once established, it is drought resistant. This shrub needs well-draining, acidic soil to look its best. It is hardy to twenty to twenty-five degrees Fahrenheit and needs to be protected from strong winds. Prune aggressively after it finishes blooming in winter to keep it dense and compact. Use this exquisite, colorful shrub for tropical effects around pools and water features for its interesting flower show. This plant also grows well in containers, raised planters, and as a foundation plant in butterfly and hummingbird gardens. It is native to Southern and Western Australia where it grows along sandy, costal plains in sand, limestone, and clay soils.

Kangaroo paw is an herbaceous evergreen that grows three to four feet or more with a two to three-foot spread. It has a grasslike, clumping growth habit with long, dark green leaves and underground rhizomes. Kangaroo Paw blooms in early spring, producing an abundance of showy, upright blossoms that are covered in velvety hairs. The wooly flowers are curved at

Anigozanthos flavidus
Kangaroo Paw

Anisacanthus quadrifidus var. wrightii

Hummingbird Bush,
Flame Acanthus
Medium-sized perennial

Anisacanthus quadrifidus var. wrightii
Hummingbird Bush, Flame Acanthus

the tip and resemble the paw of an animal. Its striking blooms are chartreuse, maroon, red and green, pink or yellowish green and are exquisite in dried or fresh flower arrangements. Birds help to propagate the plant by pushing their beaks into the flower to draw the nectar and transferring pollen to the next plant. The kangaroo paw likes full sun to partial shade and is adaptable to many soils as long as they are well draining. It also needs regular irrigation when it is actively growing and flowering. After it blooms, irrigate lightly. The plant is hardy to mid-thirty degrees Fahrenheit and tolerates a light frost. Use to attract hummingbirds, in pool areas and around ponds and fountains, in large containers or raised planters with other perennial plants. This plant is not as attractive in winter but makes its amazing presence in the spring. There are many varieties available, and some are hardier than others. It is native to Western Australia where it can be found growing in river banks, swamps, shallow water, and forests, tolerating light shade.

The deciduous, sprawling perennial shrub grows three to five feet tall and wide with an interesting irregular shape, green leaves and attractive, exfoliating bark. From midsummer to late fall, it produces slender, orange-red, tubular, flowers that attract hummingbirds and butterflies. The plant grows moderately with supplemental irrigation but is drought tolerant. Do not overwater this plant and give it well-draining soils. It likes full sun and reflected heat to help promote its prolific blooming cycle. Hummingbird bush is hardy to five degrees Fahrenheit and also enjoys extreme heat. Prune back severely in winter to encourage new growth and flower production in the spring. The plant may reseed itself in other parts of the landscape. Use it as a summer color plant in foundations, patios, or containers. Its unusual bark and fall color also provide some early winter interest. This stellar plant works well when mixed with perennials and other hardy, evergreen plants. It can also be used as an understory plant in filtered shade. Hummingbird bush grows natively on rocky streambeds and on plains in Southwestern Texas and Northeastern Mexico.

Artemisia 'Powis Castle'
Wormwood

new growth to shape but do not prune it in the fall. The plant is hardy to around twenty degrees Fahrenheit. Use it as a groundcover, in containers or in low planters mixed with other perennials, or in herb gardens and rock gardens. It can also be used as a specimen or with other low, shrubby plants. The texture and color of this plant makes a nice contrast against other green foliated and flowering vegetation. It also makes a great border accent plant. Wormwood is not susceptible to pest or problems, and it is also deer resistant. The plant is a cross between two other species of the Artemisia genus, which originated in the Mediterranean region and in temperate localities in Asia.

*Artemisia 'Powis Castle'

Wormwood
Small-sized perennial shrub

This bushy, low-growing evergreen grows two to three feet tall and wide with bluish silvery, velvety foliage that is aromatic. It spreads and grows by underground rhizomes. In late summer through the fall, it produces attractive, upright, yellow blossoms that make an amazing contrast against its colorful silvery foliage. This small shrub likes full sun or partial shade. It also needs regular to moderate irrigation and does not like to be overwatered. Wormwood is susceptible to root rot in moist soils, so plant it in well-draining locations. Prune in the spring after it produces

Asclepias linaria

Threadleaf Milkweed, Pineleaf Milkweed
Small-sized perennial shrub

This erect, shrubby perennial grows three feet tall and wide with needlelike, grayish green foliage that is covered in fine hairs. From March

Asclepias linaria
Threadleaf Milkweed, Pineleaf Milkweed

Asclepias linaria
Threadleaf Milkweed, Pineleaf Milkweed

through October, it produces showy, white flower clusters with pinkish burgundy buds. Threadleaf milkweed is a spectacular plant when it is in bloom, and its flowers last for a long time. After flowering, decorative seed capsules appear that are shaped like teardrops and are about two inches long. It is very easy to grow and maintain and does very well in our hot, dry climates. Use this shrub for its exotic character, perhaps with other showy perennial plants. A milky substance oozes from the plant when a branch is broken or pruned. The plant enjoys full sun to partial shade, well-draining soil, and moderate

irrigation to keep its nice appearance. It grows faster when given supplemental water and is hardy into the mid-twenties. Use for its exotic character with other showy perennial plants and to attract the monarch and queen butterflies. Also use in patios, around pools, and near water features. It looks nice planted along foundations and low walls with its interesting growth habit and foliage. This plant is native to rocky slopes and canyons from Southern Arizona into California and the Mexican Sonoran Desert at elevations of 1,500 to 6,000 feet.

Asclepias subulata
Desert Milkweed
Small-sized perennial shrub

Asclepias subulata
Desert Milkweed

Desert milkweed is a fast-growing evergreen that comes alive in the spring, reaching four feet tall and wide. It has slender, vertical, woody stems that produce small leaves for brief periods. In spring through the fall, it develops a showy display of yellow to creamy white, tubular blossoms followed by flat, black seedpods. Its stems are greenish gray and if broken, produce a thick, milky sap. This plant prefers well-draining soil, full sun, and reflected heat. It is drought resistant but looks better if given supplemental irrigation. Desert milkweed is hardy to twenty to twenty-five degrees Fahrenheit. Avoid overwatering to prevent aphid infestations in the spring. This plant is an important source of food for the monarch butterfly and a great plant for revegetation since it propagates easily from seed. Use it in low-water-use landscapes in front of a wall, as a foundation, in courtyards, around pools boulders, or in butterfly gardens. The plant is native to Baja California, Southern Nevada and the Sonoran Desert of Mexico and Arizona. It grows along dry, sandy, desert washes and rocky slopes and hillsides below 2,500 to 3,000 feet in elevation.

Asparagus densiflorus 'Meyersii'
Foxtail Fern

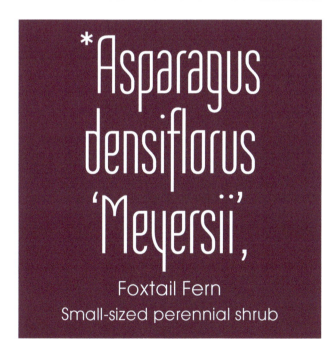

*Asparagus densiflorus 'Meyersii'

Foxtail Fern
Small-sized perennial shrub

This low-growing evergreen has feathery, upright, bright green, needlelike stems and trailing branches. It is not a true fern but has fernlike foliage and a dense growth habit, growing two to three feet tall and three to four feet wide. It has a

tall, fluffy frondlike appearance. In the summer, it produces small, white blossoms followed by bright red berries. The flowers and berries do not appear every year and the berries can be toxic if eaten. The foxtail fern takes full sun to partial shade but grows more densely in full sun. This plant likes well-draining, amended soil for optimum growth. The foxtail fern has an extensive root system with large tubers that can store water and food during periods of drought. It is easily divided by its root system to propagate and grow in other parts of the landscape. The plant is hardy to twenty-eight degrees Fahrenheit and if frozen back, it resumes growth in the spring. Prune off all of its frozen parts to the ground to hasten new growth. It is somewhat drought resistant but does better with regular irrigation. Use the foxtail fern as a groundcover, container plant, sculptural foundation, and border or courtyard plant in tropical settings or around pools and borders. Mix into beds with perennials and other lush plants. It is a native to South Africa, where it grows naturally along coastal areas of the Southeastern Cape and KwaZulu-Natal, most commonly in open areas, in rocky soils, and along coastal dunes.

Buddleja davidii
Butterfly Bush, Summer Lilac

Buddleja davidii
Butterfly Bush, Summer Lilac
Medium- to large-sized shrub

Buddleja davidii
Butterfly Bush, Summer Lilac

The medium to fast-growing semi-evergreen produces long, arching canes and grows in a weeping habit to eight to ten feet tall, spreading four to eight feet. As its name implies, it attracts butterflies as well as hummingbirds with fragrant clusters of pinkish purple or white blooms that droop downward from the plant. The leaves are greenish gray with fine-toothed edges. The underside of the leaf is white and fuzzy. From late summer to early fall, it produces amazing clusters of flowers that have orange throats. It likes well-draining, fertile soil, and handles drought conditions when mature. Plant this shrub in full sun to partial shade on north-facing walls. It often freezes to the ground when the temperatures reach the low thirties but recovers in the

spring. Every few years, the plant benefits from heavy pruning; growth re-emerges in spring. Flowers are more prolific on new wood, and spent blossoms should be removed to encourage continued flower production. This plant is easy to root from cuttings in warmer weather. Use the butterfly bush along foundations of your house. The purple flowering variety looks great as a background along a light-colored wall or other border, or in masses with other perennials. This is a great early fall color plant when in bloom. It is native to Northwestern China and Japan.

Buddleja marrubifolia
Woolly Butterfly Bush
Medium-sized shrub

This irregular, dense, rounded evergreen grows five feet tall and wide. Its small foliage is silvery white and covered in soft hairs. In early

Buddleja marrubifolia
Woolly Butterfly Bush

Buddleja marrubifolia
Woolly Butterfly Bush

water features for its interesting contrast and open, airy appearance. It can also be used in medians and or in mass groupings. This plant is native to Southwestern Texas and Northern Mexico, growing in canyons and washes and on limestone slopes at elevations of 1,800 to 3,800 feet.

Buxus microphylla
Japanese Boxwood
Medium-sized shrub

Buxus microphylla
Japanese Boxwood

spring through the summer, it produces dense, fragrant, round clusters of intricate orange flowers. This low-maintenance plant is hardy to about fifteen degrees Fahrenheit, likes full sun and heat, and is very drought resistant. It prefers supplemental irrigation during the summer. The woolly butterfly bush is susceptible to Texas root rot, so avoid overwatering or planting in clay soils. Provide once-per-year applications of ammonium phosphate fertilizer in the spring. Occasionally, this shrub could require some light selective pruning every few years to maintain its shape and rejuvenate it. Use it in low-water-use gardens as a specimen, in butterfly gardens, or around pools and other

This versatile, hardy evergreen is known for its low-growing, formal growth habit. It reaches heights of two to four feet with an equal spread. This plant can be kept trimmed to any height and has many uses as a landscape plant. It has small, bright, glossy green, oval leaves. The leaf color may change from a greenish red to bronzy color during the winter seasons. Japanese boxwood produces small, inconspicuous, whitish flowers in the spring that are slightly fragrant. Plant it in well-draining soils in full sun to light shade and avoid reflected heat. It is drought tolerant and hardy to zero degrees and can be used in low-lying, colder locations. Apply a complete fertilizer in the spring and early fall to stimulate growth.

Use for a formal pathway or hedge, bonsai, topiary, low border plant, clipped hedge, or accent for foundation plantings and in Japanese gardens. It is also deer resistant and is a great plant for open locations. This plant is believed to be native to Japan; however, it may have originated in China or Korea. It has been hybridized over the years and many different varieties are available in local nurseries.

*Caesalpinia mexicana

Mexican Bird of Paradise
Large-size shrub

Caesalpinia mexicana
Mexican Bird of Paradise

Caesalpinia mexicana
Mexican Bird of Paradise

This large size, semi-deciduous shrub grows to heights of ten to twelve feet or more and six to ten feet wide. It has a gray trunk and lush, rounded, fernlike foliage that is dark green. Spikes of bright, fragrant, yellow blooms appear throughout spring and sporadically in summer, during the monsoon. Flat, tan seedpods split open to expose small, lima-bean-shaped seeds. The seeds are highly toxic if eaten. This plant remains evergreen in warm climates but sheds its foliage in colder regions. It prefers full sun with reflected heat and good drainage, is hardy to twenty-five degrees Fahrenheit but freezes back in the low twenties. The plant is also drought resistant but prefers supplemental, weekly irrigation during the warm season to bloom and thrive. It is relatively low maintenance but needs occasional pruning to remove old pods and blooms. The Mexican bird of paradise will reseed freely in the landscape during the summer monsoon. Use this fast-growing plant as a screen, background shrub, tropical accent, or courtyard planting. It can also be used as a small patio tree or tucked into corners, and it attracts bees, butterflies, and hummingbirds. This plant is native to the extreme lower Rio Grande Valley in Texas and into Northern Mexico, where it grows in washes and on slopes.

*Caesalpinia pulcherrima

Red Bird of Paradise
Medium-sized shrub

Caesalpinia pulcherrima
Phoenix Yellow Bird of Paradise

Caesalpinia pulcherrima
Red Bird of Paradise

Caesalpinia pulcherrima
Phoenix Yellow Bird of Paradise

Caesalpinia pulcherrima
Red Bird of Paradise

Noted for its striking, orange and red flowers, this evergreen grows eight to twelve feet tall with wide, spreading branches. It has deep green, fernlike foliage and produces showy blossoms that bloom profusely in spring through summer. The flowers are bowl shaped in terminal clusters with red and orange petals and bright red stamens that extend from the bloom. After flowering, hard, flat, three-inch, brown pods appear with small, brown beans inside. The beans are toxic if eaten. This plant is easy to grow in well-draining, acidic, or alkaline soils. It is also drought tolerant and blooms profusely with supplemental irrigation. It is hardy to fifteen degrees Fahrenheit with stem damage below thirty degrees. If frost damaged, prune it back to about twelve inches above the ground during its dormant period. Cut to live wood to hasten new growth when the weather warms. The plant reseeds by itself in the landscape and in tropical locations. It likes full sun and reflected heat and can take the hottest spot in the landscape. Use it for its magnificent spring and summer color as a specimen, in masses around pools, as a tropical accent, along roadways and medians, or mixed into desert and transitional landscapes. The flower will also attract hummingbirds and butterflies. The red bird of paradise is native to the West Indies and tropical Americas. It has been naturalized in Texas and is widely cultivated throughout the warm regions of the world. The variety "Phoenix Yellow Bird" resembles the red bird of paradise except the blooms are all yellow. The "Phoenix" varieties have the same cultural requirements as Caesalpinia pulcherrima.

Calliandra californica
Baja Fairy Duster

Calliandra californica
Baja Fairy Duster

*Calliandra californica

Baja Fairy Duster
Medium-sized shrub

This evergreen grows six feet tall and wide with upright branches, light gray, somewhat hairy stems that become darker with age. Its dark green divided, tiny leaflets give this plant a lush, topical look. It produces very colorful, showy blooms with bright red stamens that explode in a mass of color in early spring and intermittently into fall. After flow-

ering, long, thin, brown seedpods appear. The pods open after a period of time and disperse seed. The plant grows in most soils as long as they are well draining. It enjoys full sun with reflected heat or partial shade. The Baja fairy duster is hardy to twenty to twenty-five degrees Fahrenheit and shows signs of frost damage when the temperatures drop in the teens. Prune dead branches back in early spring for a quick recovery; otherwise, leave it alone to grow in its natural form. Do not overprune this plant. It is extremely heat and drought tolerant but grows at a faster rate with regular irrigation. Use it as a low, informal screen, foundation plant, hedge, desert accent, or hummingbird and butterfly attraction. Plant this appealing, low-water-use accent around patios, pools, and water features. The Baja fairy duster is native to the sandy wash flats and hillsides of Baja California up to 4,000 feet in elevation.

Calliandra eriophylla

Fairy Duster
Small-sized shrub

Calliandra eriophylla
Fairy Duster

Calliandra eriophylla
Fairy Duster

The fairy duster is a low-growing, densely branching, semi-evergreen shrub with fernlike leaflets that drop during periods of drought or in cold temperatures. It gets one to three feet tall and will spread three to four feet wide. The plant produces dense clusters of pinkish white, puff-shaped blossoms in early spring that bloom sporadically throughout the warm weather. Long, pink stamens produce the magnificent color on the flower. After blooming, a legume-like seedpod appears, and when it opens, the exposed seeds fall to the ground, becoming a great food source for quail, birds, and rodents. It is hardy to fifteen degrees Fahrenheit and takes full sun and reflected heat. The fairy duster needs supplemental irrigation during the hot summer and explodes with a flush of color and new foliage during the summer monsoons. It prefers well-draining, coarse, rocky soil and is an easy plant to grow. Use it as an informal hedge, in medians, cactus and rock gardens, or for a hummingbird and butterfly attraction. This slow-growing plant can also be used on slopes for erosion control. It is native to the Sonoran Desert in Southern Arizona, as well as Western Texas, Southern California, New Mexico, and Mexico. The fairy duster can be found in grass-land areas growing at elevations of 1,000 to 5,000 feet.

*Carissa macrocarpa

Natal Plum
Medium-sized shrub

Carissa macrocarpa
Natal Plum

Carissa macrocarpa
Natal Plum

Natal plum is an evergreen that grows two to seven feet tall and can spread to ten feet. Its size depends on the particular variety. It has thick, oval, shiny, green foliage and a milky sap that appears when the stems or leaves are pulled, broken, or cut from the plant. In spring, the natal plum produces an abundance of white, highly fragrant, star-shaped blossoms that attract birds and butterflies. After flowering, small, edible, egg-shaped fruit appears and turns red when ripe. The fruit makes a wonderful cranberry-like preserve. All parts of this plant are toxic except the fruit. The shrub is also recognized by forked spines along its stems. It takes full sun to light shade and is hardy to about twenty-eight degrees Fahrenheit. The natal plum prefers sandy, well-draining soil and is also tolerant of alkaline soil. It also grows well in windy or coastal situ-

Carissa macrocarpa
Natal Plum 'Boxwood Beauty'

ations with the salty sea air. The plant responds well to pruning to keep its shape and size. It is drought resistant but prefers supplemental water to look its best. With its thorny spines, the natal plum makes a good hedge, foundation, screen, container, or barrier plant. The variety "Bonsai" grows in a compact mound to about two feet. The varieties "Prostrata" and "Horizontali" are also good low-growing varieties and make excellent ground covers. "Nana" and "Boxwood Beauty" are thornless dwarf varieties. The natal plum is a native of the South African province of KwaZulu-Natal, where it grows along the coastal bush, in forests, and on sand dunes.

Chrysactinia mexicana
Damianita

*Chrysactinia mexicana

Damianita
Small-sized shrub

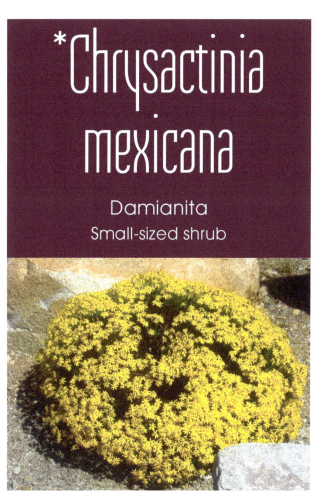

Chrysactinia mexicana
Damianita

and reflected heat and tolerates the hottest locations in the landscape. If planted in the shade it becomes leggy. It takes a variety of soil types as long as they are well draining. Prune lightly in spring after blooming to shape and remove dead wood but do not overprune. Provide supplemental irrigation during the warmer weather and keep it drier in winter. The blooms are more prolific with additional water. The plant is hardy to ten degrees Fahrenheit or lower. Use it to attract butterflies and as a border shrub in flowerbeds and entryways. The damianita can also be used as erosion control on steep slopes or a groundcover for hillsides and hot, exposed areas like medians and roadsides. It makes a nice contrast when planted with agaves, yuccas, and other low-water-use accent plants in the landscape. This plant is native to the hillsides of Western Texas, New Mexico, Coahuila, Chihuahua, Nuevo Leon, and Tamaulipas. It grows on south-facing, rocky, or limestone slopes at elevations of 1,800 to 3,000 feet.

This low-growing, compact-looking shrub with masses of spring color reaches heights of two feet or more with aromatic, dark, evergreen, needlelike leaves. It produces a beautiful bouquet of golden yellow, daisylike blossoms that appear in springtime and then intermittently into the fall. This drought-resistant plant likes full sun

*Cordia parvifolia

Little-Leaf Cordia
Medium-sized shrub

Cordia parvifolia
Little-Leaf Cordia

Cordia parvifolia
Little-Leaf Cordia

This bushy, dense-spreading shrub with arching branches grows four to eight feet tall with a three- to ten-foot spread. It is a semi-evergreen with oval, grayish green, leathery leaves that have deep margins. This attractive plant produces showy clusters of white blossoms in spring and again in the fall. Little-leaf cordia blooms profusely with high heat and humidity and during our summer monsoon. The plant is hardy to eighteen degrees Fahrenheit and suffers during severe frosts. It drops its foliage if it is drought stressed but recovers quickly during the summer monsoons. Plant it in full sun with reflected heat or partial shade. It is drought resistant but responds better with supplemental irrigation. This low-maintenance, moderately growing shrub also likes well-draining soil. Prune it heavily in early spring to shape. Use it as an informal hedge, screen, foundation planting, or flowering accent in low-water-use landscapes. It also looks nice as a background shrub with its attractive white blooms, especially when using lower growing accent plants in the foreground. This plant is native to the Chihuahuan Desert, Baja California, and Sonora, Mexico, in addition to Coahuila, Durango, Zacatecas, and other parts of Mexico, where grows in washes, flats, and rocky soils at elevations of up to 2,800 feet.

Cordyline australis 'Purpurea'

Purple Cabbage Tree
Medium-large, perennial shrub

Cordyline is an interesting evergreen that in warmer, tropical climates reaches heights of twenty feet or more. It grows upright like a yucca or palm tree, producing a crown of swordlike cranberry to reddish green foliage. Its two- to three-foot-long branches tip downward and are semistiff. In late spring through summer, the shrub produces creamy white flow-

Cordyline australis 'Purpurea'
Purple Cabbage Tree

Cuphea hyssopifolia
Mexican False Heather
Small-sized shrub

Cuphea hyssopifolia
Mexican False Heather

ers in a tall panicle. While this plant can take full sun in California gardens, plant it in partial shade in the Southwest desert to avoid sunburn of its leaves. It is drought resistant but grows very quickly with supplemental irrigation and does not like to be overwatered. Plant it in rich, well-draining soil and prune as needed to hasten new growth. The purple cabbage tree is hardy into the mid to low twenties. During our hot summer or sometimes throughout the year it will need to be cut back to the ground but will grow back very quickly. Use it in containers, atriums or in large, shady protected planters with other tropical plantings or against a pale wall for its amazing cranberry colored foliage. Purple cabbage tree looks nice in lush, tropical settings around water features and ponds. This plant is cultivated throughout Southern California but is native to New Zealand, where it reaches thirty to fifty feet tall.

This small evergreen has a compact, mounded form and interesting, textured foliage. It grows two feet tall and wide. It has green, feathery, fernlike foliage on branched stems with small, oblong leaves. This plant produces small, purple or lavender flowers throughout most of the warm parts of the year. Some varieties produce flowers in white, purple, or a deep rose. It looks best when planted in partial to full shade conditions and in well-draining soil. Provide regular irrigation to avoid flower drop. Also, apply two applications per year of ammonium phosphate fertilizer. Mexican false heather suffers severe frost damage when temperatures drop below the low thirties Fahrenheit but will resume growth when the weather warms. It is an easy plant to grow and needs little care, except protection from the frost. If it is frosted back, prune it heavily in the spring to encourage new growth. Use this attractive shrub as a border plant, in containers, or in raised beds mixed with other evergreen plants. It makes a nice groundcover in protected areas and is a wonderful butterfly attractor. This plant is native to Mexico and south to Guatemala.

Cyperus involucratus
Umbrella Plant

*Cyperus involucratus

Umbrella Plant
Medium-sized, perennial shrub

Cyperus involucratus
Umbrella Plant

Umbrella plant is a dramatic evergreen grass-like plant that reaches heights of four to six feet when given plenty of water. It is known for its upright, dark green stems that support a whorl of umbrella-like foliage. In the spring or early summer, small, yellowish brown flowers grow upright from the center of the foliage. This plant needs ample irrigation and does not like dry conditions. The wetter the roots are, the more it thrives. It produces underground rhizomes that spread sideways creating more plants. Plant it in rich soil that is full of amendments and provide ample fertilizer during the growing season. Frost damage can occur between twenty-five to twenty-eight

degrees Fahrenheit, but the plant recovers quickly in the spring with new shoots and leaves. If frosted back, prune heavily to the ground. The shrub requires a great deal of pruning every few years to control its size and removal dried out stems and leaves. It grows best in filtered or total shade but will tolerate full sun. Use it as an accent in tropical settings, oriental gardens, or small entryways. It can also be planted where its roots are submerged in water gardens and ponds. This fast-growing plant is easily propagated by root cuttings or division of the plant and can also be cut and used in flower arrangements. The variety "Gracilis" is a miniature version reaching two feet tall but produces limited flowers and seed. It makes a good container plant. The umbrella plant is native to the swamps and marshes of Madagascar, the Reunion Islands, and Mauritius.

Dalea frutescens

Black Dalea
Small-sized shrub

This small mounding, deciduous shrub grows three feet tall and four feet wide. In late sum-

Dalea frutescens
Black Dalea

Dalea frutescens
Black Dalea

mer and fall, it develops silvery green, lacy foliage and small, rose purple blooms at the end of terminal branches. It produces the most prolific flower display of all the Dalea species. Its blooms attract bees, butterflies, and hummingbirds. The black dalea grows fuller and denser in full sun and reflected heat in the hottest spot in the landscape. It prefers any soil type as long as it is well draining. This fast grower is drought tolerant but becomes fuller and produces more blooms with supplemental irrigation. It is a low-maintenance shrub that is hardy to fifteen degrees Fahrenheit or lower. Prune in late winter to encourage new growth and to help maintain its rounded, dense shape. Protect newly planted shrubs with chicken wire, because rabbits like to feed on them. Use for erosion control on rocky slopes, in parking lot medians, or in combi-

nation with other native vegetation. Also use it as a low-water-need, transitional shrub and for revegetation of disturbed areas. The variety "Sierra Negra" produces masses of purple blooms and is cold hardy to zero degrees. The plant is native throughout the deserts of Central Texas, Southern Oklahoma, and Southern New Mexico, and into Chihuahua, Coahuila, and Nuevo Leon, Mexico.

Dalea pulchra

Bush Dalea, Pea Bush, Indigo Bush
Medium-sized shrub

Dalea pulchra, Bush dalea
Pea Bush, Indigo Bush

The upright, multibranched evergreen, noted for its beautiful winter color, grows four to five feet tall with a three- to five-foot spread. It has tiny, silvery gray foliage that is covered in velvety hairs. This Arizona native produces numerous purple, pea-sized, spiked blooms with white, fuzzy heads from late winter through early spring. The flowers attract butterflies and bees. It is hardy to about to about ten to fifteen degrees Fahrenheit and is drought resistant but prefers supplemental irrigation, especially during summer months. Do not overwater this plant and plant it in well-draining soil. The bush dalea is easy to grow and low maintenance, although it needs pruning every few years to encourage foliage and flower production. It prefers full sun, reflected heat, and hot locations in the landscape. It will not bloom in the shade. Use it in borders, as an informal hedge, in medians, or as a background planting along with agave and yucca species. This shrub can also be used as a transition plant in low-water-use landscapes and needs a good amount of space to grow. The plant is native to the Sonoran Desert in Arizona, where it grows on rocky slopes in the Santa Catalina Mountains in Tucson, Arizona. The bush dalea is also endemic to Sonora and Chihuahua, Mexico at elevations of 3,000 to 5,000 feet, where it grows in the lower foothills.

Dermatophyllum secundiflorum

Texas Mountain Laurel
Large-sized shrub

Dermatophyllum secundiflorum
Texas Mountain Laurel

Dermatophyllum secunfiflorum 'Silver Peso'
Silver Peso Texas Mountain Laurel

Dermatophyllum secundiflorum
Texas Mountain Laurel

The upright, evergreen grows to heights of eight to fifteen feet and six to ten feet wide with a grayish black trunk that darkens at the plant matures. It is recognized by its beautiful, fragrant flowers that are dark lavender to purple. The plant produces leaflets that are thick, leathery, rounded, and glossy, dark green. In spring, wisteria-like flower clusters appear and hang down from the branches in a spectacular show lasting for several weeks. After the blooms die, thick, dark seedpods develop and eventually open to contain poisonous, orange seeds. Texas mountain laurel is a slow-growing plant, so it is recommended to purchase and install a fifteen-gallon plant to enjoy its immediate beauty. The plant is hardy to ten degrees Fahrenheit and likes full sun and reflected heat. It also prefers well-draining, dry, alkaline soil and supplemental irrigation during hot, dry weather. Watch for signs of the larvae of the pyralid moth or Uresiphita reversalis that can infest the plant, mainly feeding on its foliage. In spring, treat it with a systemic insecticide if needed, or handpick the larvae from the leaves. Use it as a landscape specimen in patios and courtyards, as a screen, as a small patio tree, in groupings, on medians, along roadways, and around pools and areas that get intense, reflected heat. The variety "Silver Peso" has exquisite silvery gray foliage. This shrub is native to Southern New Mexico and South and Central Texas, growing below 5,000 feet.

Dodonaea viscosa
Green Hopseed Bush

*Dodonaea viscosa

Green Hopseed Bush
Large-sized shrub

The hopseed is a versatile evergreen that reaches heights of twelve to fifteen feet with an equal spread. Its fibrous leaves appear dark green, glossy, long, and narrow, or they can be a dark crimson or purple, depending on the variety. New foliage is often covered in a fine sticky substance, while older foliage is smoother. It produces small clusters of greenish white to purple blossoms in early spring that sometimes resemble hops. Its showy fruit is greenish tan with papery wings and the seeds are eaten by birds, dove, and quail.

Dodonaea viscosa 'purpurea'
Purple Hopseed Bush

The hopseed bush is hardy to fifteen to seventeen degrees Fahrenheit, and some varieties are hardier than others. Its foliage will be severely damaged in the low teens. If frosted back, the plant recovers in the spring. The green-leafed varieties "Arizona" and "Mexico" are hardier. The plant likes full sun to partial shade and is extremely

Dodonaea viscosa
Green Hopseed Bush

Dodonaea viscosa
Green Hopseed Bush

*Duranta erecta

Sky Flower, Golden Dewdrop
Medium-large shrub

Duranta erecta
Sky Flower, Golden Dewdrop

Duranta erecta
Sky Flower, Golden Dewdrop

drought resistant. Provide supplemental irrigation during the hot season to encourage a lush appearance. The hopseed bush might suffer from iron chlorosis if given too much water and may need some supplemental iron fertilizer. It looks best in its natural appearance, so avoid overpruning. The plant grows in just about any soil but prefers well-draining, amended soil. Use it as a screen, hedge or accent in desert landscapes. It can also be used as backdrop or transitional landscape shrub to add a touch of deep green or purple color during the winter season when other plants are dormant. It is native to the warm, arid regions of Australia, New Zealand, South Africa, and the southwest deserts of Arizona, California, and Mexico at elevations of 2,000 to 5,000 feet. It can be found growing in washes, canyons, and arroyos, and on dry, rocky slopes.

Sky flower is a showy evergreen that grows eighteen feet tall and wide, if it doesn't freeze back. It is a multitrunk plant with arching branches that droop and trail in a downward appearance. Some species have spines on them, while others are spineless. The dark green foliage is thin with long leaves arranged in whorls of three and pointed at the tip. This plant produces showy, bluish purple, tubular blossoms that flower for most of the year in warmer climates. It also attracts butterflies. There are a number of varieties available, including one that produces a white flower. In the Southwest desert, the sky flower begins blooming in the spring and continues its magnificent color show throughout the fall until the first frost. It also produces a showy, golden yellow berry that hangs from the plant. The berry is poisonous to humans. It grows best in full sun or partial shade and does not like reflected heat. Sky flower prefers frequent irrigation and well-draining, rich soil but also tolerates rocky, alkaline soil and salty air. This plant will freeze in temperatures below the low thirties, but its roots are hardy into the low twenty degrees Fahrenheit. It may not fruit in colder locations. If frosted back, it recovers quickly in the spring. Use it as a large background shrub for its amazing flower color, as a screen, windbreak, or container plant around patios, pools, and water features. The plant is native to the scrubby woodlands of the West Indies and Central and South America. It has become established in Western Texas and Florida.

Encelia farinosa
Brittlebush

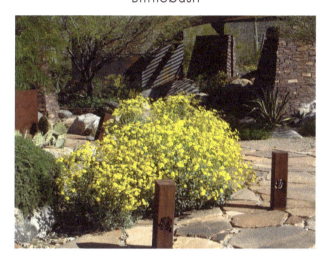

Encelia farinosa
Brittlebush

Encelia farinosa
Brittlebush
Medium-sized, perennial shrub

This rounded, herbaceous evergreen gets its name from the brittleness of its dried stems and grows three to four feet tall with an equal spread. It offers silvery, bluish gray foliage that has a thick cover of dense, white hairs. The shrub produces upright, yellow, daisylike blooms that are held high above the foliage in the spring. Brittlebush continues to bloom dramatically through spring and intermittently throughout the monsoon season. Plant it in full sun with plenty of reflected heat. While drought tolerant, its leaves turn a deeper green with supplemental irrigation during

the hot, dry season. Without water, and during colder weather, it drops foliage and becomes dormant. This native shrub is easy to maintain but looks better when cut heavily after its springtime blooming period. The plant is hardy to about twenty degrees Fahrenheit and likes well-draining soil. Its lush, new growth and flowers attract aphids in spring, so treat it with a systemic insecticide if needed and keep plants on the drier side to help control this pest. The brittlebush is easy to transplant, or it can be established by direct seeding in disturbed areas. Use for revegetation of desert areas, in hydroseed mixes, in medians, and as a desert color plant. This shrub was used by Native Americans as glue and chewing gum and the resin was burned as incense. Brittlebush is native to the Sonoran Desert in Arizona as well as Baja California. It is also indigenous to Western San Diego County, Southern Nevada, and Southwestern Utah, growing in open sandy washes, on dry, rocky slopes, and in hot, open deserts at elevations below 3,000 feet.

Equisetum hyemale

Horsetail, Scouring Rush
Small-medium, perennial shrub

Equisetum hyemale
Horsetail, Scouring Rush

Horsetail is a fast-growing, reedlike perennial shrub that gets its name from the silicon crystals in its plant tissues that have a gritty texture much like a scouring pad. Historically, early pioneers used sections of the plants as a scouring pad to clean pots and pans. It offers vertical, jointed stems that are dark green and hollow. The plant grows three feet tall or more and produces tiny, green leaflets that grow around the stem to form a narrow, green band at each joint. This plant does

not flower or seed but spreads by underground rhizomes. It does best in filtered sun to partial shade and has a higher moisture need, growing best in wet conditions. The horsetail also tolerates a wide range of soils but needs good drainage. It is hardy into the low twenties Fahrenheit and is a fast-growing plant. Horsetail can be invasive in some parts of the country. Protect it from rabbits by placing chicken wire around younger plants. Use this whimsical plant in Japanese and ornamental gardens, around ponds, in tub gardens, and around other water features as well as in shady locations. Also, use in containers and raised planters for a strong, vertical accent, or cut its stems and mix them into flower arrangements. Parts of the plant are poisonous if ingested. It is native to wetlands, lakes, ponds, and rivers in South America, Canada, and the United States.

Eremophila glabra

Common Emu Bush
Medium-sized shrub

Eremophila glabra
Emu Bush

Common emu bush grows three to five feet tall and wide, depending on the variety. *Eremos* comes from the Greek word for desert, and *phileo* means to love, which explains why the plant seems to love to grow in desert landscapes. It produces light green to silvery gray, elongated, evergreen foliage with small hairs on its leaves. The emu bush also produces orangey red or yellow, tubular flowers characterized by their bright colored petals. It blooms heavily in the spring and fall and intermittently throughout the year. Plant it in full sun to partial shade and avoid reflected heat. While drought resistant, this shrub likes occasional water and well-draining soil. It is hardy to the mid to low twenties Fahrenheit. Prune it to shape in late summer, removing dried branches or damaged wood. Use this medium to fast grower in hummingbird and butterfly gardens, or as a foundation, screen, or background planting for color and accent. Plant it in groupings with other drought-tolerant vegetation for year-round color. The common emu bush is native to inland and arid regions of Western and Southern Australia. It also is found growing in Queensland, New South Wales, and Victoria in areas with high summer temperatures and minimum annual rainfall.

Eremophila maculata 'Valentine,'
Emu Bush

show in late winter, just in time for Valentine's Day. This emu bush continues blooming through spring with an abundance of tubular, rosy red blossoms that grow along the tips of its branches to attract hummingbirds. It grows best in full sun and can take plenty of reflected heat. The emu bush likes well-draining soil but can also grow in alkaline or salty situations. It grows better with supplemental irrigation but can survive on very little water. Prune it in spring after blooming to produce more color and vigor for the following season. It is hardy to fifteen to twenty degrees Fahrenheit. Use it as an early season color accent plant along roadways and medians or as a foundation planting, backdrop, or focal point. The Eremophila family is a large genus of more than two hundred different species of plants that are all native to the lakes and waterways in the inland part of Australia. This particular species is endemic to deep, sandy, or rocky soil where it grows in salt lakes, dry watercourses, and dry, arid inlands areas.

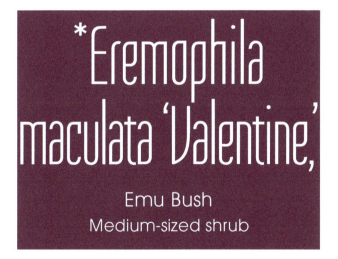

*Eremophila maculata 'Valentine,'

Emu Bush
Medium-sized shrub

This evergreen has small, rounded, lush, green leaves and a dense, rounded growth habit reaching three to six feet tall and four feet wide or greater. It produces a magnificent, prolific flower

Euonymus japonicus 'Aureo-marginata,'

Gold Spot Euonymus
Medium-sized shrub

Euonymus japonicus 'Aureo-marginata,'
Gold Spot Euonymus

The gold spot euonymus is a compact evergreen prized for its colorful, dense foliage and form. It is a moderate grower that reaches heights of five feet or more with a three- to six-foot spread. It produces glossy, dark green foliage mixed with bright yellow colorations. In late spring or early summer, greenish white blossoms appear followed by a pink-orange fruit capsule. Plant the gold spot euonymus in filtered sun or full shade. It needs moderate water but does not like to be overwatered. It also prefers well-draining soils and is tolerant to salt spray and salty conditions. Watch for infestations of aphids, powdery mildew, or scale during the warmer weather. Treat it as needed for insect and disease problems. It can be pruned at any time to shape and train. This plant is hardy to thirteen to fifteen degrees Fahrenheit. It produces a poisonous sap and parts of this plant can be toxic if ingested. Always wash your hands if you come in contact with the sap. It benefits from applications of ammonium phosphate fertilizer in the spring to induce new growth. Use it as a hedge, screen, foundation, or border plant. It looks nice in woodsy situations with its interesting, showy leaf color. It does well on the north side of a house or building and can also be grown in containers. The variety "Aureo-marginata" was introduced into the Netherlands in the mid-1800s and has been cultivated in Japan, and later, in other parts of the world. There are many varieties and variegated forms of the euonymus available at local nurseries.

Euryops pectinatus

Yellow Bush Daisy, Euryops Daisy
Medium-sized, perennial shrub

Euryops pectinatus
Yellow Bush Daisy, Euryops Daisy

The fast-growing, multi-stemmed evergreen reaches four to five feet high and wide with dark green to greenish gray, lacey, fernlike leaves,

Euryops pectinatus
Yellow Bush Daisy, Euryops Daisy

Gardenia jasminoides

Gardenia, Cape Jasmine
Medium-sized shrub

depending on the variety. It produces upright, bright yellow daisylike flowers in late winter through early spring. Once the hot summer weather appears, it ceases blooming. Plant it in full sun and reflected heat or some filtered shade. It likes frequent irrigation and needs well-draining soil. The yellow bush daisy is hardy to about twenty degrees Fahrenheit. Prune off dead blooms after it finishes flowering and prune it heavily every few years. Parts of this plant are poisonous if ingested. Plant it in masses for its amazing winter color. Use it in rock gardens, along borders, as a foundation plant, in containers, or as a border or background planting. This shrub is a great choice to use around pools, ponds, and water features in tropical landscape settings. It is also a great butterfly attraction, and birds may feed on the seed if the flowers are allowed to dry on the plant. The plant is native to South Africa, growing in rocky, sandstone slopes.

Gardenia jasminoides
Gardenia Cape Jasmine

Gardenia jasminoides
Gardenia Cape Jasmine

This medium-sized evergreen, which is prized for its highly fragrant, white, cream, or ivory flowers, reaches heights of four to six feet with an equal spread. Mature shrubs are round in appearance with dark green, glossy leaves that have pointed tips. In spring and intermittingly throughout the warm weather, gardenia flowers add a wonderful fragrance to the garden. Sometimes, flower buds drop or flowers die from too much hot air or plant stress. Gardenias like well-draining, slightly acidic soils that are high in organic material. When planting in the ground, mix mulch and organic compost with the soil. In the spring, add ammonium phosphate fertilizer to the soil and water it in thoroughly. Use a light amount of iron fertilizer at the same time to prevent iron chlorosis. Fertilize it again in the summer during the monsoon season to encourage blooms. Avoid fertilizing it in fall to prevent stimulating new growth that would be susceptible to early winter frosts. Gardenias prefer filtered sun to shade. They can sunburn if planted in full sun. The plant is hardy into the low twenties Fahrenheit and should be protected during prolonged periods of frost. Provide ample to moderate irrigation and good air circulation to help prevent infestations of diseases and insects. Use it in containers in protected areas or on patios and porches or use it as an understory plant beneath trees for woodsy or tropical effects or in oriental gardens. Many different varieties are available. The plant is native to Southern China, Japan, and Taiwan.

Hamelia patens
Firecracker Bush, Fire Bush

Hamelia patens

Firecracker Bush, Fire Bush
Small- to medium-sized, perennial shrub

The multitrunk evergreen matures quickly up to six feet tall and wide with bright green foliage that has a pointed tip and grows in clusters along the branches. During the warmer weather, the leaves are covered in fine hairs. With cooler temperatures, the foliage turns crimson-green. Tubular, orange-red blossoms appear in the spring and continue to bloom into the heat of the summer, attracting hummingbirds. In fall, small, blackish purple fruit appears, attracting birds. The firecracker bush defoliates when temperatures drop into the high twenties to low thirties; however, the roots of this colorful plant are hardy to twenty degrees Fahrenheit. If frosted back, the plant recovers quickly in warm weather. It likes full sun, reflected heat, and ample to moderate water. It is a good water indicator plant because its leaves wilt when drought stressed and revive with a deep irrigation. This plant tolerates a variety of soils as long as they are well draining. Prune it back as needed in late winter and apply a light fertilizer in early spring. Use it in mixed perennial gardens for summer color or as a foundation plant on patios, in courtyards, or around water features, ponds, and pools. This plant is native to Florida, the Caribbean, the West Indies, Central and South America, and into Bolivia and Paraguay.

*Hibiscus rosa-sinensis

Chinese Hibiscus
Medium-large shrub

Hibiscus rosa-sinensis
Chinese Hibiscus

Hibiscus rosa-sinensis
Chinese Hibiscus

Hibiscus rosa-sinensis
Chinese Hibiscus

Hibiscus is an amazing tropical, flowering evergreen that grows upright to six feet tall or more, with a five- to eight-foot spread. It has glossy, green-toothed foliage that is alternately arranged on the leaf. During warm weather, it produces beautiful, showy flowers in colors of red, pink, yellow, apricot, white, and orange that attract butterflies and hummingbirds. The flowers are edible and used in salads and for decoration and offer some medicinal uses. The blooms are six inches in diameter and may be single or double flowers. The single-flowering varieties perform much better in the Southwest desert, although many different varieties are available with different blooming habits, foliage, and flower color. The hibiscus needs full sun to partial shade to produce ample blooms as well as well-draining, rich soils that are full of amendments. It is hardy to twenty-eight degrees Fahrenheit and should be planted in protected areas, where winter frosts are prevalent. If this shrub does freeze to the ground, it recovers quickly in the spring. This fast grower also needs ample water and shows signs of water stress if not given enough irrigation. It also likes occasional applications of ammonium phosphate fertilizer during the warm weather. Prune it to control shape and size and remove dead blossoms. The plant is susceptible to aphids, wind damage, and Texas root rot. Use it for bold, tropical effects as a hedge, screen, or foundation, in containers and entryways or on patios for its flower show. It is native to Southern Asia and is the national flower of Malaysia.

*Hibiscus moscheutos 'Moy Grande',

Texas Giant Hibiscus
Medium-large shrub

it in full sun with well-draining soil and provide plenty of irrigation. It is salt tolerant and a good choice for coastal locations. Use it in mixed borders, as a foundation planting, in containers or as a conversation piece. The brilliant flowers make great table decorations and last a day before wilting without being in water. The Texas giant hibiscus was bred and introduced to the San Antonio Botanical Gardens by Ying Doon Moy. It is a genetic cross between two other stunning hibiscus species, both native to the Americas.

Hibiscus moscheutos 'Moy Grande'
Texas Giant Hibiscus

The Texas giant hibiscus has an upright, bushy growth habit reaching four to five feet tall and almost as wide. This showy plant has grayish green foliage and during warm weather, produces striking blooms in rose pink, hot pink, raspberry, mauve, plum, deep red, and dusty rose colors that attract hummingbirds and butterflies. The blossoms are huge and delicate and bloom continuously from late spring throughout the warm growing season, into fall. This is a tender plant and usually freezes back to the ground during the winter but recovers quickly in the spring when the temperatures warm up. It should be cut to the ground each year for optimum growth. Plant

Ilex vomitoria 'Stokes Dwarf'

Stokes Dwarf Yaupon Holly
Medium-sized shrub

Ilex vomitoria 'Stokes Dwarf'
Stokes Dwarf Yaupon Holly

The dwarf variety of the Yaupon holly grows three to four feet tall and wide, maturing into a dense, rounded evergreen with shiny, olive green, lightly toothed leaves. It develops attractive purplish green new growth, and the male

Ilex vomitoria 'Stokes Dwarf'
Stokes Dwarf Yaupon Holly

Justicia brandegeeana
Shrimp Plant
Small- to medium-sized,
perennial shrub

Justicia brandegeeana
Shrimp Plant

plant produces an insignificant white spring flower. Red berries form after blooming and are usually eaten by birds and rodents. This dwarf shrub grows best in either full sun to partial shade, is drought tolerant but likes frequent irrigation during its growing season. Do not overwater this plant. It is also tolerant of sandy, salty, or clay soils as long as they are well draining. The Stokes dwarf yaupon holly is hardy into the low twenties Fahrenheit. It is low maintenance but does best with an application of fertilizer in early spring. Use it in raised beds, as a screen, foundation, low hedge or border plant, in parking lot medians, or as a background plant for gardens and flowerbeds. This versatile shrub makes an excellent bonsai, topiary, or espalier plant and is resistant to deer. It is native to the Southeastern United States, where it is found growing along coastal plains from Virginia to Florida and west to Texas.

The shrimp plant is an exotic, fast-growing evergreen reaching four feet high and three feet wide with a thick mass of oval, light green, veined foliage. The underside of the leaf is soft and tender. In spring and during warm seasons, it produces spikes of orange-red showy bracts that surround its less conspicuous long, white, tubular blossoms. The flowers resemble a shrimp, giving this plant its common name. It blooms continuously until the first frost and attracts butterflies and hummingbirds. There are a number of cultivars available with different flower bract colors, including yellow, bright red, pink, and lime green. Plant it in filtered shade in a protected area for best flower production. Provide lots of moisture to young plants and additional irrigation during the hot, dry season. This plant will drop its leaves and show signs of stress if not given enough water. It needs well-draining, loamy, fertile soils for lush growth. Apply ammonium phosphate fertilizer in the spring to promote blooms and prune leggy plants to keep a nice, mounded appearance and to control its height. This shrub is not very hardy and will freeze into the low thirties Fahrenheit but recovers in the spring. Use it with other perennials and annuals in beds and borders, containers, raised planters and small foundation beds around patios and entryways for tropical effects and bold statements. The shrimp plant is native to Mexico and has naturalized in parts of Florida.

Justicia californica
Chuparosa

*Justicia californica

Chuparosa
Small-sized shrub

Justicia californica
Chuparosa

The chuparosa, which means hummingbird in Spanish, is an attractive, open, arching plant noted for its profuse flowers that bloom over an extended period of time. It grows three feet tall and spreads to four feet wide, producing medium green, succulent, heart-shaped foliage. The plant produces bursts of color in spring and again in fall. As its name implies, its showy, tubular blossoms attract hummingbirds. The flowers are also edible and can be eaten raw or cooked. The plant is hardy to about twenty-eight degrees Fahrenheit. If frosted back, wait until spring to prune. During periods of drought or extreme cold temperatures, it will drop leaves to minimize evaporation loss. Even though this plant is drought tolerant, it looks better when given extra water, especially during the hot, summer months. The chuparosa will also grow at a faster rate with irrigation. Plant it in full sun with reflected heat and well-draining soil. Use it as a color and accent plant, hedge, foundation, or specimen shrub. It works well in medians and along streetscapes, in courtyards or mixed into perennial gardens for its attractive color and accent show. This showy plant continues to bloom and produce color throughout the winter months. It is native to washes, rocky slopes, and sandy soils below 2,500 feet in Arizona, Baja California, Sonora, and Sinaloa, Mexico.

*Justicia spicigera

Mexican Honeysuckle, Orange Plume Flower
Small- to medium-sized shrub

native to Mexico, Belize, Costa Rica, El Salvador, Guatemala, Honduras, and Nicaragua.

*Lantana camara

Bush Lantana
Small-sized shrub

Justicia spicigera
Mexican Honeysuckle, Orange Plume Flower

Lantana camara
Bush Lantana

Mexican honeysuckle is an evergreen with a rounded shape that grows three to five feet tall and about four to five feet wide. It has green, soft, velvety foliage that gets larger when planted in partial shade. Clusters of orange-red, tubular blossoms appear in spring and throughout fall at the end of its branches and attract hummingbirds. Plant it in full sun to light shade in loose, amended, well-draining soil. It is drought and heat resistant but likes supplemental irrigation to look its best during the warm weather. Mexican honeysuckle is hardy to the low twenties and recovers quickly in the spring if frosted back. Prune it as needed to shape and remove woody branches. Use it as a low foundation planting in containers, as a desert accent plant, in groupings, or in hummingbird gardens. It can also be used for tropical effects in pool areas, as a courtyard planting, or as a specimen plant under palms or other trees. This low-maintenance plant is

Lantana camara
Bush Lantana

The lantana is a prolific bloomer growing two to four feet tall and wide with sprawling branches that produce dramatic color during the warm

Lantana camara
Bush Lantana

Lantana camara
Bush Lantana

cations of ammonium phosphate fertilizer in the early spring. Irrigate it during the hot summer weather. If stressed for water, the plant will wilt, indicating that it needs moisture. It often reseeds itself in areas of the landscape where water is available, and in some areas of the world it can be an invasive plant. In our Southwest deserts, however, it is a reliable, colorful shrub that provides enormous amounts of color in spring, summer, and fall. Lantana can also be used as an accent, border, and foundation or container plant for dramatic color. It works well as a transition shrub in desert gardens and around pools and water features. The bush lantana is native to Australia and South Africa, where it has become an invasive plant. It also grows naturally in the Gulf Coast region of Florida, warmer parts of Texas, and tropical areas all over the world.

Larrea tridentata

Creosote Bush
Medium-sized shrub

Larrea tridentata
Creosote Bush

season. The foliage is green, rough, and sometimes has prickly stems and leaves with rough hairs that emit a pungent aroma when crushed. This plant produces prolific flower clusters in an array of colors—yellow, orange, fuchsia, pink, white, and many multicolor varieties. Many hybrids are available. This nonstop bloomer produces flowers from early spring until the first frost. The bush lantana likes full sun with plenty of reflected heat. It needs well-draining soils to look good and will respond well to applications of fertilizer. The plant is hardy to twenty-eight degrees Fahrenheit. It likes full sun with plenty of reflected heat and needs amended, well-draining soils. The lantana also responds well to appli-

The Southwest native is a slow- to moderate-growing evergreen that reaches a height of four to twelve feet and spreads six to eight feet wide. It produces flexible, twisted stems and small, waxy grayish green leaves that have a distinctive scent after a rainstorm. The foliage contains a resin that helps the plant conserve water. The creosote bush has been used by Native Americans of the Southwest and Mexico for many medicinal treatments. The shrub provides a safe haven for crickets, grasshoppers, and other insects. After the summer monsoons, it is green and lush looking. Throughout the year and especially after a rain, it produces a small, bright yellow flower with five twisted petals. In late spring, small, white rounded capsules appear. While it survives in its native habitat with only natural rainfall and can go many years without water, newly planted shrubs should be irrigated infrequently. The creosote bush likes full sun and reflected heat and is hardy to five degrees Fahrenheit. Use for revegetating disturbed areas, as a mass planting, in low-water-use landscapes, in medians, along streetscapes, or as a single accent planting. It will live for a long time and is low maintenance. This plant is native to western parts of Texas, Southeastern California, Southern Mexico, and into Utah and Nevada. It also grows natively in Mexico in loose, well-draining soils. In the wild, the creosote bush covers large areas and its roots produce chemicals that inhibit the growth of other plants nearby.

Lavandula stoechas subsp. pedunculata
Spanish Lavender

Lavandula stoechas subsp. pedunculata
Spanish Lavender

Lavandula stoechas subsp. pedunculata

Spanish Lavender
Small-sized, perennial shrub

Spanish lavender is an attractive, fragrant evergreen that grows eighteen inches to two feet tall. It has smooth, silvery gray foliage and dark purple, pineapple-shaped flower spikes with violet bracts that attract bees, butterflies, and hummingbirds. The flowers appear in spring providing a wonderful fragrance in the air. Lavender is from the Latin word *lavare* which means to wash. This plant was used by the ancient Greeks and Romans to scent their bath water, and today is also an ingredient in soaps, shampoos, and body oils. It thrives in full sun and has few pest problems. Spanish lavender does well in poor soils but prefers them to be well draining. It tolerates salt and hot, humid conditions. This plant is drought tolerant when established but will also take regular irrigation. It is hardy to about ten degrees Fahrenheit. While low maintenance, it likes occasional, light pruning after it finishes blooming. Use it in perennial gardens, containers, and raised planters or as a border or edging plant for spring color and fragrance. The flowers can also be used in dried arrangements. It is native to the Middle East from Northeast Spain to areas of Turkey, Southern France, and Northern Africa.

Leucophyllum candidum
'Thunder Cloud' Texas Silverleaf
Medium-sized shrub

Leucophyllum candidum
'Thunder Cloud' Texas Silverleaf

This stunning, irregular-shaped shrub grows five feet high and four to five feet wide with small,

hairy, silvery white foliage. The stems are twiggy when young and become woodier with age. Small clusters of bluish violet blooms appear in abundance after the summer monsoon and again in the fall. It may bloom periodically after a hard rain. The fast-growing plant is extremely hardy to about fifteen degrees Fahrenheit. It is also drought resistant and does not like to be over-watered. If it begins to decline in the landscape, the cause is usually too much water. Do not plant this shrub in areas with water runoff or where water accumulates, as it is susceptible to root rot. The "Thunder Cloud" sage likes full sun with plenty of reflected heat and performs well when planted in the hottest spot in the landscape. This plant grows best in well-draining soil and does not need any extra amendments added at planting. Spring is best time to plant it after flowering is completed. Do not ever shear this plant; allow it to remain in a natural shape. Use it as a hedge, screen, or backdrop in medians, along roadways, in parking lots, and in masses for color display. The plant is native to the southern portions of Texas and into Central and Southern Mexico in the states of Durango, Zacatecas, Chihuahua, and Coahuila, growing at elevations of 2,000 to 5,000.

Leucophyllum frutescens
Texas Ranger
Medium-sized shrub

The evergreen, rounded shrub grows from four to eight feet tall with an equal spread. It has small, velvety, greenish gray foliage with fine hairs and an attractive silver trunk. Mature trunks become

Leucophyllum frutescens
Texas Ranger

Leucophyllum frutescens
Texas Ranger

flower production in spring. The fast-growing shrub does not like added amendments. Use it as an accent in low-water-use situations, in medians, as a screen, in masses, along foundations, and as a border or hedge planting. The shrub is native to Texas and grows from Northern Mexico through the Rio Grande Plains and Trans-Pecos area. It also grows along the Western Edwards Plateau, into New Mexico in dry, rocky limestone slopes at elevations of 1,000 to 4,000 feet.

*Leucophyllum laevigatum

Chihuahuan Sage
Medium-sized shrub

woody and grayish brown. The plant blooms in response to the summer monsoon with a massive, fragrant cluster of purple, magenta, lavender, or white blossoms. The color display may last two weeks or more and is extremely showy. There are many varieties of this plant that bloom in different colors with variations in leaf size and color. The plant takes full sun, reflected heat, and just about the hottest spot that you can give it in the landscape. It needs light to moderate water and likes to dry out between irrigation cycles. The Texas Ranger is tolerant of most soils as long as they are well draining. It is also tolerant of high winds, salty sea air, and deer. The plant is hardy to about fifteen degrees Fahrenheit. It is easy to grow and requires little maintenance. When pruning, do not use hedge trimmers since shearing this plant will ruin its natural shape. Also, prune it in late fall to encourage

Leucophyllum laevigatum
Chihuahuan Sage

Chihuahuan sage is an evergreen with an upright growth habit and interesting shape. It reaches heights of four feet tall with a five-foot spread. This plant produces small, oval leaves that are a half inch to a quarter-inch wide. Its foliage is the

Leucophyllum laevigatum
Chihuahuan Sage

Leucophyllum zygophyllum

Blue Ranger, Cimarron
Dwarf Sage
Small-sized shrub

Leucophyllum zygophyllum
Blue Ranger, Cimarron Dwarf Sage

smallest of all the rangers, in colors varying from a bluish green to olive green color. This shrub is less reliant on the summer monsoon to produce its flowers. The blooming period starts in the spring and continues until the fall. It is the longest bloomer of all the Texas rangers. The blossoms are fragrant, showy spikes of blue, lavender, purple, or violet, and they attract butterflies, bees, and hummingbirds. Chihuahuan sage likes full sun and reflected heat but also takes some filtered shade. It is drought resistant but needs supplemental irrigation until the summer monsoons arrive. This plant prefers well-draining, alkaline, and limestone soil but can take most other soil conditions. Do not overwater it since it is susceptible to root rot. It has a moderately fast growth rate and may need occasional, light pruning once a year in the spring. It looks its best, however, when it is left to grow naturally as an open, sprawling plant. This plant is hardy to about eighteen degrees Fahrenheit and may defoliate at fifteen degrees. Use it as a foundation planting, in medians, along roadways, as an informal hedge, in background plantings or as a desert accent around pools and patios. It is native to hillsides and rocky limestone soils in Chihuahua, Coahuila, Zacatecas, San Luis Potosi, and Durango, Mexico growing at elevations from 4,000 to 7,800 feet. It is also found growing in the Big Bear County of Texas.

The blue ranger is a petite evergreen and one of the smallest of the Leucophyllum species. It has a rounded form and grows three feet tall and wide with slightly cupped, thick, velvety grayish blue foliage that forms a soft silhouette. In summer and fall, it produces bell-shaped, purplish blue, fragrant blooms in response to rain. The blue ranger likes full sun and can take plenty of reflected heat. It is a moderate- to slow-growing shrub that is hardy to about ten degrees Fahrenheit. This ranger is drought resistant but likes regular irrigation, especially during the hot, dry seasons. Once established, it needs occasional irrigation to develop an extensive root system. It does not like to be overwatered and requires a well-draining soil. This shrub does not need any pruning and is easy to grow with minimal maintenance. Use this shrub as an accent in small, tight spaces. It can also be used in masses, as a foundation in borders or as an informal, low hedge. Its attractive blue foliage looks nice when planted with deep green foliated plants. Blue ranger is native to Nuevo Leon, Tamaulipas, and San Luis Potosi, Mexico where it grows in rocky and limestone soils at elevations of 4,000 to 6,900 feet.

Loropetalum chinensis var. rubrum

Chinese Witch Hazel, Chinese Fringe Flower
Medium- to large-sized, perennial shrub

Loropetalum chinensis var. rubrum
Chinese Witch Hazel, Chinese Fringe Flower

The fast-growing evergreen reaches five to eight feet and grows four to six feet wide. It has an open, irregular growth habit with whiplike shoots. The new foliage is reddish to deep burgundy and older leaves are a darker greenish burgundy. The flowers are colorful, blooming sporadically throughout the year, prolifically in late winter through springtime, and then again in the fall. The blooms are long, tubular, and pinkish rose to mauve. Both the flowers and foliage of this plant work well in indoor flower arrangements. Plant it in full sun to partial shade conditions. It likes moist, acidic, well-draining soils that are high in organic matter. Chinese witch hazel is hardy to the mid teens and may become semideciduous in cold locations. Give this colorful shrub moderate water. Do not let it dry out but be careful not to overwater it either. It responds well to heavy shearing and grows back quickly during the warm weather. This plant requires frequent applications of ammonium phosphate fertilizer during the spring and again in late summer. The showy foliage and blooms make it a great plant for containers, raised beds, foundation planting, or mass planting. Use it in oriental or Japanese gardens or in that special area of your landscape that needs a touch of drama. The plant is native to China, Japan, and Northeast India. It is a common plant that grows in medians and along roadways in China.

Lycianthes rantonnetii

Blue Potato Bush, Paraguay Nightshade
Medium- to large-sized, perennial shrub

Lycianthes rantonnetii
Blue Potato Bush, Paraguay Nightshade

This interesting, multibranched evergreen grows from four to six feet tall with an equal spread. It has smooth, dark green foliage with waxy margins along the leaves. In spring, this colorful shrub produces a mass of showy, fragrant, cup-shaped, purple-blue flowers with a yellow center. It blooms prolifically and continuously from early spring throughout the fall, during hot weather. After blooming, the plant produces a small, decorative, round, reddish fruit, which is poisonous. This tropical looking shrub likes full sun and grows in the hottest locations. It is drought tolerant but likes regular irrigation to keep its lush appearance. The blue potato bush prefers well-draining, fertile soils and is hardy into the mid-twenties Fahrenheit. Use this plant in protected, hot locations. If it is frosted back, prune it in early spring and give it a slow-release fertilizer of ammonium phosphate to hasten new growth. It recovers quickly as soon as the weather warms up. Use for a splash of color or accent in raised beds or containers. Use the blue potato bush on the south or west side of a house or building as a tall foundation plant or around pools, ponds, and water features. It is native to the tropical and subtropical regions of Brazil, Bolivia, Paraguay, and Argentina.

Melaleuca citrina 'Little John'

Dwarf Bottlebrush
Small- to medium-sized shrub

Melaleuca citrina "Little John"
Dwarf Bottlebrush

This dense, low-growing evergreen reaches three feet with an equal spread. It has dark green to bluish green foliage with a fuzzy, reddish tip of new growth in the spring. The plant is noted for its

Melaleuca citrina "Little John"
Dwarf Bottlebrush

beautiful blooms. In spring, it produces showy, crimson red, feathery stamens that resemble a bottlebrush. This plant likes full sun to partial shade and reflected heat. It is drought resistant when established but prefers regular irrigation and will show signs of water stress in hot weather. Plant it in well-draining, rich soils and provide applications of ammonium phosphate fertilizer in early spring to promote growth. Dwarf bottlebrush is hardy to about twenty degrees Fahrenheit and does not need much pruning or care to look good. Use it in groupings as a landscape accent, along foundations, as a border plant, in medians, as a hedge, as a hummingbird attraction, or in planters around pool areas and water features. This plant brings a tropical, lush statement to any location. Its versatile, dwarf size also makes it perfect for smaller gardens or containers or mixed into low-water-use landscapes as a green contrast against cacti and succulents. The plant is native to Australia.

Musa x paradisiaca

Edible Banana, Plantain
Large-sized, perennial shrub

Musa x paradisiaca
Edible Banana, Plantain

The banana is a large, tropical plant with dramatic, glossy, dark green sheaths that form along its slender trunks. It grows from underground rhizomes, reaching ten to fifteen feet tall at maturity. Its trunk develops from an underground root that grows upward. Many varieties are available. It is admired for its large, bold foliage with distinctive veins that run from the middle of its rib straight to the outer edge of the plant. The leaves can grow to four feet long and about two feet wide. The banana flower appears as a long, tapering purple bud that opens revealing slim, nectar-rich, tubular, white flowers. Each cluster is covered with a waxy, thick, hooked bract that is purple on the outside and deep red in the inside. In frost-free locations, the female plant produces fruit, which develops from a deep green color to yellow or red, and ranges in length from three quarters to two inches long. In the Southwest desert, the banana usually freezes back each year. It will freeze at twenty-five to twenty-eight degrees Fahrenheit but recovers in spring. Plant it in warm, protected areas in partial to filtered sun, and provide rich, well-draining, amended soil. Fertilize it with ammonium phosphate in early spring to encourage new growth. This lush-looking shrub requires a great deal of irrigation, especially during the warm weather. Also, remove tattered, older leaves that can shred in high winds. Use it for tropical effects in large containers or covered atriums and around pools, water features, and protected patios. The banana is native to India, Southern Asia, and Central America. Portuguese Franciscan friars are thought to have introduced this plant into the Caribbean and parts of Americas.

*Myrtus communis 'Boetica'

Twisted Myrtle
Medium- to large-sized shrub

Myrtus communis 'Boetica'
Twisted Myrtle

This twisted, irregular evergreen grows to heights of nine to twelve feet with dark green, glossy leaves that have a slight sharp point on the tip and are clustered around the branches. The foliage produces an aromatic scent when the plant is touched. Its growth habit is interesting in appearance, with a twisted branching pattern. The plant has tan bark, and when mature, it peels and becomes papery. In spring through summer, twisted myrtle produces fragrant, white, star-shaped blossoms in small clusters on its branches followed by bluish black fruit. The bitter fruit can be eaten, and the flowers attract birds, butterflies, and bees. This plant likes full sun to partial shade. It prefers regular irriga-

Myrtus communis 'Boetica'
Twisted Myrtle

tion but will take some drought conditions. If it is overwatered or is grown in poorly draining soils, the plant could become chlorotic. Treat this with iron chelated fertilizers as needed. Twisted myrtle does best when planted in amended soil with organic mulch. It is hardy from sixteen to twenty degrees Fahrenheit. Use it as a focal point, accent, screen, background planting, barrier, container or informal hedge. It also is an excellent plant choice for oriental or Japanese gardens. When it reaches maturity, prune off the branches to expose its exquisite trunk. This plant is native to Iran and Afghanistan and has been cultivated throughout Mediterranean gardens for many centuries.

Nandina domestica

Heavenly Bamboo
Medium- to large-sized shrub

Nandina domestica
Heavenly Bamboo

Nandina domestica
Heavenly Bamboo

The woody evergreen with distinctive foliage and lacy appearance grows six to eight feet. It is noted for its beautiful winter leaf color in shades of green, red and maroon. In spring, it produces small, creamy white flowers at the tip of each stem. Its flowers are followed by clusters of bright green berries that turn an exquisite red in the fall. The berries stay on the plant for months, producing a nice winter color and attracting birds. This plant prefers rich soils that are well draining. It likes full sun, reflected heat, and supplemental irrigation, although it takes some drought conditions. The plant is hardy to ten degrees Fahrenheit. Use it in a group as a

Nandina domestica 'Nana'
Dwarf Heavenly Bamboo

screen, background, or hedge or as an accent or container plant up against a pale wall or building. It looks nice in courtyards and oriental or tropical settings. Do not shear or heavily prune this plant. Let it keep its natural appearance to look its best. The variety "Compacta" is a slower-growing,

Nandina domestica
Heavenly Bamboo

more compact plant with lacy foliage that grows to four feet. The variety "Nana" grows under two feet and works best in shade. The plant is native to China and Japan but has naturalized in parts of Florida and other areas.

Nerium Oleander
Oleander

Nerium oleander

Oleander
Large-sized shrub

This fast-growing, evergreen shrub grows to twenty feet tall and is noted for its colorful clusters of single or double blossoms in white, hot pink, pink, red, and salmon that bloom during the warm season. It has dark glossy, green leaves with a prominent vein running along the entire leaf. The plant can be trained into a single or multi-trunk tree or shrub. It is fast growing, hardy to twenty degrees Fahrenheit and likes full sun with plenty of reflected heat. Oleander can survive under drought conditions but grows quickly with supplemental irrigation. It is also salt tolerant and does well in coastal situations. Oleander is toxic to humans and animals if eaten. It also produces a milky substance that can be a skin irritant to some

Nerium Oleander
Oleander

people. The smoke from burning the wood of the oleander is also very toxic. Prune it in early spring to control its size. Some varieties, especially the double pink bloomers, have a tendency to become leggy and need occasional pruning. Many vari-

Nerium Oleander 'Petite Dwarf'
Dwarf Oleander

eties are available. One variety "Petite Salmon" grows three to six feet with salmon flowers and is hardy to twenty-six degrees. Prune off damaged foliage when temperatures warm up in the spring. In recent years, the bacterial disease, oleander leaf scorch, has become a problem. Additionally, oleanders may suffer from the disease Xylella fastidiosa, which is spread by the sharpshooter insect (Homalodisca liturata). The disease inhibits the flow of moisture though plant tissue. The insect, which moves from plant to plant, feeds on plant tissue. The bacteria are passed by the insect and get into the plant's vascular system, causing it to become blocked. This inhibits the flow of water or moisture though the plant tissue. The insect is about a quarter of an inch long, winged and brown, and has an arrow-shaped head. It is small and moves very quickly throughout the plant. The symptoms look like severe salt or chemical damage on the leaf or severe iron chlorosis. The leaf veins will become more prominent, and the outside band of the leaf will turn yellow with brown edges that appear to be scorched. This disease will make its appearance during the warm season, affecting one branch, twigs, or sections of the plant. As the disease continues, the plant will continue to decline and eventually die. There is no control or treatment for this disease. Sharpshooters are hard to manage because they move quickly, and insecticidal treatments are ineffective. One method of treatment may be to prune infected plants to the ground while infestations are still mild and hope that when new growth appears, the insect will be gone and the plant can regrow with healthy foliage. This disease first appeared in Southern California in the early 1990s. Use the oleander as a single-specimen planting, screening plant, informal hedge, foundation planting, or colorful accent. It is a great choice to plant along roadways, windbreaks, or medians. It can also be used in containers and as a streetscape planting. The oleander is native to Northern Africa, Southeast Asia, and the eastern Mediterranean regions. It has naturalized in warmer, dry climates around the world.

Perovskia atriplicifolia
Russian Sage
Medium-sized, perennial shrub

Perovskia atriplicifolia
Russian Sage

The interesting landscape perennial has upright, white stems and finely textured, silvery gray, scented foliage, growing four to five feet tall and wide. Older stems become woody, and the younger stems are more herbaceous. In late summer and early fall, it produces long lasting, tall spires of tubular, lavender blue flowers that attract butterflies and bees. After flowering, the plant should be cut heavily for the next season's growth since the best flowering occurs on new growth. The plant goes dormant in the winter. It likes full sun and hot, exposed spots of the landscape with reflected heat. If planted in shade, it becomes leggy and requires staking. It also should be cut back hard in the fall. While drought tolerant, it prefers moderate water. Russian sage likes well-draining, alkaline soil to look its best. This fast-growing shrub is tolerant to salty soils and resistant to rabbits and deer. Russian sage is hardy to zero degrees or lower. Use this showy, versatile, fall color plant in containers, tubs, and mass plantings, or mix it into colorful borders and perennial gardens. The grayish stems and leaves are a nice backdrop for other plantings. Russian sage is native to Iran, Pakistan, Tibet, and Afghanistan.

Philodendron bipinnatifidum
Split-Leaf Philodendron

Philodendron bipinnatifidum
Split-Leaf Philodendron

Philodendron bipinnatifidum

Split-Leaf Philodendron
Medium-sized, perennial shrub

The split-leaf philodendron is a tropical evergreen with extremely large, deeply lobed, glossy, green leaves and large aerial roots. The drooping leaves are about three feet long and two feet wide. It gets its name from the leaf shape that is split into many sections and held onto long, green, fleshy stems. In its native habitat and in regions where temperatures remain mild year round, it develops small, petal-less flowers surrounded by a greenish red bract. This plant also grows a thick, woody trunk and reaches heights of fifteen feet with an equal spread. In the Southwest desert, it grows three to six feet high and wide. Split-leaf philodendron likes moist, fertile, well-draining soils, and partial to full shade. It tolerates drought but prefers supplemental irrigation. This plant is the hardiest of all the philodendrons, but temperatures into the low thirties will damage the leaves. Therefore, plant it in protected areas. Prune it lightly to remove yellow or frost-damaged leaves and fertilize monthly during the warm weather. Use it as a container plant or accent under patios and porches or in protected entryways, courtyards, atriums, and raised beds in tropical settings for bold foliage or to soften up a wall or an open space. When planting, provide plenty of room for this lush shrub to grow and spread. There are many varieties and hybrids of the philodendron that vary in leaf size and shape. Philodendrons are extremely poisonous if eaten, and the sap may irritate skin. The plant is native to the rainforests of Paraguay, Brazil, Bolivia, and Argentina.

Phlomis fruticosa
Jerusalem Sage
Medium-sized, perennial shrub

Phlomis fruticosa
Jerusalem Sage

Phlomis fruticosa
Jerusalem Sage

Jerusalem sage is a fast-growing, warm-season plant that reaches three to four feet tall with an equal spread. The semiwoody evergreen plant has fuzzy, grayish green, textured leaves and bright yellow, wooly blossoms in late spring through early summer. The blooms form a cluster of rings around the stems on a vertical stalk arranged with one flower on top

of another, producing an interesting effect. Its flowers attract butterflies and hummingbirds. This plant likes full sun to light shade and becomes leggy if planted in deep shade. It prefers adequate irrigation and well-draining soil. Jerusalem sage is also drought tolerant and can be planted in hot, exposed areas of the landscape. This attractive plant is hardy to about twenty-three degrees Fahrenheit. It should be heavily pruned in late winter and given applications of ammonium phosphate fertilizer in spring. Use it in an herb garden as an accent, in raised planters or containers or in vegetable gardens. The flower heads and seeds can be dried and used in flower arrangements. Jerusalem sage looks nice when combined with Salvia greggi, Salvia leucantha, and Salvia clevelandii. It is native to the Mediterranean regions of Turkey and Syria but has been naturalized in the United States.

Photinia x fraseri

Fraser's Photinia, Red-Tip Photinia
Medium- to large-sized shrub

Photinia x fraseri
Fraser's Photinia, Red-Tip Photinia

This fast-growing evergreen grows twelve to fifteen feet tall and eight to twelve feet wide. It has lush, glossy green leaves with new growth appearing bright red. This plant produces small, creamy white blossoms in the spring that have a light fragrance. It can be grown in full sun to partial shade and likes to dry out between irrigation cycles. The plant prefers alkaline soils and tolerates most soils as long as they are well draining. It is also hardy to about five degrees Fahrenheit. This shrub is susceptible to iron chlorosis, fire blight disease, and Texas Root rot. Fertilize it in the spring with ammonium phosphate to promote new spring growth and add iron chelate, if needed. Use it as a large specimen planting, tall hedge, or background in containers or in an aboveground planter for its striking red leaf color. It can also be used as a screen or barrier plant in parking lots and medi-

ans or in transitional areas. If the branches are pruned, it can also be trained into an attractive patio tree. This plant makes a colorful splash of spring color with its striking red leaf foliage. Photinia is a hybrid that was created at Fraser's Nursery in Birmingham, Alabama and was formerly known as the variety "Birmingham." It is a cross between Photinia glabra and Photinia serrulata, which are both native to Japan and China.

Phyllostachys aurea

Fish Pole Bamboo, Golden Bamboo
Medium- to large-sized shrub

Golden bamboo grows upright to heights of ten to fifteen feet with distorted, green, ornamental stems. It has stiff, hollow, yellow canes and is one of the strongest of the bamboos. Its foliage is dark green and about six inches long. When the canes are exposed to direct sunlight, they fade with age. This plant grows slowly at first, and when established, it sends out runners to moist areas and grows rapidly in the spring. It is a hardy, evergreen plant that will survive in temperatures of five degrees Fahrenheit or below. Golden bamboo takes about three years to become established and produce an underground system of rhizomes or roots. It likes full sun, reflected heat, and prefers well-draining, rich soil, and ample water to grow. To encourage fast growth, add a high-nitrogen fertilizer once or twice each year. It requires some cleanup and maintenance from leaf drop. Use bamboo as a privacy screen, hedge, sound barrier, or accent around ponds,

Phyllostachys aurea
Fish Pole Bamboo, Golden Bamboo

Pittosporum tobira 'Variegata'
Variegated Pittosporum, Variegated
Japanese Mock Orange

Pittosporum tobira, 'Compacta'
Dwarf Pittosporum,
Dwarf Japanese Mock Orange

water features, and oriental or tropical gardens. It can stabilize embankments and is a great plant for erosion control. Bamboo is a member of the grass family and is native to China. It has been planted as an ornamental in warm Mediterranean climates and has naturalized in those regions of the world.

Pittosporum tobira

Japanese Mock Orange
Medium- to large-sized shrub

The Japanese mock orange is a durable, broad-leaved evergreen that grows ten to twelve feet or more with dense, green, glossy foliage. The leaves tend to curl down and are alternately arranged in circular patterns around the stem. It produces small, fragrant, creamy white blossoms in the spring that last for several weeks. The fragrance of the blossom is like that of citrus blooms. The flowers are pure white until they open, turning more yellow with age. Blossoms tend to be more noticeable on the nonvariegated varieties. This moderate- to fast-growing plant likes moist, well-draining soil with supplemental irrigation.

Pittosporum tobira
Mock Orange

*Plumbago auriculata

Cape Plumbago
Medium-sized shrub

Plumbago auriculata
Cape Plumbago

It is drought-, heat-, and salt-tolerant and hardy into the low teens. The Japanese mock orange can be maintained at any desired height by selective hand pruning. Use it as an ornamental, screen, specimen or informal hedge in shade to partial shade or sunny locations, for woodsy effects or in coastal situations. It can also be trained into a multitrunk tree or used as an understory plant in filtered sun. The variegated and dwarf varieties are great for oriental and Japanese gardens. The variety "Wheeleri" has a more compact, dwarf growth habit reaching three to four feet tall and is great for smaller spaces. The variety "Variegata" produces creamy, whitish gray, variegated foliage that is used in floral arrangements. The plant is native to China, Korea, and Japan.

Plumbago auriculata
Cape Plumbago

The evergreen is admired for its brilliant sky blue flowers with a loose, sprawling growth habit and grows four to six feet tall and four to ten feet wide. It has arching branches, long, skinny stems, and thin, green foliage with grayish green on the underside of its leaves. New growth is bright green growing darker as the leaf matures. When the weather warms up in spring, it produces sky blue flower tubes with five assorted petals to form clusters of showy blossoms. The plant blooms from late spring into the fall and attracts butterflies. The variety "Alba" has white flowers, and "Royal Cape" has blooms that are cobalt blue. It needs full sun, reflected heat, and well-draining soil with ample water for optimum growth. The plumbago also requires pruning to keep its shape and stimulate blooms since it produces flowers on the new season's growth. It is hardy to thirty-two degrees Fahrenheit, but if frosted to the ground, the plant will recover very quickly in the spring. Use it as a foundation or accent planting, in containers, along borders, in raised beds and flowerbeds, around pools and ponds or in oriental gardens. The plumbago has traditionally been used for headaches, warts, broken bones, and wounds. In South Africa, it is thought that by placing a stick or piece of the plant in the thatch part of the roof, it may ward off lighting. It is native to the subtropics in South Africa from the Southern Cape and Eastern Cape into KwaZulu-Natal, where it grows as a large thicket or scrambling shrub.

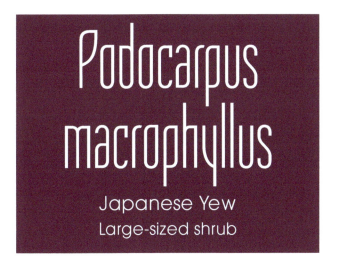

Podocarpus macrophyllus

Japanese Yew
Large-sized shrub

Podocarpus macrophyllus
Japanese Yew

This tall, narrow, upright evergreen reaches heights of twenty feet and grows to ten feet wide or more in the southwest desert. In warmer locations, it can reach heights of thirty to forty feet. Japanese yew produces long, thin, dark green, needlelike, leathery leaves with attractive light brown, peeling bark and inconspicuous flowers. Following the flower cycle, it develops fleshy, purple, inedible fruit on female plants. The seed from the fruit is eaten and dispersed by birds. It likes fertile, well-draining soil and full sun to shade but develops a looser appearance when grown in the shade. This plant does well on the north side of buildings with little or no direct sunlight. Japanese yew prefers ample water with a deep irrigation either once per week or every two weeks but will not tolerate soils that are constantly wet. It is hardy to thirteen to sixteen degrees Fahrenheit. This is a good plant for coastal areas since it tolerates salt spray and hot conditions.

When pruning this shrub, use hand pruning shears rather than electric or gas-powered trimmers. Use it as a dense screen and hedge along the foundation of a house or building. Also use it near a deck or patio in oriental gardens or to achieve woodsy or vertical effects. Foliage from the plant can also be used in floral arrangements and lasts a long time when cut. The variety "Maki" is not as tall and is a good choice for narrow locations in the landscape where some height is needed. The plant is native to Japan and Southern China.

Psilostrophe tagetina
Woolly Paper Flower
Small-sized, perennial shrub

Psilostrophe tagetina
Woolly Paper Flower

The herbaceous, mounding shrub grows moderately to two feet tall and wide, producing prolific, long lasting, fragrant blooms in spring and summer. The small, yellow flowers turn a papery texture and can be used in dried flower arrangements. The foliage is narrow, grayish green with

a velvety texture and its stems are covered with wooly hairs. This plant is short-lived but reseeds itself every year if moisture is available. It prefers full sun, reflected heat, and well-draining soil. The woolly paper flower does not like to be overwatered. It is hardy to below ten degrees Fahrenheit. The plant is also mildly poisonous. Remove unattractive vegetation that may become scraggly with age. Use it as a border or color plant in perennial spring gardens or combine with other low-water-use plants in disturbed or revegetated areas. Plant the woolly paper flower around water features and fountains. It is native to open spaces in New Mexico, Texas, Eastern Arizona, and Northern Mexico between 4,000 to 7,000 feet.

*Punica granatum or Punica granatum 'Nana',
Pomegranate and Dwarf Pomegranate
Large-medium-sized shrub

Pomegranate is a fast-growing, deciduous plant noted for its berrylike fruit that grows six to fifteen feet tall with a multiple or single trunk. "Nana" is the dwarf variety, and it reaches just one to three feet. The species produces slender, upright branches that gracefully weep if left unpruned. It has skinny, shiny green foliage and bright, orangey red, trumpetlike flowers with ruffled petals that are two inches long and bloom in spring for several weeks. After three to four years, pomegranates begin bearing a wonderful fruit

Punica granatum
Pomegranate.

Punica granatum
Pomegranate Showing Fall Color

Punica granatum 'Nana'
Dwarf Pomegranate with Fruit

Punica granatum 'Nana'
Dwarf Pomegranate With Fruit

that is about the size of an apple. It is reddish to pink and filled with crunchy, sweet seeds that are encased in a juicy, membranous skin. The seeds, pulp, and juice are eaten, but the membrane part of the fruit does not taste good. Juice from the fruit is used in jellies and wines. There are many varieties of pomegranates commonly cultivated in the Southwest desert, including "Papago," "Chico," "Wonderful," and "Angel Wings." This plant likes hot, dry climates with long summers and cool winters. It also prefers sandy, acidic, or alkaline soils and is fairly salt tolerant. It needs full sun and reflected heat as well as ample water but will become more drought tolerant as it matures. Pomegranate is hardy to about fifteen degrees Fahrenheit. Use it as an attractive shrub, small tree, hedge, screen, or accent in the landscape. It can also be used in landscapes with other fruit trees or citrus. The dwarf form can be used as an edging or small foundation plant and in courtyards, containers, raised planters, and patios. The pomegranate is a native to Asia from the Middle East to the Himalayas, where it grows in sandy or rocky soils and scrublands. It has been cultivated in Mediterranean climates and tropical areas throughout the world.

Rhapiolepis indica
Indian Hawthorn
Medium-sized shrub

Rhapiolepis indica
Indian Hawthorn

This evergreen shrub is admired for its showy, fragrant flowers and compact growth habit, reaching four to five feet with a spread of four feet. It forms a round, loose shape that makes it a perfect foundation planting. Indian hawthorn has green, oblong, leathery foliage that has slightly serrated edges. New growth appears bronzy red in color. In early spring, it develops fragrant blossoms in clusters of pink to light pink with five petals that attract bees, butterflies, and birds. After flowering, the plant produces small, bluish black berries that are eaten by birds. Many varieties are available, including "Ballerina" with pink blossoms and "Clara" with white blossoms. All varieties of this shrub prefer full sun to partial shade. Avoid planting it in reflected heat because it can sunburn in the southwest desert. This plant prefers regular irrigation and is drought tolerant when established. Do not overwater and do not give it overhead water. This plant prefers well-draining, rich, acidic soil and is hardy to zero degrees. The Indian hawthorn is susceptible to white grub damage and fire blight. Do not prune or shear this plant; let it maintain its natural growth and shape to look its best. Fertilize with ammonium phosphate in early spring. Use it as a low, informal hedge or background, accent, or divider plant along walkways and low walls. It also works well near patios, in containers, or trained as a bonsai plant. The Indian hawthorn is native to India and Southern China.

Rhus ovata
Sugar Bush, Sugar Sumac
Medium- to large-sized shrub

Sugar bush is a dense, mounding evergreen that grows eight to twelve feet tall and eight to ten feet wide with a dark brown, sometimes shaggy bark. It has rich, leathery, deep green foliage that is large, oval, and pointed at the tip. In early to late spring, it produces pinkish white buds that open to expose showy clusters of dense, white blossoms. In late fall through winter, it develops small, reddish berries that are coated with a sugary, lemon-flavored substance. The berries are edible and can be used to make a lemonade-like beverage. Fruits are eaten by birds and other small rodents and wildlife. The sugar bush is

Rhus ovata
Sugar Bush, Sugar Sumac

Rhus ovata
Sugar Bush, Sugar Sumac

hardy to about ten to fifteen degrees Fahrenheit but can freeze in lower temperatures when the plant is young. It is susceptible to sunburn, so plant it in an area where it will receive afternoon shade. Avoid reflected heat. In higher elevations or closer to the California coast, it can be planted in full sun. This plant is very drought resistant but likes supplemental irrigation, especially during the hot weather. It prefers well-draining soil and does not like to be overwatered. Also, it does not need any additional pruning and should be left to grow naturally. Plant it in the ground during

the cooler seasons of fall and winter. It should be allowed to acclimatize in warmer weather to look its best. Use it as a screen, informal hedge, or barrier plant, in groupings or as a specimen planting around pools and foundations. With its lush green foliage, it looks nice when planted with low-water-use or drought-resistant shrubs or as an understory plant beneath a deciduous shade tree. The sugar bush grows natively in chaparral areas or dry slopes in Southern California, Central Arizona, Baja California, and Mexico at elevations of 3,000 to 5,000 feet.

Rosmarinus officinalis
Rosemary
Small- to medium-sized shrub

Rosemary is a hardy evergreen with needlelike, deep green, fragrant foliage that grows three to five feet high and three to eight feet wide. It is popularized as a landscape plant and offers edible leaves that when dried are used in cooking and for medicinal purposes. In the spring and again in fall, it produces attractive blossoms in blue, lavender, white, or purple. Bees, butterflies, and some birds are attracted to its small blossoms. Rosemary likes well-draining soil with full sun and reflected heat. It is extremely drought resistant but likes additional irrigation during the hot, dry season and does not like to be overwatered. This plant is very hardy into the teens and below. New growth may freeze if exposed to low temperatures. It benefits from occasional fertilizer applications of ammonium phosphate in early spring. When needed, prune woody growth out of mature plants to keep them lush and increase side branching. Use this versatile shrub as a foundation,

Rosmarinus officinalis
Rosemary

Rosmarinus officinalis
Rosemary

Ruellia californica subsp. peninsularis
Desert Ruellia, Baja Ruellia
Medium-sized shrub

Ruellia californica subsp. peninsularis
Desert Ruellia, Baja Ruellia

Ruellia californica subsp. peninsularis
Desert Ruellia, Baja Ruellia

border, low growing hedge, culinary herb, and transition or container plant. It is a good choice to use against a hot wall or in dry locations for erosion control on steep slopes and in rock gardens. Its attractive green foliage makes it a nice winter contrast plant. Use the dwarf cascading variety "Prostratus" to creep over walls and drape over surfaces. Other varieties grow upright and have variations in flower color and taste. Rosemary works well as an herb in vegetable gardens. Oils extracted from the plant have been used for many centuries for antibacterial and holistic purposes, and the leaves give a nice scent to lotions, perfumes, soaps, and sachets. Rosemary originated in the Mediterranean region where it grows in dry, sandy, or rocky soils.

This medium-sized evergreen shrub has bright green, oval foliage and grayish brown, twisted stems. It reaches heights of four feet with a six-foot spread, developing delicate, dark purple, funnel-shaped blossoms throughout the warm growing season, but mostly in the spring. After the summer monsoons, it blooms again, producing a massive flower show. The desert ruellia is drought resistant, grows lush with supplemental water, and it likes full sun or partial shade and reflected heat. The plant suffers leaf dieback at twenty-five degrees Fahrenheit and freezes when the temperatures reach the mid teens but recovers quickly in the spring since it is a fast grower. Prune frozen plant parts as needed. Use it for tropical effects near pools, ponds, and fountains. It also works well as a transitional specimen along roadsides, as an informal hedge, color accent plant, background plant, and in groupings. The desert ruellia works in containers and along the foundation of a house or building. This plant is native to Baja California and the lower Sonoran Desert in Mexico, where it grows on dry, gravelly slopes, rocky arroyos, and washes.

Ruellia tweediana

Dwarf Ruellia, Mexican Petunia
Small-sized, perennial shrub

Ruellia tweediana
Dwarf Ruellia, Mexican Petunia

Ruellia tweediana
Dwarf Ruellia, Mexican Petunia

Ruellia tweediana
Dwarf Ruellia, Mexican Petunia

The dwarf ruellia is a beautiful flowering, low-growing perennial with long, narrow, glossy green, foliage that grows one to three feet, depending on the variety. The semiwoody stalks of the plant grow in an upright pattern. This plant produces bright, vibrant, bluish purple, trumpet-shaped blossoms that flower through the warm growing season. Other varieties bloom in white, pink and many other shades of blue. The plant is very showy when it is in bloom and can be a great butterfly and bird attraction. This shrub will naturalize and reseed in moist areas of the garden. It is hardy to thirty-two degrees Fahrenheit and will freeze to the ground when temperatures drop into the mid-twenties. In spring, prune it back to remove any frost damage and encourage new growth. The ruellia likes full sun and reflected heat. It prefers ample water and well-draining, fertile soils and will take some drought once established. Fertilize with Ammonium phosphate in early spring, to encourage flower production. Use it as a flowering border plant in perennial gardens, near patios, around ponds and water features, in courtyards or as a showy container plant. The variety "Katie" is more compact and refined and has purple flowers, "Chi Chi" and "Rosa" both produce pink blooms and "Blanca" has white flowers. The ruellia is native to Mexico but has naturalized throughout the Southeastern United States.

*Russelia equisetiformis
Coral Fountain
Medium-sized, perennial shrub

Russelia equisetiformis
Coral Fountain

Russelia equisetiformis
Coral Fountain

Russelia equisetiformis
Coral Fountain

The coral fountain is a flowering perennial plant with long, slender, arching, fountainlike branches that form a dense mound to four feet tall and six feet wide. Its weeping branches produce dark green, scalelike leaves on stems. The plant has showy, one- to two-inch coral red, tubular flower clusters through the fall and into the winter. The blooms attract hummingbirds and butterflies. It likes full sun or shade. During the hot months, the plant may become stressed if exposed to reflected heat. It is a moderate to fast grower and likes plenty of supplemental irrigation and can take some drought during the cooler season. The coral fountain is hardy to the low thirties Fahrenheit and will suffer frost damage in the high twenties but recovers quickly in the spring when daytime temperatures start to warm up. This plant is salt tolerant and likes yearly fertilizer applications.

The coral fountain needs rich, fertile, well-draining soil, and some protection from rabbits when young; use chicken wire for this purpose. The shrub works well in pool areas, around ponds and water features, or cascading over banks, walls, and planters. Also, plant it in containers, as a foundation or color plant for tropical effects, and in hanging baskets, or train it to spill over a raised planter. It is an excellent plant to use in floral arrangements. This fast-growing plant is native to the humid, tropical areas of Central Mexico, and has become established in areas of Florida.

*Salvia clevelandii

Chaparral Sage, Cleveland Sage
Medium- to large-sized shrub

Salvia clevelandii
Chaparral Sage, Cleveland Sage

Salvia clevelandii
Chaparral Sage, Cleveland Sage

This rounded evergreen with highly aromatic foliage and exotic flowers grows four to five feet tall and six feet wide. It has soft, fuzzy, wrinkled, small, grayish green foliage. The underside of the leaf is lighter in color. The best features of this plant are its striking fragrant flower spikes that appear above the plant with clusters of bluish purple blossoms. As the plant matures, the flower displays become more spectacular. It likes fertile, well-draining soil with supplemental irrigation. Allow the soil to dry out between irrigation. This plant will take full sun and reflected heat. When planting, leave plenty of room for it to grow quickly, as it takes up a lot of space in the landscape. Prune it back heavily each season after the blooms are spent to keep its size manageable. This plant is hardy to the low teens and is a great butterfly, bee, and hummingbird attraction. It also makes an excellent habitat for quail and other desert birds. Use it as a foundation or low-water-use plant in perennial gardens or for spring color on roadsides and medians, and for revegetating large areas. Also use around water features, pools, and ponds. The blossoms make excellent dried flowers and can be used in potpourris. It is native to the rocky slopes and hills in San Diego County, the central coast of California, and Baja California.

*Salvia greggii

Red Salvia, Autumn Sage
Medium-sized, perennial shrub

Salvia greggii
Red Salvia, Autumn Sage

This amazing evergreen color plant has a compact, mounding appearance with dark green foliage that is slightly sticky to the touch and mildly aromatic. It grows two to three feet high and wide, producing long spikes of small, tubular hot pink, fuchsia or red blossoms that flower for a long period of time. The nectar-laden flowers attract hummingbirds and butterflies. It begins to bloom in early spring and then enters dormancy in summer, coming alive again in the fall with a flush of growth and color. Newer varieties offer purple and cherry red flowers. It is hardy to fifteen degrees Fahrenheit but can survive temperatures much lower. This fast-growing plant does best in full sun but prefers filtered sunlight or shade. It grows best as an understory plant in the shade of a large tree. The red salvia is tolerant of drought, although looks healthier with supplemental irrigation during the hot, dry summer. Plant it in well-draining soil and avoid overwatering. Add light applications of ammonium phosphate fertilizer during the summer months to stimulate new growth in the fall. Prune periodically in midsummer or early fall to prevent it from becoming woody. Use it in masses, in desert landscapes, as a foundation planting, low hedge, small shrub or as a nice addition to a perennial garden. It is an excellent choice to use in areas with heavy rabbit infestations, as they do not bother to eat it. The foliage of this plant is also resistant to deer and javelina damage. The red salvia is native to rocky hillsides of the Chihuahuan Desert in Mexico as well as New Mexico and Western Texas, growing at elevations between 2,500 to 8,000 feet.

*Salvia leucantha

Mexican Bush Sage, Mexican Sage
Medium-sized, perennial shrub

Salvia leucantha
Mexican Bush Sage, Mexican Sage

Salvia leucantha
Mexican Bush Sage, Mexican Sage

Salvia leucantha
Mexican Bush Sage, Mexican Sage

It will freeze in the low thirties and recovers quickly in the spring. Prune frozen growth back in late winter. This plant needs plenty of room to grow and likes a good pruning in early spring to keep its shape and prevent it from getting top-heavy when it blooms. Use it as a summer and early fall color accent plant, and as a border, foundation, or background plant. You can also use it around pools, ponds, and water features in English and perennial gardens. In the landscape, plant it next to yellow or orange lantana for an interesting contrast. The flowers can be dried and used in flower arrangements. It is native to Central America and Mexico.

*Schefflera arboricola

Dwarf Schefflera, Dwarf Umbrella Plant
Medium- to large-sized shrub

The colorful herbaceous plant grows in a mounded shape to four feet tall and wide with willowy, slender, arching stems that have soft, grayish green to silvery, wrinkled-looking foliage. In late summer through the first frost, it produces elongated, lavender clusters that attract hummingbirds. The purple clusters send out white, tubular flowers that extend beyond the plant to create an amazing landscape accent. It likes full sun to produce its magnificent color but tolerates light shade. Provide supplemental irrigation throughout the growing season but allow the plant to dry out between each watering. It does not like to be overwatered. Mexican sage prefers well-draining, slightly alkaline soils.

Schefflera arboricola
Dwarf Schefflera, Dwarf Umbrella Plant

Schefflera arboricola
Dwarf Schefflera, Dwarf Umbrella Plant

Schefflera arboricola
Dwarf Schefflera, Dwarf Umbrella Plant

This easy-to-grow, tropical, treelike plant reaches ten to twelve feet with a three to four-foot spread and develops an extensive root system. It is known for its upright umbrella-shaped leaves with five to seven glossy, green leaflets on each leaf stalk. The leaves are oval, pointed and variegated forms have yellow, gold or cream colorings mixed with green. In tropical locations, it produces a panicle of small flower stalks and small, yellowish orange fruit. This plant likes partial to full shade. Avoid planting it in full sun or its foliage will sunburn. Provide ample irrigation but let it dry out between watering and do not overwater. The plant prefers well-draining, fertile soil, and humidity. It is hardy to twenty-five degrees Fahrenheit. All parts of this plant are poisonous if ingested. Selectively prune it to

shape and remove dead foliage. Use it in raised planters, containers or enclosed patios. This shrub works well as a foundation plant in shade situations, as a showy accent or as an understory plant in protected, shady locations. The variegated form "Gold Capella" has golden yellow and green leaves. "Trinett" has variegated cream and green leaves. There are numerous varieties available with variations in leaf, color, pattern, and size. This plant is native to Taiwan and the Pacific Islands.

Senna artemisioides

Feathery Cassia
Medium-sized shrub

Senna artemisioides
Feathery Cassia

Feathery cassia is an upright, rounded evergreen growing four to six feet tall and wide with fine, needlelike, feathery leaflets. This fast grower develops prolific, yellow, pealike blossoms in late winter through early spring that cover the plant in amazing color. It blooms for an extended time and is usually one of the first flowering plants of the spring season. After blooming, long, flat, green seedpods appear and hang off of the plant. The pods eventually turn brown and papery as they mature. The plant is hardy into the low twenty degrees Fahrenheit and is the least cold hardy of all the cassia species. If water-stressed, the foliage will dry up and shed from the plant. Cassia likes full sun and reflected heat. It is drought resistant but enjoys supplemental irrigation every few weeks. Do not overwater as it is susceptible to iron chlorosis. This plant needs well-draining, alkaline soil and will not live long in poor growing conditions. Every few years, prune the older, woody branches to encourage new growth. This fast-growing plant will reseed in other parts of the landscape during summer monsoon or if supplemental water is available. Use this shrub as a foundation planting; in groupings, masses, borders; or as a hedge or transitional plant. The feathery cassia also works well in medians and along roadways. Feathery cassia is native to Central Australia.

Senna artemisioides subsp. x coriacea
Desert Cassia

green, one-inch needlelike leaflets. It blooms in late winter through early spring with aromatic, yellow buttercup blooms. The blossoms are one of the first desert shrubs to flower. Following the bloom cycle, desert cassia produces long, brown seedpods that hang down from the plant. Sometimes, the seedpods can be unsightly and need to be pruned. This shrub also needs light pruning and shaping in early spring to look its best. The plant is hardy to twenty degrees Fahrenheit and is one of the hardiest of all the cassia species. It is also highly drought tolerant but likes supplemental water during our hot, dry summer season. Avoid overwatering to prevent chlorosis. Apply light applications of ammonium phosphate fertilizer in spring. Plant the cassia in full sun and reflected heat or partial shade. This plant may reseed itself after the summer monsoons. Use desert cassia as a screen, in groupings, along medians, as a background or foundation planting along streetscapes and roadsides or in groupings. This is a great choice for its early spring color and fragrance. Desert cassia is native to arid areas of Australia.

Senna artemisioides subsp. x coriacea
Desert Cassia
Medium-sized shrub

This dense, fast-growing, evergreen shrub grows six feet tall and wide with attractive grayish

Senna artemisioides subsp. petiolaris

Silver Leaf Cassia
Medium-sized shrub

ammonium phosphate and use iron chelated fertilizers if needed. This shrub also needs good drainage and is hardy to twenty degrees Fahrenheit. Prune dead wood and old seedpods as needed. It will not reseed itself like the feathery cassia. This plant may need shaping or pruning in the fall or after blooming. Use this shrub in foundations; as a hedge, mass planting, or screen; in transitions or low-water-use landscapes; around pools and roadways; and in hot locations, medians, and parking lots. Mix the silvery foliage of this species with deep green plants for an interesting contrast or as a late winter color plant. It is native to arid regions of Southern Australia, New South Wales, and Queensland Australia where it grows at elevation from sea level to 2,500 feet.

Senna artemisioides subsp. petiolaris
Silver Leaf Cassia

Silver leaf cassia is an airy, rounded evergreen with shiny, silvery blue foliage that grows five to six feet tall with an equal spread. In late winter through early spring, a mass of showy, yellow buttercup blossoms appear in branched, terminal clusters over the entire plant. After the blooms fade, flat, curved, green pods appear, becoming papery brown as they mature. The pods develop in abundance all over the plant and when they open, the seed is dispersed by wind. It likes full sun and reflected heat, is drought resistant but prefers supplemental irrigation during the hot summer months. Overwatering may cause it to become chlorotic. Fertilize in the spring with

Simmondsia chinensis

Jojoba
Medium- to large-sized shrub

Simmondsia chinensis
Jojoba

Simmondsia chinensis
Jojoba

The jojoba is a slow-growing, irregular-shaped evergreen that grows six to eight feet tall and wide with oblong, leathery, bluish green foliage that is stiff and has pointed tips. It has become popularized by the seed it produces and is used in lubricants and cosmetics. Native Americans also have used the seed as a food source. It is a tough, durable, low-maintenance plant. The leaves are arranged on the plant in such a way as to allow it to adapt to the intense heat of the sun and effectively pollinate the flowers. The shrub produces small clusters of inconspicuous, yellowish white blossoms in late winter through early spring. Female plants produce a brown acornlike nut that holds the seed, which is harvested for the coveted oil. The fruit and oil of this plant also serve as food to wildlife. The jojoba likes well-draining soil, full sun, and reflected heat and is highly drought resistant. It prefers supplemental irrigation during its first year to get started, and then irrigation can taper off. Water it every two weeks during the dry season and avoid overwatering, or the plant can become chlorotic and eventually die. It is hardy to twenty degrees Fahrenheit. Prune lightly only during the cooler season; do not ever shear the plant. Use it as an informal privacy screen, hedge, or foundation plant in low-water-use landscapes, and along medians, interstates, and highways. It is native to dry, rocky

slopes and along washes of Southern California and Southern, Eastern, and Central Arizona, as well as in Baja California, where it grows from 1,500 to 5,000 feet.

Strelitzia reginae
Bird of Paradise
Medium-sized, perennial shrub

Strelitzia reginae
Bird of Paradise

This bold, tropical evergreen produces large stalks from the base of the plant, reaching heights of four to five feet tall and wide. It has glossy, bluish green, banana-shaped leaves, and in late winter, early spring it develops a brilliant flower that stands high above the foliage. The blooms, which have the appearance of a bird head, are brilliant orange and yellow with blue petals. The plant does not produce flowers until a few years after planting. There are several varieties that differ in leaf and flower color as well as plant size. This slow grower prefers light shade and needs protection from the hot afternoon sun. It likes rich, loamy, fertile soil with ample water in order to thrive. Do not overwater it and keep it on the drier side during the winter months. This plant likes applications of ammonium phosphate

Strelitzia reginae
Bird of Paradise

fertilizer during the growing season. The bird of paradise is wind resistant and tolerant of salty, coastal air. However, it is sensitive to cold and will freeze at thirty degrees Fahrenheit and suffer severe leaf damage at twenty-eight degrees. Plant it in protected areas and prune affected plant tissue. It will recover quickly in the spring. Use for bold, tropical statements, as a border shrub, in masses with perennials and annuals, in containers or in raised planters on the north side of a building or home. Its showy flowers can also be used in cut flower arrangements. This plant is indigenous to South Africa, where it grows along the Eastern Cape.

Tagetes lemmonii
Lemon Marigold, Mountain Marigold, Copper Canyon Daisy
Medium-sized, perennial shrub

Tagetes Lemmonii
Lemon Marigold, Mountain Marigold,
Copper Canyon Daisy

Lemon marigold is a large, sprawling perennial that grows four to six feet tall, spreading to four feet. It is admired for its rich, distinctive, aromatic foliage and flowers that attract butterflies and hummingbirds. The daisylike flowers are golden yellow and appear at the end of each branch in late summer until the first frost. It is hardy to about thirty-two degrees Fahrenheit and suffers frost damage in low-lying areas. This shrub recovers in the spring as soon as the weather warms up. The plant grows rapidly during the warm summers and likes full sun, reflected heat, and hot locations. It is resistant to deer feeding. The lemon marigold needs well-draining soil and prefers ample water to thrive. Once established, it is drought tolerant. This plant likes yearly applications of ammonium phosphate fertilizer in early spring. Prune it heavily as needed in late winter to shape and remove any spent blooms or frozen foliage. When working around this plant, wear gloves and protective clothing, especially if you have sensitive skin or allergies. It can cause an itching reaction. Prune it in late winter to shape and remove any spent blooms or frozen foliage. Use it for fall and early winter color, in perennial and butterfly gardens, or along rocky slopes. It can also be planted in herb gardens. This plant is native to mountains and canyons of northern and Southern Arizona, growing in mountain canyons between 4,000 to 8,000 feet. The lemon marigold got its name from a husband and wife team who were plant collectors in the late nineteenth century. They found the plant growing in Southeastern Arizona.

Tecoma alata
Orange Jubilee

*Tecoma alata

Orange Jubilee, Orange Esperanza
Large-sized shrub

Tecoma alata
Orange Jubilee

Tecoma alata
Orange Jubilee

This fast-growing hybrid evergreen grows quickly to heights of twelve feet and eight feet wide. It has lush, lacy, glossy green foliage with serrated edges on each leaf. Its long stems are green and then turn brown as they mature. Large, brilliant orange, trumpet-shaped blossoms appear in springtime and continue to bloom throughout the fall, attracting butterflies and hummingbirds. This hybridized plant produces very little seed-pods. The shrub is hardy to the mid-twenties Fahrenheit. If frost damaged, it grows back very fast in a single growing season. The plant is partially drought resistant and requires regular irrigation to look good and stimulate blooms. The orange jubilee can grow in a variety of soils and is a low-maintenance plant that is relatively easy to maintain. Plant this colorful shrub in full sun and reflected heat. Prune anytime during the growing season if it grows too large. Use it as a screen, barrier, and foundation plant or in masses. The orange jubilee looks great around pools, ponds, and water features, in streetscapes and parking lots or as a transitional planting. Orange jubilee is a great choice for tropical landscapes and looks attractive when planted in groupings with the yellow bells. There are many different variations of this plant.

Tecoma capensis
Cape Honeysuckle
Medium-sized shrub

Tecoma capensis
Cape Honeysuckle

Tecoma capensis
Cape Honeysuckle

The fast-growing, scrambling, vinelike evergreen reaches heights of five to ten feet tall and four to five feet wide, but if left unpruned, it can grow twenty-five feet high. It has long, sprawling, dense stems and glossy foliage. In the fall and early winter, it produces showy clusters of orangey red, tubular blossoms that attract butterflies and hummingbirds. The variety "Apricot" is smaller and more compact growing. The powdered bark of this plant is used as a traditional medicine for sleeplessness and to relieve pain. In the landscape, it likes full sun and reflected heat but will take partial shade. While drought tolerant, provide it with ample water, especially during the hot season. It is hardy to about twenty-eight degrees Fahrenheit, is salt-tolerant and can grow in many soil types as long as they are well draining and fertile. This plant benefits from applications of ammonium phosphate fertilizer in the spring. Prune it in early spring to train and remove any frost-damaged branches and foliage. Use it for fall or early winter color, as a barrier, screen, hedge or as a specimen for tropical effects around pools, ponds, and other water features. Train it to cascade over large boulders, walls, and planters, or plant it in masses as a bank cover. It also can be trained as an espalier or vine or used in cut flower arrangements. The plant is native to Swaziland on the KwaZulu-Natal coast and in Mozambique in South Africa. It has naturalized in parts of Florida, Hawaii, and the tropics.

*Tecoma stans 'Gold Star',

Yellow Bells, Gold Star Esperanza
Medium- to large-sized, perennial shrub

Tecoma stans 'Gold Star'
Yellow Bells, Gold Star Esperanza

Tecoma stans 'Gold Star'
Yellow Bells, Gold Star Esperanza

The lush, broad-leaved evergreen grows quickly to four to five feet with a three to four-foot spread but gets much taller in warmer, tropical areas. The variety "Gold Star" blooms the earliest of all Tecoma species and continues to flower prolifically throughout the summer and early fall. It produces large clusters of brilliant yellow, trumpet-shaped blossoms that attract hummingbirds and butterflies. In late summer, its brownish tan seedpods appear and remain on the plant for a long time. It is hardy to about twenty degrees Fahrenheit. If frost-damaged, prune it back frozen growth in early spring. The yellow bell will grow in a wide variety of soils with good drainage. This plant likes an application of ammonium phosphate fertilizer in the spring. This will help promote blooms and lush foliage. It is drought resistant when established but needs supplemental irrigation during our hot, dry summers. The yellow bell also likes full sun and reflected heat. Sometimes after the summer monsoon, foliage can fall, and carpenter ants attack the plant. To control insects, treat it with a systemic insecticide around the base of the plant. Use it in masses or as a tropical color plant around pools, ponds, and water features, and in containers, courtyards, patios, and landscapes for summer color and accent. The variety "Gold Star" was hybridized at Texas A & M University, and many more selections and hybrids of this plant exist.

Tithonia diversifolia

Mexican Sunflower
Medium-sized, perennial shrub

Tithonia diversifolia
Mexican Sunflower

Tithonia diversifolia
Mexican Sunflower

Mexican sunflower is an outstanding, shrubby, perennial with large, pointed, velvety, olive green foliage and upright, hollow stems. It grows quickly to nine to twelve feet tall with equal spread. In late spring and again in the fall, it produces large-petaled, brilliant, orangey yellow sunflower-like blooms that attract butterflies. When the flowers dry up at the end of their blooming season, they leave behind a golden brown, rounded seed head with many narrow, black seeds. It takes full sun or lightly filtered shade and does not like reflected heat. The Mexican sunflower requires well-draining soil and needs protection from strong winds since it has soft, hollow, brittle stems that can be damaged. The shrub also likes supplemental water for continued blooms and does not like to dry out. It is hardy to thirty-two degrees, and if frosted back will recover quickly in the spring. Remove dead blooms regularly and cut it back heavily in late winter. Use it in protected areas and warm microclimates against a south-facing wall for its interesting silhouette and blooms. Also plant it around ponds, pools, and water features, or where butterflies are abundant. The blossoms also make excellent cut flowers. It is native to Sonora and Sinaloa, Mexico and down into Chihuahua and Durango, through Central Mexico. The Mexican sunflower grows in sandy, desert, native soils at elevations of 800 to 4,800 feet. This plant may be hard to find in local nurseries but can be found for sale at botanical gardens.

Ungnadia speciosa
Mexican Buckeye
Large-sized shrub

Ungnadia speciosa
Mexican Buckeye

The Mexican buckeye is a densely branched deciduous shrub growing from ten to twelve feet tall with a spread of six feet. This plant has glossy green, oval leaflets that are long and very showy with a paler color on the underside of the leaf. Its dark gray bark is an interesting contrast to the dark green foliage. The bark is smooth when young and darker as it matures. Its leaves turn a colorful yellow in the fall before dropping to the ground. In spring, before the leaves reappear, this shrub produces colorful clusters of small, pale pink to dark pink blooms, which are very fragrant. A woody seed capsule with poisonous black seeds appears in late spring. Plant the Mexican buckeye in full sun to light shade. It is very drought tolerant once it is established, but water it at least every other week during the hot, dry season before the summer monsoons arrive. It will take most soils as long as they are well draining. The plant is hardy to about five degrees Fahrenheit and is fast growing. Allow this shrub to develop naturally into a large plant and do not overprune or shear it. As it matures, the lower branches may be pruned to allow it to develop into a smaller tree that provides summer shade. Use it as a specimen with other evergreens in a courtyard or patio or plant it on the west or south side of a residence or building. It grows natively in Southern New Mexico and into Texas. This plant can also be found growing in the Northeast Chihuahuan Desert and through North and Central Mexico. It grows in canyons, ridges and on rocky slopes elevations of 1,000 to 6,500 feet.

*Vauquelinia californica
Arizona Rosewood
Large-sized shrub

The large, vase-shaped, densely branching evergreen grows to fifteen feet or more. It is a moderate-growing shrub with leathery, dark olive green foliage. The underside of the leaves can have bronzy red coloration. The younger stems are reddish with fine hairs that become smoother and darker as they mature. In later May through June, it produces tiny, dense, slightly fragrant clusters of snowy white to cream blossoms at the end of terminal branches. After the plant blooms, dark brown to tan colored, oval and

Vauquelinia californica
Arizona Rosewood

Vauquelinia californica
Arizona Rosewood

locations. It is a good alternative to oleanders. When it is mature, the lower branches can be pruned to train it as a small patio tree. The Arizona rosewood is native of canyons and rocky hillsides of Southern Arizona into Southwestern New Mexico, where it grows at elevations of 2,500 to 5,000 feet. It also is found growing in Central Mexico, Southern Baja California, Northern and Eastern Mexico. It grows natively into Sonora and Durango, Mexico at elevations of 5,000 feet.

Xylosma congestum
Xylosma
Medium-tall-sized shrub

Xylosma congestum
Xylosma

woody seed capsules form and last on the plant for a long time. It likes full sun and reflected heat but will take some shade. While extremely drought resistant and able to live on natural rainfall in its native habitat, it does much better when given supplemental, deep irrigation at least once a month. Young plants should be watered more frequently. It prefers well-draining soil but tolerates rocky or alkaline soil. Arizona rosewood is hardy to fifteen degrees Fahrenheit. Watch for spider mites and aphids on the flowers as well as powdery mildew outbreaks, and treat them as needed. This plant is slow to grow when young, but when its roots mature, its growth rate increases. Use it as a hedge, transition plant, privacy screen, or noise barrier in medians, streetscapes, low-water-use gardens, or hot, exposed

The fast-growing evergreen shrub reaches heights of twelve feet or more with an eight- to twelve-foot spread. It is valued for its bright, glossy, green foliage pointed at the tip. New growth in the spring is bronzy red. The tree has slender branches with an upward spreading form and produces a graceful canopy if left unpruned. The

Xylosma congestum
Xylosma

natural leaf drop, especially in the springtime. The xylosma is susceptible to iron chlorosis, so treat it with applications of iron chelate fertilizer as needed. Watch for infestations of spider mites in the spring. This versatile plant can be pruned as a hedge or espalier or used as a specimen tree on a patio. It also works well as a screen, garden accent, topiary, or background planting. The tree can also be used in an oriental garden with other interesting plants and works well in large containers. This handsome plant is native to China and Asia.

Xylosma in tree form

bark is dark brown to brownish gray and either furrowed, scaly, or smooth. This plant is attractive when trained as a multitrunk tree. It produces an inconspicuous flower and small, bluish berries in the spring. The xylosma likes full sun but tolerates partial shade and prefers moist, well-draining soil. It has low water needs but grows faster with supplemental irrigation. This tree is hardy to ten to fifteen degrees Fahrenheit, but its leaves will defoliate and twigs and can die back if temperatures drop into the mid teens. It produces some

4 Ornamental Grasses
for Southwest Landscapes

Ornamental grasses are meant to grow, not be cut, mowed down, or used as groundcovers. When you incorporate grasses into your desert gardens, you will be amazed by how many varieties, sizes, shapes, textures and colors are available for landscape use. They also add movement and sound as they rustle in a morning breeze. Once established, they are drought resistant and easy to maintain. I have added some of my favorite grasses into this chapter.

Arundo donax

Giant Reed
Ornamental grass

Arundo donax
Giant Reed

Arundo donax
Giant Reed

The giant reed is a tall, robust perennial that grows up to twenty feet, and it has thick, spreading clumps of grasslike foliage. Its numerous leaves are long and smooth, tapering to a fine point and resembling the leaves of a corn plant. This plant spreads by underground rhizomes to form large stands. Its stems are hollow, and the rhizomes are tough and fibrous and spread beneath the soil to form a dense underground rooting system. The margins of the leaves can be sharp to the touch. It produces exquisite, white, one- to two-foot-tall plumes in late summer. The giant reed grows best in full sun with supplemental water during the hot season. It likes soils moist, fertile, and well draining. This plant can also tolerate some standing water. It also handles drought conditions and is hardy to twenty-eight degrees Fahrenheit but recovers in the spring if frosted back. Prune back old stems and dig out rhizomes to control its size. Propagate it by rooting portions of the stems in water and replanting them in other areas of the landscape. Use the giant reed for erosion control on wet slopes and banks or as an ornamental for its striking appearance around water features and ponds. The large flower plumes can be used in flower arrangements. It is excellent as a windbreak or screen for blocking anything that is unsightly. This plant is native to the Mediterranean region but has been introduced to temperate parts of the world, including the United States. It grows naturally along riverbanks and disturbed sites and in wetlands and riparian habitats.

Cortaderia selloana

Pampas Grass
Ornamental grass

Pampas grass is a graceful-looking ornamental grass noted for its spectacular, whitish pink

Cortaderia selloana
Pampas Grass

*Muhlenbergia capillaris 'Regal Mist'

Gulf Muhlygrass, Mist Grass
Ornamental grass

Muhlenbergia capillaris 'Regal Mist'
Gulf Muhlygrass, Mist Grass

flower plumes that cover the plant. It grows about eight to ten feet tall. Its leaves are serrated, narrow, and razor sharp at the edges. The genus name, Cortaderia, originates from the Spanish verb "to cut," best describing its dangerous leaf edges. The blooms appear in late summer as fountainlike clumps that stand about four feet above the mounding plant. Its flowers can be used in dried arrangements, and the female plants generally produce a prettier bloom. Plant the pampas grass in fertile, well-draining, loamy or sandy soil in either full sun or partial shade. This plant can handle some drought but prefers supplemental irrigation and reflected heat. Its foliage often suffers from frost damage during the winter but recovers quickly in the spring. Pampas grass is hardy into the low twenties and requires pruning of frozen foliage in early spring. Mature plants may need heavy pruning every few years to remove dried leaves and to reduce the size if the plant becomes too large. Use it as a focal point or specimen plant for its architectural beauty or in groupings and wide-open spaces. Since it is a fast grower, it can be used as a screen or barrier plant and looks good when used next to tall palms in a tropical setting. The blooms are extremely dramatic when grown in front of darker background shrubbery. Do not plant too close to walkways or pedestrian areas. Pampas grass is native to the grasslands of Chile, Brazil, and Argentina.

The regal ornamental grass grows four feet tall and wide with glossy green foliage and upright flower spikes from late September into November. In cooler climates, the blooms appear earlier. Its flower spikes form a dense, purplish red, upright plume. This attractive perennial grass is easy to grow and needs very little care. It tolerates a wide variety of soils and habitats. While drought resistant, it benefits from supplemental irrigation during the hot weather into the fall. Gulf muhlygrass can also take plenty of water and periodic flooding. If plants start to look stressed or turn brown, they most likely need more water. This

Muhlenbergia capillaris 'Regal Mist'
Gulf Muhlygrass, Mist Grass

plant is hardy to about ten degrees Fahrenheit. The fast-growing accent takes full sun to partial shade. It needs a light pruning in the winter to remove old, spent blooms. Heavy pruning can be done in early spring to rejuvenate the plant, if needed. Protect it from rabbits with chicken wire when young. It is great as an accent or in groupings and masses for its whimsical effects. Use this plant in street medians, roadways, and golf courses, or around water features and pools. It is native from Kansas to Massachusetts and south into Florida. Gulf muhlygrass also grows widely in Texas and Mexico.

Muhlenbergia emersleyi 'El Toro,'

Bull Grass
Ornamental grass

Bull grass is a perennial, evergreen grass noted for its textural quality, its graceful, eye-catching plumes, and its bluish green, course-textured foli-

Muhlenbergia emersleyi 'El Toro'
Bull Grass

age. It grows three to five feet tall with an equal spread. In fall, it produces lacey, upright, reddish purple plumes that grow above the mass of foliage, up to five feet tall. In the winter, the plumes turn an ivory white and keep their color for a long time. This plant produces a showy dense mass of foliage. It likes full sun and reflected heat and also takes some shade. It is one of the most drought tolerant of all the landscape grasses but likes supplemental water during the hot, dry season. The plant is hardy to ten degrees Fahrenheit or lower. It is a low-maintenance grass but needs to be cut back severely in late winter or early spring before new growth emerges. Do not cut it back during the summer months. Use it as an accent planted with agaves and yuccas for its structural interest. It is a great plant to use for revegetation and erosion control on slopes and hillsides and around pools and water features. Butterflies and birds are attracted to its flower stalks. Bull grass is native to rocky slopes and dense, woodland areas, mostly from Arizona into Texas and throughout other parts of the United States.

Pennisetum setaceum 'Cupreum'
Purple Fountain Grass
Ornamental grass

Pennisetum setaceum 'Cupreum'
Purple Fountain Grass

Pennisetum setaceum 'Cupreum'
Purple Fountain Grass

The showy grass has graceful, arching foliage that grows in dense clumps to four feet tall with a two- to three-foot spread. Its slender, curving foliage is dark plum or cranberry, providing a dramatic accent in the landscape. In late summer through the fall, it produces a fountain of purple plumes that stand in spikes about one foot or more above the plant. It takes full sun and some partial shade, is drought resistant and needs little water to survive. Plant it in well-draining soil and provide weekly irrigation during the hot, dry seasons. It is hardy into the low thirties Fahrenheit and turns brittle and strawlike after a winter freeze. Purple fountain grass will die back completely in the low twenties. If severe damage occurs, prune it to the ground and the plant will resprout quickly in the spring. Use it as a foundation or accent mixed with deep green plants around fountains, ponds, and other water features for tropical effects. It can also be used in medians, borders, and parking lots for erosion control, or as a colorful accent along roadways or in medians. The plumes of this plant can be used in dried flower arrangements. The varieties "Rubrum" and "Purpureum" are larger, while the variety "Eaton Canyon" is a miniature plant. Purple fountain grass is sterile and does not produce any seed. It is native to open, scrubby locations and the tropics of Northern Africa, the Middle East, Southwest Asia, and the Eastern Mediterranean, and has naturalized in warmer, dry climates around the world.

Stipa tenuissima
Mexican Feather Grass
Ornamental grass

Mexican feather grass grows from one to three feet tall and wide. It produces a mass of long, graceful, green foliage that grows in dense

Stipa tenuissima
Mexican Feather Grass

Stipa tenuissima
Mexican Feather Grass

clumps. In a gentle breeze, its narrow leaves will sway back and forth, creating an interesting effect. The silky seed heads may glow brightly when they catch the sunlight. Flowers mature to a golden brown color in late summer through the fall. This grass likes full sun and prefers amended, well-draining soils. It will take our hot summers and prefers moderate irrigation to look its best. Mexican feather grass is hardy to thirty degrees Fahrenheit. It will become drought tolerant as it matures and does not like to be overwatered. Prune it back in later winter or early spring. This ornamental is considered a cool season grass because most of its growth occurs during the cooler months. It will go dormant during the hot,

bone-dry summers in its native range. This grass will reseed itself and is not a pest, but some consider it to be invasive at times. It is a good idea to cut back the seed heads before they ripen to keep the plant from reseeding. Run a rake through it in late winter to early spring to take out any dead foliage. This ornamental grass looks nice when mixed in with boulders, planted in masses, or used as a specimen. Plant it in beds or use it in borders along with perennials and annuals. It can also be grown in containers and used in dried flower arrangements. Mexican feather grass is an exceptional choice to use for erosion control on sunny slopes. It can be found growing naturally on rocky slopes, dry open woods, and dry prairies, growing from New Mexico and Texas, and south through Central Mexico.

Typha latifolia

Broad-Leaved Cattail
Aquatic, perennial plant

The broad-leaved cattail is a perennial plant that will reach heights of nine feet or more. It has stiff, long, green stems with erect, swordlike leaves. The plant is connected by thick underground roots called rhizomes. Once established, it spreads quickly and is sometimes considered a weed due to its aggressive growth habit. The stems are topped with dense cylindrical spikes of tiny brown flowers that resemble sausages or cattails. The plant produces its flowers during the summer through late fall. The cattail needs full sun to light shade and requires a lot of moisture. It likes areas that are rich in organic matter and does not need supplemental fertilizer or nutrients. This perennial does best when grown at the water's edge and tolerates only brief periods of drying out. Divide plants in the early spring, making sure that roots are attached to the

Typha latifolia
Broad-Leaved Cattail

Typha latifolia
Broad-Leaved Cattail

pools, ponds, or lakes. This invasive plant will spread if not contained by pond liners or deep water. Cattails add an architectural element to large ponds and lakes, and the flower heads can be used in dried arrangements. The plant is not suitable for growing in small areas. It can be found growing natively in dense stands of fresh or brackish marshes and around the margins of lakes, ponds, and streams throughout most of North America, Europe, Asia, and Africa.

plant. It is extremely hardy to well below zero degrees. Many parts of this plant are edible. The rootstocks and rhizomes were an important food source for native peoples when other food was scarce. These roots are quite nutritious, containing more starch than potatoes and more protein than rice. The young shoots can be cooked like vegetables, and the pollen can be used in baked goods. In addition to food, cattails have also provided people with building materials. The dried leaves were woven into furniture and mats, and their pulp and fibers can be made into paper and string. They also have medicinal value and many cultures have used the roots to treat bruises and burns. Cattails are best suited for use in large

5 Groundcovers
for Southwest Landscapes

Groundcovers are low-growing plants that spread quickly to form a dense cover. They add beauty to the landscape and can also provide protection to the soil from erosion and drought. Groundcovers are a great alternative for lawn, especially in low light areas. They can transform a dull space with a mixture of leaf shapes, textures and colors. Groundcovers can also be used for filling in spaces between flagstone or pavers and help to spruce up challenging areas under trees.

Acacia redolens

Prostrate Acacia
Groundcover

Acacia redolens
Prostrate Acacia

Acacia redolens
Prostrate Acacia

This sprawling evergreen with woody stems grows two to four feet tall and spreads six to twelve feet, covering a large area of ground very quickly. It has long, leathery, dark greenish olive leaves. In spring, a mass of ball-like, golden yellow, spiked flowers appear followed by narrow, thick, brown seedpods. The plant is extremely drought resistant and needs little water. During hot, dry summers, it responds to supplemental irrigation but does not like to be overwatered.

The prostrate acacia handles most soils, including those that are alkaline, as long as they are well-draining. The plant is hardy to fifteen to twenty degrees Fahrenheit, likes full sun and takes reflected heat. When young, it is slow to take off and then grows at a quicker rate when its roots become established. This plant is maintenance free and easy to grow. Prune it in early spring, if needed, by making small cuts. Do not heavily prune. The variety "Desert Carpet" is a more compact, lower growing plant. "Low Boy" is a variety popularized in California and is used to cover large areas. Use this plant for soil stabilization or plant it in masses to quickly cover expansive areas. This groundcover works well as a low shrub or bank cover in landscapes or along freeways, for erosion control, or to stabilize a sloping area. It also works in masses to create a continuous groundcover. Prostrate acacia is native to the inland areas of Western Australia, where it grows in saline and alkaline soils.

Aptenia cordifolia

Hearts and Flowers,
Baby Sun Rose
Perennial groundcover

This sprawling plant forms a dense mat that grows in flat clumps along the ground from six to twelve inches tall. It has bright green, heart-shaped, succulent leaves and small, reddish purple to pinkish purple, buttonlike flowers with yellow centers. Its flowers bloom from early spring until summer. The blossoms attract bees, opening during the daylight hours and closing at night. The variety "Red Apple" has bright red flowers. This variety is a much faster and more vigorous growing plant. The hearts and flowers prefer a well-draining, rich, sandy, or loamy soils and partial shade to filtered sun. It also tolerates

Aptenia cordifolia
Hearts and Flowers, Baby Sun Rose

*Asparagus densiflorus 'Sprengeri'
Asparagus Fern
Groundcover

Aptenia cordifolia
Hearts and Flowers, Baby Sun Rose

Asparagus densiflorus 'Sprengeri'
Asparagus Fern

drought conditions but prefers regular irrigation, especially during the hot summer months. This plant is relatively easy to propagate from cuttings and spreads vegetatively by rooting from its branches. It is hardy to twenty-three degrees Fahrenheit. Lightly fertilize it two to three times each year with ammonium phosphate to keep it looking healthy. Use it as a bank cover, along a retaining wall, in containers, rock gardens, or hanging baskets, cascading down a wall, or around boulders. It looks nice when used on the north sides of buildings or in north-facing planters. The hearts and flowers plant is native to the eastern coastal regions of South Africa.

Asparagus fern is a mounding, spreading, evergreen that grows one to two feet with a three-foot spread. It is a fast-growing plant with bright green to yellow green, airy, fernlike, delicate leaves, and tiny thorns. It's arching stems and branches cascade and trail, making this a great groundcover to use in the landscape. In spring, it produces small, waxy, white, inconspicuous flowers that bloom sporadically. After flowering, small clusters of red berries appear that are toxic to humans but are eaten by birds and rodents. It is hardy to about twenty-four degrees Fahrenheit. If frost damaged, prune aggressively to the ground, and this fast-growing plant will recover quickly in the spring with spikes of new foliage. When pruning, wear gloves and long sleeves to protect against its small, aggressive thorns. It takes full sun, partial shade, and some reflected heat. This plant needs regular water, especially during the warm growing season. Fertilize it in the spring with a nitrogen-based fertilizer. Use it as an understory plant, in coastal areas, containers, planters, and hanging pots with its foliage spilling over the sides, or cascading over rocks, boulders, or embankments. Also, plant it as an informal groundcover in tropical landscapes and around pools, water features, and fountains. This is a great filler plant to use for a splash of green, lush foliage. Asparagus fern is very hard to remove because it produces underground tubers and has an extensive root system. This plant can be invasive in some locations but is a tough, pest-free groundcover that is very easy to grow. It is native to South Africa.

Baileya multiradiata
Desert Marigold
Perennial groundcover

Desert marigold grows twelve inches tall and wide with fuzzy greenish gray leaves and a compact, mounded shape. While a short-lived plant, it beautifies the landscape by producing bright yellow, daisylike blossoms that grow on long stems. The plant blooms through the early spring and into the summer months and may intermittently bloom all year, except during the

Baileya multiradiata
Desert Marigold

cold weather. Cut flowers can last for a long time, and a large amount of seed is present in the flower heads; collect the seeds when the flowers fade and allow seeds to dry. Desert marigold is hardy to about ten degrees Fahrenheit and drought tolerant, needing little rainfall or irrigation to thrive. Do not overwater this plant. If given too much water, it will rot and die very quickly. Plant the desert marigold in well-draining, rocky soil with no organic mulch. It likes full sun conditions and reflected heat. Lightly prune it and remove spent blooms to encourage additional flowers. This plant can also take hold and germinate in disturbed areas along roadsides. Use it as a summer color or revegetation plant, in containers or in desert rock gardens with cacti to add a touch of color to an area. It is a good companion plant to verbena and penstemon. The plant is native to the Southwest and into Northern Mexico, where it grows on desert plains, mesas, and rocky slopes at elevations below 5,000 feet.

*Bulbine frutescens

Shrubby Bulbine
Groundcover

Bulbine frutescens
Shrubby Bulbine

The succulent evergreen with fleshy, smooth, aloe-like green leaves is low maintenance and easy to grow. It spreads by underground rhizomes, creating clumps of growth that reach heights of eighteen inches and spreads of three feet across. In the fall through spring, it produces delicate, six-petaled, star-shaped, yellow flower spikes that grow twelve to eighteen inches above the plant, toward the sky. The variety "Hallmark" produces orange blossoms. Bees and butterflies are attracted to the blooms. The fruit is a small, rounded capsule containing many black seeds that disperses in the wind when the fruit dries out. In addition to its landscape value, the plant is cultivated in some parts of the world for it medicinal properties. The sap inside the leaves is used to treat chapped lips, insect bites, bee stings, sunburn, and other skin disorders. A tea can be made from the leaves to treat coughs, colds, and arthritis. This fast-growing plant is hardy to about twenty degrees Fahrenheit. It may suffer some leaf damage in a hard frost but recovers quickly in the spring. It is drought resistant and can withstand long periods without water. It grows moderately and likes supplemental irrigation during the hot, dry season. Plant it in full sun or partial shade and avoid reflected heat. It grows best in well-draining soil and is not very particular about soil type. Remove the spent flowers after they bloom to encourage more blossoms. It is easily propagated by dividing its tubers and offsets, and then replanting them elsewhere in the landscape. This groundcover likes light applications of ammonium phosphate fertilizer in the spring. Use it as a groundcover in rock gardens and as a foundation plant, border, or understory plant with other succulents and cacti. It can also be grown in raised planters along narrow sidewalks and entryways. The plant is native to South Africa, where it grows throughout the dry valleys in parts of the Northern and Eastern Cape.

Calylophus harwegii subsp. fernleri

Sundrops
Hartweg Evening Primrose
Perennial groundcover

Calylophus harwegii subsp. fernleri
Sundrops, Hartweg Evening Primrose

This fast-growing, bushy, perennial with linear, green foliage and showy flowers grows one foot high and two inches wide. During the spring and early summer, it develops small, yellow, buttercup-like blossoms. The flowers are present for only one day, but the plant continues to produce new blooms; the blooms open at night and start to fade by the next day. It grows best in well-draining soil and is hardy to twenty degrees Fahrenheit or lower. The calylophus may die back during the winter but resprouts quickly it early spring. During winter months, the foliage may turn dull in color or fall from the plant. This groundcover is drought resistant and needs only weekly irrigation during the warm weather. Be careful not to overwater this plant. When needed, remove old flowers and growth to prolong the blooming period. Prune it back in the fall to reshape. It likes full sun and reflected heat. The calylophus can also be grown in partial shade but will not bloom as prolifically. Use it in raised beds, as an understory plant in filtered shade, with other perennials in rock gardens for early spring color, or with other drought-resistant plants. It is native to the hillsides, valleys, roadways, plains, and open woods in Wyoming, Nebraska, Arizona, Texas, and Mexico.

Carpobrotus chilensis
Common Ice Plant, Sea Fig
Perennial groundcover

Carpobrotus chilensis
Common Ice Plant, Sea Fig

The succulent evergreen with brilliant blooms has three-sided leaves that form a thick, fleshy green mat. The common ice plant grows six inches to one foot, spreading three feet through an aggressive rooting system. Its bold foliage and warm season color makes it a great choice as a groundcover. The common ice plant produces small, asterlike flowers in shades of red, pink, purple, or magenta, depending on the variety. The blossoms are showy from early summer into the fall. Its flowers are sterile and do not produce any seed. This fast-growing, perennial groundcover spreads quickly and requires minimal maintenance. While drought tolerant, it requires occasional water at least once per month. It needs full sun and good drainage and is easy to propagate. Prune off fleshy stems and replant them in amended, well-draining soil. Provide irrigation, and they will regrow in other parts of the landscape. The plant can be walked on and will bear a great deal of human disturbance and foot traffic. It is hardy into the low twenties Fahrenheit. Use it in sunny gardens, train it to trail down a vertical wall, or plant it in rock gardens or around pools and water features. The common ice plant can also be used in heavily eroded areas to root into the soil as a bank cover. It is an excellent choice for beachfront landscapes because it tolerates salty conditions. Rabbits may eat the plant, so when it is young, place chicken wire for protection. The ice plant is native to the Pacific coastline from Oregon down to Baja California, as well as in Chile and South Africa. It species name, Chilensis, comes from the Latin name for Chile. The plant can become highly invasive in some areas.

Cephalophyllum alstonii

Red Spike Ice Plant
Perennial groundcover

Cephalophyllum alstonii
Red Spike Ice Plant

This creeping evergreen with spectacular red flowers has succulent, triangular-shaped, slightly curving leaves with a smooth, greenish, silvery gray surface. When wet, the foliage glistens and looks like ice. Its trailing stems grow quickly to form low clumps that reach six inches and spread to about fifteen inches. It produces small, showy, blood red blossoms that appear mainly from late winter until early spring. The red spike ice plant can also bloom intermittently throughout the year. The flowers open during the middle of the day to attract many insects, and will only bloom in bright sunlight. At night or on cloudy days, the flowers do not open. The plant takes full sun to partial shade. It is drought resistant and likes well-draining soil. This groundcover prefers additional irrigation during the hot summer but does not like to be overwatered. Provide regular applications of fertilizer during the warm seasons. It is moderately tolerant to frosts and is very maintenance free. The red spike ice plant will not tolerate any foot traffic unlike the common ice plant. It is easy to propagate by cuttings and can be reestablished any time of the year. Use this moderate-growing groundcover to prevent erosion, as a soil stabilizer plant or color plant in the landscape in small, tight spaces, containers, raised planters, and rock gardens, or mixed in with other blooming succulent plants. It is native to South Africa.

*Dalea capitata

Lemon Dalea
Groundcover

The sprawling, aromatic plant grows eight inches tall and three feet wide with lush, fine-textured, light green foliage and small, yellow flowers. It is fast growing and forms a mound of dense foliage that makes it a great plant for many locations.

Dalea capitata
Lemon Dalea

Dalea capitata
Lemon Dalea

The foliage and flowers have a lemony fragrance. Small, pealike, yellow flowers appear on short spikes in spring and fall and attract bees and butterflies. It likes full sun and reflected heat. The lemon dalea is drought resistant but responds to moderate irrigation and needs well-draining soil. Do not overwater this plant. The variety "Sierra Gold" is an extremely durable groundcover that withstands more moisture and can be planted near a lawn that receives daily irrigation. The species is hardy to five degrees Fahrenheit but loses all of its foliage when temperatures drop in to the low twenties. Prune back in late winter and give it a light application of ammonium phosphate fertilizer for a quick recovery in the spring. It is a very low-maintenance plant but

can be susceptible to infestations of white flies. Treat it with a systemic insecticide if needed. It can also be eaten by rabbits and needs protection in heavily infested areas. Use along walkways and street medians, in planters, as a groundcover tucked into large boulders or in small, narrow spaces for a lush splash of green. This plant looks great when mixed with agave or tall yucca plants. It also works well around fountains, ponds, and water features. It is native to Coahuila, Mexico.

Dalea greggii
Trailing Indigo Bush
Groundcover

Dalea greggii
Trailing Indigo Bush

This durable, long-living evergreen has a mounding, creeping growth habit reaching two to three feet tall and spreading three to eight feet wide. It is known for its silvery, bluish gray foliage and pea-sized, lavender to deep purple blooms in early spring through the summer. The flowers attract butterflies and bees. It is hardy to thirteen to fifteen degrees Fahrenheit and may suffer some dieback and root damage at those temperatures. The trailing indigo bush is drought tolerant and prefers full sun and can take plenty of reflected heat. Irrigate once per week during the warm weather but do not overwater or over fertilize this plant. It needs well-draining soil but is tolerant of most soil conditions. This fast-growing plant needs minimal maintenance and should be allowed to grow naturally. Do not prune or shear except to remove dead or woody growth. Use it in rock gardens or planters or train it to cascade over a wall. Plant it as an understory specimen, use for erosion control, as a soil stabilizer, in medians, and along roadways. It works well in drought-resistant landscapes. This groundcover is native to rocky and limestone hillsides of Western Texas, Southeastern New Mexico, and Mexico, ranging across Chihuahua, Coahuila, Tamaulipas, Nuevo Leon, Hidalgo, Durango, San Luis Potosi, Puebla, and Oaxaca at elevations of 2,000 to 4,500 feet.

Delosperma cooperi
Trailing Ice Plant

groundcover enjoys full sun and thrives in our hot, dry locations. It prefers well-draining soils but will grow in just about any soil condition. The trailing ice plant is very drought tolerant but prefers occasional irrigation during the hot, dry season and needs to dry out between watering cycles. This groundcover is very easy to propagate by stem cuttings and will grow very quickly to create a sprawling plant. The fast-growing plant works well mixed into containers as a perennial, in terraces, and as a bank cover for erosion control. It also works well in medians, parking lots, and exposed situations with other cacti and succulents. It is native to South Africa.

Delosperma cooperi

Trailing Ice Plant
Hardy Ice Plant
Perennial groundcover

This trailing perennial groundcover has an upright growth habit and fleshy green foliage that is two to three inches long and flat on the top. It produces a mass of brilliant blooms in late spring through the fall. The magenta, daisylike flowers are very long lasting and will cover the entire plant in a showy display. The blossoms will close up in the evening and then open again as soon as the sun is high. This hardy plant will take temperatures below twenty degrees Fahrenheit, and in the winter the foliage will turn an attractive red color with the cold weather. The attractive

*Gaillardia x grandiflora

Blanket Flower, Indian Blanket, Gaillardia
Perennial groundcover

Gaillardia x grandiflora
Blanket Flower, Indian Blanket, Gaillardia

Gaillardia x grandiflora
Blanket Flower, Indian Blanket, Gaillardia

The perennial continuous-flowering, rounded plant grows two to three feet tall from a taproot and spreads by underground rhizomes. It produces striking flowers and linear, dark green leaves that are serrated with coarse, grayish white hairs. If the upper stems of the plant are destroyed, the plant regrows from its rhizomes. It is a member of the sunflower family, developing large, brilliant, daisylike flowers in colors of gold, red, orange, or bronze. Many varieties are available, including shorter dwarf forms and various flower colors. Blooms last over a long period from early spring into the fall and attract butterflies and birds. Wild birds feed on the flower seeds, dispersing them to other parts of the landscape. The plant freezes in the low thirties but recovers quickly in the spring. It prefers full sun, moist, well-draining soil and

drought conditions. Do not overwater this plant. Fertilize it with a light application of ammonium phosphate in spring. Prune it lightly to encourage further blooming and prevent the plant from becoming too weedy. Use it in beds, borders, raised planters, perennial gardens, and low-water-use landscapes. The gaillardia also makes a beautiful cut flower for indoor arrangements. Its brilliant red and yellow colors add a great addition to any garden. Plant the blanket flower from seed or nursery transplants. It is a hybrid created by crossing North American wildflowers.

Gazania rigens
Gazania
Perennial groundcover

Gazania rigens
Gazania

The gazania has a compact, mounding growth habit and produces beautiful flowers and dark blue or green dandelion-like leaves that grow one foot high and wide. In spring, large, daisylike blooms appear that come in a variety of colors: red, orange, bright yellow, and bronzy yellow. The flowers attract bees, butterflies, and hummingbirds. There are many different hybrids available. The flowers close at night and

Gazania rigens
Gazania

Glandularia peruviana
Peruvian Verbena
Perennial groundcover

Glandularia peruviana
Peruvian Verbena

reopen during the day. This plant blooms prolifically in spring and again in fall. While beautiful, this short-lived species should be replanted every few years. All parts of the plant are poisonous if ingested. Plant this groundcover in full sun or in an area that gets some late afternoon shade. It is drought resistant but likes supplemental irrigation during the hot weather. Do not overwater it since it could lead to root rot. Let the plant dry out between irrigation cycles. It will freeze in the low twenties Fahrenheit but recovers if pruned heavily to the ground. The gazania prefers sandy to average, well-draining soils. Do not plant it in areas heavily infested with rabbits, since they love this plant. Protect new plants with chicken wire. Apply light applications of ammonium phosphate fertilizer in the spring and late summer to encourage growth and blooms. Use it as a mass planting for color in containers and rock and perennial gardens, and as a border plant. This groundcover is great as a soil stabilizer for erosion control. It is native to South Africa.

Glandularia peruviana
Peruvian Verbena

The fast-growing groundcover with its colorful flowers reaches six inches or taller with a three- to six-foot spread. It trails and spreads along the ground, producing new herbaceous roots as it grows to form a dense mat. It has finely cut and lightly serrated deep green foliage. The Peruvian verbena produces tiny clusters of colorful flowers on its terminal ends in fuchsia, pink, red, white, or purple, depending upon one of the many varieties available. Flowers appear in early spring, taper off during the summer, and then bloom again in the fall, attracting butterflies and bees. The plant needs ample to moderate water to produce flowers. The Peruvian verbena can be planted in full sun, reflected heat, and well-draining, fertile soil. It is hardy to about twenty-four degrees Fahrenheit. Verbena is not a long-lived plant and will need to be replanted every few years. Provide a light application of ammonium phosphate fertilizer in the spring to encourage new growth and flowers. Lightly prune after it blooms to keep it neat and compact. Use it as a transitional plant, in rock gardens, cascading over containers or in low planters. It combines nicely with wildflowers and other perennial groundcovers. The Peruvian verbena is a great choice for low-water-use landscapes. This plant is native to South Africa where it grows at elevations of 800 to 2,500 feet.

Glandularia rigida
Sandpaper Verbena

*Glandularia rigida
Sandpaper Verbena
Perennial groundcover

Glandularia rigida
Sandpaper Verbena

As its name indicates, this prolific bloomer, one of the hardiest of all the verbenas, has dark green foliage that feels like sandpaper. The plant develops tuberous roots that spread underground and grows two feet tall and three to four feet wide. This fast-growing perennial develops bright clusters of vivid purple blossoms in early spring that continue to bloom during the warm weather.

During the hot, summer months, it stops blooming and looks somewhat ratty. However, it bounces back in the fall with vivid color. In history, the plant was considered a sacred herb, and its stems were made into wreaths for rituals and healing. It is hardy to fifteen degrees Fahrenheit and will regrow quickly in the spring if frozen back. This groundcover is drought tolerant when established but likes moderate irrigation during the hot summer to produce blooms in the fall. The sandpaper verbena can be planted in well-draining, moist soil and in areas that receive lots of sun. Prune it moderately in early spring to promote blooming and shape, and give it light applications of ammonium phosphate fertilizer. Use it in borders, planters, containers, butterfly gardens, and wildflower gardens, and around pools, fountains, and water features. Also, use the sandpaper verbena in masses on banks and slopes for erosion control. It looks nice when planted with larger agave species and tall yucca plants. This plant is native to Argentina, Southern Brazil, and Paraguay. It has been naturalized in the United States from Southeastern North Carolina to Florida.

Hedera canariensis

Algerian Ivy, Canary Ivy
Groundcover/vine

Hedera canariensis
Algerian Ivy, Canary Ivy

This fast-growing evergreen has thick, shiny, deep green, lobed leaves with reddish stems. New growth is a light green color. It rarely produces flowers, but if it does, they are whitish green in color. Algerian ivy can take over an area very quickly, making this plant an appealing groundcover. It likes well-draining soil with amendments but will grow in most soil conditions. Algerian ivy can also be used in coastal situations since it is very salt tolerant. The variety "Variegata" has green, lobed foliage surrounded by white and is less hardy than the green variety. There are many cultivars available of this plant. It likes some morning sun but prefers partial to full shade. Established plants are drought tolerant but like moderate to ample irrigation. It is hardy to ten degrees Fahrenheit. The plant is susceptible to Texas root rot, and it may sunburn if exposed to full sun during the summer months. Prune it heavily during the winter months and trim lightly any other time.

Hedera canariensis
Algerian Ivy, Canary Ivy

This plant likes fertilizer applications in early spring. Use it for its bold foliage in tropical settings or plant it beneath deciduous trees, in shady areas of the landscape and in raised plant-

181

ers under covered patios. It can also be trained as a self-climbing vine in shady locations or northern exposures. Algerian ivy is native to Northwestern Africa and the Canary Islands and is widely cultivated in warm, tropical areas of the world.

Hedera helix
English Ivy
Groundcover, vine

Hedera helix
English Ivy

Hedera helix
English Ivy

English ivy is a hardy evergreen with dark green, glossy, lobed leaves growing six to eight feet when used as a groundcover. It climbs to fifty feet when used as a vine. The plant climbs and creeps by above ground roots that cling to most surfaces. When mature, it creates a lush, green carpet effect. Variegated varieties are also available. In its native environment, the plant is highly valued for attracting wildlife. The flowers and fruits can be eaten, and the foliage provides a great retreat for deer and other wildlife. The plant has also been used as a medicinal treatment for coughs and colds, in addition to bloodshot and watering eyes. However, it contains many tox-

ins, and the leaves can cause a skin irritation or allergic reaction. In late summer, it may produce a small greenish yellow umbel that is very rich in nectar. In its native habitat, the nectar is an important food source for bees and other insects. After flowering, purplish black to orange-yellow berries appear. The berries are poisonous to humans, but an important food source for birds. English ivy can be planted in partial sun to full shade with rich, fertile, well-draining soil and ample moisture. It can sunburn if planted in full sun in our southwestern deserts. The plant is hardy to well below ten degrees Fahrenheit. It needs occasional pruning and maintenance to keep it from taking over an area. Apply fertilizer in the early spring to boost growth. Use it as an understory groundcover in shady conditions for woodsy effects or mix it into containers with taller plants for a cascading effect. The plant is native to Europe, Western Asia, and Northern Africa.

*Ipomoea batatas
Sweet Potato Vine
Perennial groundcover

Ipomoea batatas
Sweet Potato Vine

Ipomoea batatas
Sweet Potato Vine

Sweet potato vine is fast growing reaching heights of six to twelve inches with a spread of one to three feet. It has dark green or deep purple, heart-shape, lobed leaves. The variety "Blackie" has the darker purple foliage and the variety "Margarita" has green foliage. Both varieties look nice when used together in combinations for their interesting, contrasting, colored foliage. The plant produces tuberous roots that are similar in appearance to the sweet potato, but they are not edible. It takes filtered sunlight to deep shade and likes regular irrigation. Plant it in well-draining, fertile soil and do not allow it to dry out. Prune it lightly as needed to control its size. Sweet potato vine is hardy to thirty degrees Fahrenheit and should be protected from frosts. It recovers quickly in the spring if frozen to the ground. Use it in beds, raised planters, window boxes, and hanging baskets; in foundations and borders; trailing or cascading over a wall; or in a container. Use this groundcover in perennial and annual gardens for it amazing, exotic foliage. This lush groundcover is a great plant for warm seasons and loves our hot, dry weather. It is easy to propagate by cuttings and is easy to transplant. Sweet potato vine is native to the tropical areas of South America.

Jacobaea maritima
Dusty Miller
Perennial groundcover

The shrubby perennial grows one to two feet tall and wide in a mounding form. It is known for its silvery blue, velvety-textured foliage that is intricate and lacey. The stems are covered with long, white, matted hairs. Its foliage provides an attractive contrast to other boldly colored flowering plants. In late summer to early fall,

183

Jacobaea maritima
Dusty Miller

Jacobaea maritima
Dusty Miller

perennial gardens. The dusty miller is native to the Mediterranean regions of Northern Africa, Western Asia, and Europe, where it grows in arid locations

*Lantana montevidensis

Trailing Lantana
Groundcover

Lantana montevidensis
Trailing Lantana

it produces upright flower stalks with mustard yellow spikes. The flowers are pretty, but the plant is mainly grown for its foliage. There are many varieties available. Pinch off flowers and lightly prune the plant to encourage bushy leaf production. The flower makes a nice addition to a cut or dried arrangement. This plant takes full sun to partial shade. It is drought tolerant but likes occasional irrigation, especially during the hot weather. The dusty miller also likes rich, well-draining soil and is hardy to twenty degrees Fahrenheit. Rabbits may feed on its foliage but the plant is deer proof. This plant may be toxic if ingested. Use it in containers, raised planters, and rock gardens, as edging or a backdrop, or mixed into annual and

The trailing lantana is a majestic flowering evergreen that reaches two feet and spreads six to ten feet with dark green, oval, and coarsely toothed foliage. It has sprawling stems covered with fuzzy growth. The plants emit an aroma when crushed and can be a skin irritant or produce an allergic reaction. Clusters of small, funnel-shaped blooms appear in lavender, white, and purple, depending on the variety. Flowers attract hummingbirds and butterflies. The fruit is a small, fleshy, dark blue berry that is very toxic if eaten. There are hundreds of subspecies

Lantana montevidensis
Trailing Lantana

of lantana, and all are fast-growing and easy to grow. The plant can freeze back in temperatures below thirty degrees Fahrenheit but recovers quickly in the spring. Lantana likes to be planted in full sun to enhance its blooms. The trailing lantana needs less water when humidity levels are high. Its leaves may yellow between the veins (called chlorosis) when trailing lantana is overwatered. It likes moderate irrigation to look its best and prefers well-draining soils. The trailing lantana benefits from yearly pruning to keep its shape. Prune frost-damaged foliage when the weather warms up in early spring. Fertilize it in spring with ammonium phosphate fertilizer to promote blooms. The plant is deer resistant, and the foliage can be toxic to livestock. Use it as a groundcover in lush gardens, for transitional landscapes, in planter beds, as a border, as a groundcover, in hanging baskets, or cascading over a large container. It can also be mixed with other plants for an amazing accent. The trailing lantana will grow near hot pavements, parking lots, and driveways, in medians, on slopes, and as erosion control on banks. It is native to Argentina, South America, and Uruguay.

Liriope muscari
Lily Turf
Groundcover

Liriope muscari
Lily Turf

The dense, grasslike evergreen spreads by underground rhizomes and is not actually a grass but a member of the lily family, growing upward to ten to eighteen inches. It has dark green, ribbonlike foliage that curves downward toward the ground. There are also variegated varieties available. The plant produces attractive spikes of purplish lavender or white blooms in the spring. After flowering, pea-sized, black berries form in late summer through early fall. Plant it in partial shade or filtered sun since it will sunburn in full sun. It is moderately drought resistant but prefers supplemental irrigation in hot weather. The plant tolerates any soil that is well draining and fertile. Groom it by removing old flower stalks and dried foliage. Lily turf is hardy to about twenty degrees Fahrenheit. Fertilize it in spring with ammonium phosphate. The groundcover can be easily divided to thin out or propagate. Use it in mass plantings, as an understory plant, in narrow spaces, and as an edging plant. It can also be used in perennial gardens, rock gardens, small planters, atriums, entryways, walkways, and courtyards. This groundcover is a great choice for oriental and tropical effects. It is native to shady forests in Japan, Taiwan, and China.

Melampodium leucanthum

Blackfoot Daisy
Perennial groundcover

Melampodium leucanthum
Blackfoot Daisy

This low-growing plant with aromatic, daisy-like flowers has a mounded appearance with narrow grayish green foliage. It grows to about one foot tall and eighteen inches wide. Small, abundant, white, daisylike flowers with a yellow center appear on terminal stalks. The color of this plant can be seen from a distance because of the density of the blooms. Its flowers have a light honey fragrance and attract butterflies and birds. The plant is also resistant to deer. The perennial produces the most color during the spring and fall seasons. Plant it in full sun and reflected heat. It also likes well-draining soil and some moisture, but be careful not to overwater it. This groundcover is very hardy and will take temperatures well below freezing. Prune it back heavily in late summer or fall as needed to keep the plant compact. It reseeds naturally throughout the landscape and does not require any fertilizer. Use it in perennial and wildflower gardens, in masses or in rock gardens. This plant looks great in the springtime planted next to penstemon and verbena. The blackfoot daisy is a short-lived specimen groundcover but is worth planting for its color and interesting qualities. It is native to gravelly, dry, desert slopes, rocky soils, pastures, plains, and meadows, and on prairies in Arizona, Texas, New Mexico, Oklahoma, Colorado, and Kansas.

Myoporum parvifolium

Prostrate Myoporum
Groundcover

This fast-growing, glossy evergreen forms an even mat as it gracefully spreads along the ground, to one feet high and six feet wide. Its leaves are small, lush, and serrated. In spring, a profusion of small white or pink starlike blossoms appear. The flowers may attract

Myoporum parvifolium
Prostrate Myoporum

Myoporum parvifolium
Prostrate Myoporum

bees. In late spring, small berries cover the plant and are sweet and edible. It likes full sun and reflected heat. This groundcover has low to moderate water needs and does not like to be overwatered. Because it forms such a dense cover, it suppresses weeds. The plant grows in a variety of soil from clay to salty or alkaline conditions but prefers amended, well-draining soil. It will freeze below twenty-five degrees Fahrenheit. If frosted back, prune it heavily in the spring. It also needs replacing every few years when older plants become woody and die back, and mass plantings may require some refurbishing in early spring. Use it on sloping sites for erosion control and as a bank cover by grouping several plants together as

a continuous groundcover. The prostrate myoporum is a great substitute for lawns since its appearance from a distance is green and lush. Use it in xeriscape or transitional landscapes. It is native to New South Wales, Victoria, and Southern Australia.

*Oenothera speciosa
Mexican Evening Primrose
Perennial groundcover

Oenothera speciosa
Mexican Evening Primrose

The showy, semi-evergreen is admired for its magnificent pink, four-petal, bell-shaped flowers. It spreads in the landscape by underground rhizomes or seed to form extensive colonies growing from eight to twelve inches tall, and spreading to three feet. The leaves are small and bright green turning crimson to deep red in colder weather. Showy, pink blossoms with yellow veins appear in spring and bloom over a long period.

Many insects and moths eat the flower nectar. This plant is resistant to deer, though the seeds attract birds and other smaller rodents. Varieties are also available with white and yellow flowers. In winter, this groundcover freezes to the ground in temperatures below twenty degrees Fahrenheit but recovers quickly in the spring. It grows best in full sun with regular irrigation and moisture but does not like to be overwatered. Mexican evening primrose prefers amended, rich soils that are well draining. This groundcover grows aggressively and sometimes can be difficult to eradicate. Prune it back in spring as needed to control its size. Use it as a mass planting in perennial or rock gardens, for erosion control or as a ground stabilizer. The plant is native to Texas, Southern New Mexico, and Mexico but has naturalized elsewhere in the United States. In its native habitat, it grows in open meadows, pastures, hillsides, and slopes, and at the edges of woodland areas.

Osteospermum fruticosum
Trailing African Daisy

full sun to partial shade. Give this groundcover ample to moderate water but do not overwater it. The plant takes any soil but prefers those that are well draining. It is frost tolerant to twenty degrees Fahrenheit and tolerates salty coastal situations. Apply a light application of ammonium phosphate fertilizer in early spring to help promote blooms. Lightly pinch tips to keep the plant lush and encourage bushy growth. For most of the summer, the species will become dormant during the hot, summer months. Use it on retaining walls and banks or in borders, raised beds, or containers. Use it in masses for early spring color. Mix in with spring annuals and perennials as a whimsical accent. This plant will thrive in hot, dry places. The trailing African daisy is native to Southern Africa and Southwestern Arabia.

Osteospermum fruticosum

Trailing African Daisy
Perennial groundcover

The colorful evergreen with its striking, daisy-like flowers is used to cover large, open areas, spreading by green stems that root into the ground to form a dense carpet of groundcover. The fast-growing plant reaches heights of eighteen inches with long, greenish blue, fleshy leaves. It produces large, showy, daisylike flowers in white, deep purple, and lavender, depending upon the variety. The flowers open during the daylight and close at night and on overcast days. The trailing African daisy should be planted in

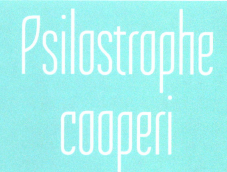

Psilostrophe cooperi

Paper Flower
Perennial groundcover

Psilostrophe cooperi
Paper Flower

plant to use and naturalize into revegetated areas. This plant is native to gravelly hillsides and washes of the Sonoran Desert in Mexico and Arizona, and in desert regions of California, New Mexico, and Utah, growing at elevations of 2,000 to 5,000 feet.

*Tetraneuris acaulis

Angelita Daisy
Perennial groundcover

The clumping perennial grows to about two feet high and wide in hot weather with supplemental irrigation. Its green stems are covered with fuzzy, white hairs, and are silvery gray on the underside of the leaves. The plant produces bright yellow flowers in late spring and continues to bloom periodically throughout the fall. The flowers have a papery texture and are held on the ends of stems for a long blooming period. This moderate grower likes well-draining soil, full sun and tolerates light shade. It is drought resistant, preferring a deep irrigation at least once a month in the winter and weekly during the hot summer. However, avoid overwatering or the plant will not produce vibrant blooms. It is hardy to about eighteen or nineteen degrees Fahrenheit. Use the paper flower for color in perennial and wildflower gardens. It looks great when planted in masses, along walkways, and around water features with its long lasting, colorful, flower show. The paper flower is a good

Tetraneuris acaulis
Angelita Daisy

This perennial resembles the desert marigold with it daisylike, golden yellow blooms that grow on tall, tightly clustered, leafless stems. It has small, fragrant grasslike leaves and grows one foot tall and eighteen inches wide. The plant produces pale to bright yellow, buttonlike flowers periodically throughout the year with prolific blooming occurring during the spring. It will naturalize anywhere if the conditions are optimum. The angelita daisy likes full sun, reflected heat and handles most soils but prefers them to be well draining. This plant can survive on monthly irrigation but looks best with weekly irrigation during hot, dry weather. It is hardy to ten degrees Fahrenheit and is resistant to deer and rabbits infestations. Remove spent blossoms and scatter seed to help it reproduce. Use the plant in rock gardens, transitional desert gardens, and raised beds. Mix with other colorful perennial plants, such as penstemon and verbena. It is native to rocky, dry, open, slopes in Arizona, New Mexico, Colorado, Nevada, and Southern California, growing at elevations of 4,000 to 7,000 feet.

Thymophylla pentachaeta
Golden Fleece
Golden Dyssodia
Common Dog Weed

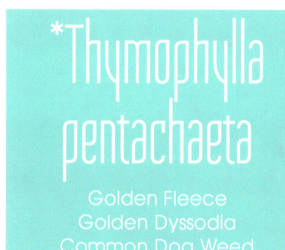

*Thymophylla pentachaeta

Golden Fleece
Golden Dyssodia
Common Dog Weed
Perennial groundcover

Thymophylla pentachaeta
Golden Fleece
Golden Dyssodia
Common Dog Weed

This low-growing, tufted, herbaceous perennial is a short-lived plant that grows seven inches tall and wide. It reseeds itself each year during the summer monsoon and regrows each season with warm weather. The plant has long, threadlike, lacy, bright green foliage with leafless stalks. It produces bright clusters of yellow, daisylike flowers on long, slender stems above the foliage. The plant blooms continuously throughout the spring and summer until the first frost, attracting bees, butterflies, and birds. It likes supplemental irrigation to remain lush and reseed. The plant requires full sun and reflected heat and is hardy to ten degrees Fahrenheit. It prefers sandy, well-draining soil but will grow and reseed in any soil. Use it in butterfly and wildflower gardens, containers, raised planters, and rock gardens. The golden dyssodia can also be used for erosion control, on slopes, as an edging plant, and along sidewalks and patios. This showy groundcover is very easy to propagate from seeds. Allow the seed heads to dry out on the plants and then remove and collect the seed. This plant can also be planted in flats or pot packs and used for quick color. It is native to New Mexico, Arizona, Texas, and Northern Mexico, growing in desert areas and rocky plains at elevations of 2,500 to 4,500 feet.

Trachelospermum asiaticum

Star Jasmine
Groundcover

Trachelospermum asiaticum
Star Jasmine

The trailing evergreen admired for its fragrant, starlike flowers, grows one to two feet tall and spreads to twenty feet wide with moderate to fast growth. It has small, dark green, leathery foliage with smooth reddish brown stems. Star jasmine produces waxy, white flowers with a golden yellow star in the center. The blossoms are highly fragrant throughout the spring. An interesting variegated variety of this plant is available in some local garden centers. It has green foliage tinged with creamy white colorations and new growth that is pink. Plant the star jasmine in full shade or partial shade, as it may sunburn in full sun. This plant does not like reflected heat. The groundcover also prefers well-draining, amended soil to look its best. It needs ample water but does not like to be overwatered. Star jasmine is hardy to about twenty degrees Fahrenheit and may be damaged by severe cold. Plant the hardy groundcover on northern or eastern exposures for best growth. This plant can suffer from iron chlorosis; if needed, treat it with an iron chelate fertilizer. Provide some light pruning to encourage new growth. Use it in shady beds for woodsy, oriental, and tropical effects; or in raised planters or cascading over a container. Star jasmine also looks good in small courtyard beds and in atriums or entryways when planted in shady, microclimate conditions. The foliage can be used in flower arrangements. This plant is native to Korea and Japan.

Tradescantia pallida

Purple Heart, Wandering Jew
Perennial groundcover

This attractive perennial is noted for its violet purple leaves and low-growing habit to one foot with an almost equal spread. The undersides of its narrow, oblong leaves are deep violet to pink. The plant is a vigorous grower with a trailing habit and produces dainty, pink blooms in small clusters that are only open in the morning. It takes full sun to partial shade, but the foliage may be a richer color in full sun. Purple heart also likes rich, moist, well-draining, sandy soil

Tradescantia pallida
Purple Heart, Wandering Jew

Tradescantia pallida
Purple Heart, Wandering Jew

and is drought tolerant. This groundcover prefers regular irrigation and freezes below thirty-two degrees Fahrenheit. If frosted back, prune it to live growth. The plant recovers quickly in the spring. To maintain a nice shape and stimulate growth, remove flower stems and prune after the groundcover finishes blooming. This plant may cause a skin irritation or allergic relation from the juices in its stems. Wear protective clothing and gloves when working around it, especially if you have sensitive skin. Use it for its excellent colored foliage, which makes a nice contrast against other green plants in containers, hanging baskets, rock gardens, raised planters, narrow beds, and borders, and as an understory plant. This plant is very easy to grow and easy to propagate by cuttings. The purple heart is native to tropical and semi tropical areas of Mexico, from Tamaulipas to the Yucatan.

Tulbaghia violacea
Society Garlic
Bulbous Groundcover

Tulbaghia violacea
Society Garlic

Society garlic is a fast-growing, clumping, bulbous evergreen that reaches two feet tall. It has grayish green, grasslike foliage that grows out of a bulbous whorl of greenery. Its fat, tuberous roots will propagate to form many clumps. The variety "Silver Lace" has variegated foliage with creamy stripes. In spring through early summer, the plant produces upright clusters of lavender purplish blossoms that form a star shape and grow on a tall flower stalk above the plant. The foliage and flowers have a distinct garlic smell, especially when crushed. Its flowers also have a sweet fragrance that is more prominent during the evening. After flowering, a fruit with triangular capsules

Tulbaghia violacea
Society Garlic

Eastern Cape, KwaZulu-Natal and Limpopo in South Africa and north towards Zimbabwe.

Vinca major
Periwinkle
Groundcover

Vinca major
Periwinkle

Vinca major
Periwinkle

appears. The fruit eventually splits open when ripe to release flat, hard, black seeds. This plant needs full sun in order to produce its bloom. The leaves and bulbous parts of the plant are edible and taste like garlic-flavored chives. Its crushed leaves can be used to help treat a sinus headache or for cooking. The smell from this plant can be a deterrent for fleas, ticks, and mosquitoes when the foliage is dried and crushed on the skin. Fresh bulbs can be boiled in water and made into a tea to treat coughs and colds. The plant likes light, sandy, well-draining soils and ample water, especially during the growing season. It can take some drought when mature and needs applications of fertilizer to enhance its bloom. Society garlic will tolerate light frosts and freezing temperatures to about twenty-eight degrees Fahrenheit before suffering damage. Use it in containers with annuals and perennials, in borders, as an edging plant, and in rock gardens, herb gardens, and raised planter beds. It is native to the rocky, grassland areas of

The low-growing evergreen spreads and roots along the ground with its trailing, arching stems, forming a dense mat. It has dark glossy green, slightly hairy foliage with pointed tips. In early spring, it produces purplish blue, starlike, funnel-shaped blossoms. The variety "Alba" has white flowers, and many other varieties are available. This lush plant needs an ample amount of water to look good but will tolerate deep, periodic irrigation. It will wilt if it becomes water stressed. This groundcover likes to be planted in rich, well-draining soil. Periwinkle will show foliage damage at temperatures below fifteen degrees Fahrenheit but recovers quickly if frosted back. It tolerates full sun but looks best planted in filtered sun in the Southwest desert. It may become invasive with its greedy roots and is difficult to eradicate. All parts of this plant are poisonous if ingested. Use it as a bank cover, in containers, window boxes, and planters and as an understory plant for woodsy effects. Use periwinkle for erosion control, as filler for bare areas, or mixed into rock gardens. Try the variety "Variegata" for its variegated leaves with yellowish white leaf margins. The species is native to Southern Europe, Central Asia, and Northern Africa.

Viola odorata

Sweet Violet
Perennial groundcover

Viola odorata
Sweet Violet

The fast-growing, long-lived evergreen reaches four inches tall with aromatic, violet flowers and small, heart-shaped foliage that is slightly serrated and dark green in color. It grows in a rosette with creeping runners that root and spread. The plant produces fragrant, five-petal flowers in deep purple, blue, violet, lavender, pink, or white, depending on variety. The flowers are edible and last from late winter through late spring. Historically, both the flowers and foliage have provided medicinal benefits and have been used to treat respiratory problems and other ailments. The flowers can also be used to decorate salads and deserts. The ancient Greeks used the violet as a symbol of love and fertility. It was also used in love potions. Sweet violet goes dormant in the Southwest desert during the hot weather but looks beautiful other times of the year. It likes partial shade to light shade conditions. Give it regular irrigation but do not overwater. This plant is hardy into the low twenties Fahrenheit and prefers rich, well-draining soil and good fertilization in the spring. Sweet violet spreads quickly by short runners or can be propagated by seeds. Use it for color or a woodsy effect under the shade of a tree, as a border plant, and in planters and containers. It is native to Europe, Asia, and Africa and has naturalized all over the world.

Zephyranthes candida

White Rain Lily
Bulbous groundcover

Rain lily is a clumping, grasslike plant that grows from an underground bulb to six to twelve inches tall and one to two feet wide. Its lush, evergreen

Zephyranthes candida
White Rain Lily

foliage is dark and glossy green. The plant produces white flowers with light pink shading that last for several days, but close up at night. The rain lily gets its name by its characteristic flowers that bloom immediately following a rainstorm, usually after a dry period in the spring and fall. It grows best in rich, well-draining soil and likes to be fertilized during the summer to enhance new growth. This plant grows in full sun or partial shade but prefers shady conditions in the southwest desert. It does not like reflected heat. It withstands some drought conditions but likes weekly irrigation and is hardy to fifteen to twenty degrees Fahrenheit. The white rain lily is easily propagated by division of its bulbs or by seed. Use this groundcover along walkways, as a border plant, in containers with other perennials, mixed in with color plants in atriums, in entryways, in rock gardens, and in raised beds. The species looks its best when clumped together in large, irregular masses. This groundcover originated in the Rio de la Plata region of South America in Argentina and Uruguay. It is also native to moist, woodland areas, marshes, and bogs in Chile and Paraguay.

6 Vines and Climbers
for Southwest Landscapes

A vine is a plant that has a long, flexible, green stem that requires support or training to climb up a wall or trellis. It can also creep along the ground and climb by clinging to a support with its leafstalk or tendrils. Fast growing, climbing vines can help to cover unwelcome features, hide bare walls and fences and offer color and texture to the landscape.

*Antigonon leptopus,

Queen's Wreath, Coral Vine
Vines and climbers

Antigonon leptopus
Queen's Wreath, Coral Vine

Antigonon leptopus
Queen's Wreath, Coral Vine

The fast-growing, tender perennial climbs thirty to forty feet tall with curled tendrils and bright green, heart-shaped leaves. The undersides of the leaves have pronounced green veins. The plant flowers prolifically with beautiful red, coral, light pink or white clusters from branching, terminal stalks. It blooms continuously from late summer until the first frost, attracting bees, butterflies, and humming-birds. After flowering, dark seeds that are enclosed in a light tan, papery sheath appear. The plant is a self-climber that clings to walls and wooden or metal trellises with its curled, strong tendrils. Its underground tubers are edible. The plant freezes at thirty-two degrees Fahrenheit but grows back vigorously during late spring and summer from its roots. The underground roots are hardy to twenty degrees. Prune it heavily in spring if it freezes back, or at other times, prune it lightly to train. The plant likes full sun and reflected heat and thrives growing up hot walls. Provide deep irrigations during the hot season to promote growth and vigor. Plant the queen's wreath in well-draining soil improved with amendments. Use on arbors, fences, and walls as a screening plant in pool areas and other water features. It is native to Mexico from Baja California, Sonora, and Chihuahua down into Oaxaca, Mexico and Central America.

*Bignonia capreolata

Cross Vine
Vines and climbers

This fast-growing, evergreen climber reaches ten to thirty feet or more with dark green foliage and long, slender tendrils. This vine produces showy clusters of long, orangey red, trumpet-shaped blossoms throughout spring and summer. The tubular flowers hang from the vine to produce a mass of magnificent color and attract hummingbirds. After

Bignonia capreolata
Cross Vine

amended soil and is hardy from thirteen to fifteen degrees Fahrenheit. Once established, the plant is drought tolerant. The cross vine is also easy to grow since its suckers will root in the ground and regrow. Use it as a warm-season color plant since it doesn't look great in the winter months. Prune it back heavily in late winter and train young plants. Use it to cover fences, trellises, archways, south- or west-facing walls or structures. It makes a great screen when properly trained. The plant is native to the Southeastern United States from Maryland to Florida, west to Missouri, and into Texas. This vine is found growing in low-lying areas, forests, and open clearings.

Bignonia capreolata
Cross Vine

*Bougainvillea hybrids
Bougainvillea
Vines and climbers, shrub

blooming, the plant develops flat seedpods, containing winged seeds. It's climbing tendrils and stems become woody as the plant matures. The variety "Tangerine Beauty" is popular and widely available. This vine enjoys full sun with some filtered shade; however, it blooms more profusely in the sun. It also likes moist, well-draining,

Bougainvillea
'Barbara Karst' Variety

Bougainvillea
'Barbara Karst' Variety

Variegated Bougainvillea

Bougainvillea
'Barbara Karst' Variety

Bougainvillea is a sprawling vine grown for its beautiful flower bracts in fuchsia, pink, orange, rose, white, or purple, depending upon the variety. Inside the center of each flower bract is a small white, waxy flower. This evergreen to semi-evergreen plant has bright green, heart-shaped foliage and reaches fifteen feet tall or more. Older vines produce more color than younger plants and bloom best when water stressed. The vine is thorny and the tips have a blackish, waxy substance. "Barbara Karst" is a popular variety for the Southwest desert since it loves the heat. "Torch Glow" has a different shape than the other varieties and its blossoms appear at the ends of stiff, erect stems. Bougainvillea needs full sun with plenty of reflected heat. Locate on the south or west side of a building or house, as the plant prefers the hottest, sunniest spot in the landscape. Plant it in fertile, organic soils that are well draining. This plant sprawls and needs training as it grows. Bougainvillea is frost sensitive and suffers foliage damage at temperatures below thirty degrees Fahrenheit. However, it recovers quickly in the spring after pruning back any dead or damaged branches. It needs ample water when young but is somewhat drought tolerant when mature. If overwatered, this plant many not flower and the roots could decay. When transplanting, be very careful to avoid disturbing the root ball. The plant can go into shock and take a long time to recover if the roots are broken or pulled apart. Use it as a warm season, color accent vine. Plant this vine to cascade over walls, banks, fences, trellises, arbors, and container rims. It can also be used as a cut flower or a security barrier. Plant the bougainvillea in tropical and Mediterranean gardens and around pools, ponds, and water features. It is native to South America from the coast of Brazil, west to Peru, and south to Southern

Argentina. There are two distinct species of this plant, Bougainvillea glabra and Bougainvillea spectabilis. B. glabra is a smaller plant with fewer thorns and grows more like a shrub. B. spectabilis is a faster-growing plant that is more sprawling, growing like a vine. There are many hybrids of these two species that show a wide variety in leaf forms and growth characteristics. It is sometimes called the paper flower since its bracts are very thin and papery.

Dolichandra unguis-cati

Cat's Claw
Vines and climbers

Dolichandra unguis-cati
Cat's Claw

Dolichandra unguis-cati
Cat's Claw

This self-climbing, self-attaching evergreen is a fast, aggressive grower that climbs to heights of twenty-five feet or higher with an equal spread. The foliage has with two green leaflets and an interesting three-pronged claw. Its tendrils work as an appendage, clinging onto most walls. In late spring, the vine produces a bright yellow, showy, funnel-shaped bloom with five petals. After flowering, it develops a thin seedpod that opens, dispersing winged, brown seeds. Its stems are reddish brown aging to a dark green color. The cat's claw is hardy to about twenty degrees Fahrenheit. This vine does best in full sun with reflected heat. It is drought tolerant but grows quickly with regular irrigation and likes sandy or clay soil that is well draining. Prune aggressively to the ground in late spring every few years to prevent it from becoming too woody and heavy on the wall. It will grow back quickly after major pruning and will start to reattach itself to any wall surface. The cat's claw produces extensive underground tubers that are hard to eradicate. This long-living vine is a great choice for covering an unsightly or hot wall in a hurry. Use it to soften a wall or side of a building. It can also be used as a screen on walls, lattice, or trellises, and on slopes for erosion control. This plant is native to the West Indies, Mexico, Brazil, and parts of Argentina. The cat's claw vine is considered an invasive plant in many parts of the world.

*Ficus pumila
Creeping Fig
Vines and climbers

Ficus pumila
Creeping Fig

Use to create a cool, green splash of foliage against a wall of wood, masonry, or block, or to soften a wall in an atrium, building, or house façade. It is native to Japan, Eastern China, and Vietnam.

Ficus pumila
Creeping Fig

The self-climbing evergreen has unique, attractive foliage and can quickly scramble up the side of a wall with its lacy stems and leaves, climbing to twenty feet or more. The creeping fig has small, heart-shaped, juvenile leaves when young, and large, leathery dark green mature foliage. It produces a pale greenish yellow figlike fruit on its horizontal stems that is inedible. Its flowers are inconspicuous or are not present. Several different varieties are available including a variegated form. It likes shady to partial shade conditions and also prefers well-draining soil. When the plant is young it requires regular irrigation, but as it matures, it becomes more drought resistant. Creeping fig tolerates freezing conditions for short periods of time and is hardy to about fifteen degrees Fahrenheit. It needs to be pruned regularly from growing into roofs, eaves, and windows. Mature vines will need to be tied or reanchored to the wall if they get too heavy. This vine is difficult to remove from walls and leaves a marking on painted surfaces and walls. If a mature vine dries out and dies, prune it heavily to its roots to stimulate new growth. When the vine is young, it is slow growing. As it matures, its growth rate dramatically increases. For best results, plant it on a north- or east-facing wall.

Gelsemium sempervirens
Carolina Jessamine
Vines and climbers

This attractive, fast-growing, compact evergreen vine climbs to heights of ten-twenty feet. Its foliage is glossy green with pointed tips, and its stems are smooth and reddish brown. In early spring, the plant produces small clusters of fragrant, yellow, trumpet-shaped blossoms with five short lobes. This vine likes full sun and ample irrigation to look its best but can withstand short periods of drought. Plant it in well-draining soil that has a high content of organic matter or mulch added to the soil mix. Lightly prune

Gelsemium sempervirens
Carolina Jessamine

Gelsemium sempervirens
Carolina Jessamine

it after blooming to remove any dead or broken branches. The Carolina jessamine is hardy to twenty-five degrees Fahrenheit. It is an easy vine to grow and can be kept in control with minimum care. Fertilize with ammonium phosphate in the early spring. All parts of this plant are toxic if ingested. The plant can sometimes cause an allergic skin reaction to some people. Use it to cover trellises, fences, and arbors in a sunny location. Also use it in a large container or as a ground-

cover along steep banks. This plant looks nice in smaller patios and entryways. This vine is native to warm temperate climates from Guatemala to the Southeastern United States, and grows into the coastal plains of North and South Carolina. It grows naturally in open woodlands, thickets, and along roadsides.

Hardenbergia violacea

Purple Coral Pea
Vines and climbers

Hardenbergia violacea
Purple Coral Pea

The twining, woody evergreen climbs slowly to ten to twelve feet tall and about five feet wide with long, grayish green, leathery leaves with prominent veins. In early spring, the vine produces showy clusters of lavender-purple, pea-shaped blossoms that cascade down from the plant. Varieties are also available that produce white or pink blossoms. This showy vine is hardy to twenty-three to twenty-five degrees Fahrenheit and takes full sun to light shade conditions but prefers to grow on north facing walls. It tolerates most soils as long as they are well draining. Apply light applications of ammonium phosphate fertilizer once or twice a year to keep it blooming and healthy. The plant is drought tolerant once established but do not allow it to dry out between watering cycles. Provide extra irrigation during the hot, dry seasons. It is also tolerant of wind and responds well to pruning, especially the older, mature plants. The purple coral pea needs some training and support if grown as a climbing vine. Use this rambling plant on trellises, walls, arbors, or fences for its amazing early spring color show. There are many available cultivars of this plant. It is native to Australia, growing in sandy soils, forests, on rocky outcrops and in woodland areas.

Jasminum mesnyi

Primrose Jasmine
Vines and climbers

Jasminum mesnyi
Primrose Jasmine

The rambling, lush evergreen with long, arching stems sprawls as it climbs to ten feet or more, forming a fountainlike, mounded appearance. The foliage grows in sets of three leaflets and is glossy green and pointed at the tip. The plant produces slightly fragrant, trumpetlike, semidouble or double yellow blossoms in early spring and then blooms intermittingly through the summer. Its flowers are edible and can be used as a garnish in recipes, such as fresh garden salad. This fast-growing vine likes full sun but takes some filtered shade, especially during the hot summer months. It prefers regular irrigation and does not like to dry out. Plant it in well draining, fertile soils and provide an application of fertilizer in the spring. Its canelike branches will root into the ground and continue to grow and propagate. Prune it back after it flowers in late spring to control its size and growth habit. The plant is deer resistant and tolerant to heavy pruning. It gets bushier when pruned and can form

Jasminum mesnyi
Primrose Jasmine

a nice, dense mound of dark green foliage. Use hand pruners and avoid electric hedge shears. It tolerates light frosts and is hardy to the high twenties Fahrenheit. If frozen, prune its long canes to live growth and let it recover in the spring. Provide some trellis support. Use it for its cascading effect in the landscape or as a screen or bank cover for erosion control. It can also be trained as a hedge or as a rambling vine on trellises, arbors, and fences. The primrose jasmine looks interesting spilling over archways and trained on walls. This versatile vine is native to Southwestern China.

Jasminum polyanthum
Winter Jasmine, Pink Jasmine
Vines and climbers

Jasminum polyanthum
Winter Jasmine, Pink Jasmine

The fast-growing, tropical evergreen climbs to heights of twelve to fifteen feet or more with fine-textured, deep green foliage with five to seven leaflets and slender, twining, woody stems. The underside of its leaves is a lighter green. It produces lightly scented, delicate, white-petaled, tubular blossoms in clusters with emerging pink buds. When the flowers open, they are star shaped and pure white. Blossoms appear in early spring and bloom prolifically until the hot weather. This vine does best on east- or north-facing walls rather than on fences or on free-standing vine frames. It handles full sun but prefers some light shade and will burn with reflected heat. Plant it in rich, well-draining, moist soil and provide weekly irrigation to ensure lush growth. However, do not overwater this plant. Apply light applications of ammonium phosphate fertilizer in early spring. This vigorous growing vine should be lightly pruned after flowering to keep the plants thinned and shaped. The winter jasmine is hardy to twenty degrees Fahrenheit and is low maintenance. Use it on a trellis, wall, or arbor, or train its twining branches along a roof or eave of the house. It can also be used as a groundcover plant or in containers for tropical effects. It is native to Western and Southern China.

Lonicera japonica 'Halliana'
Hall's Japanese Honeysuckle
Vines and climbers

The dense, vigorous evergreen or semideciduous vine has twining stems and climbs fifteen to thirty feet tall to cover a large area quickly with its sprawling branches and dense foliage. It has deep green, medium-sized, oval leaves with a brownish colored back. In spring and

Lonicera japonica 'Halliana'
Hall's Japanese Honeysuckle

Lonicera japonica 'Halliana'
Hall's Japanese Honeysuckle

Use it as a bank cover or on slopes for erosion control or train it on an arbor, trellis, or garden posts for color. Also use it as a screening plant to hide an unsightly area in the landscape. Plant this fast-growing vine near entryways to enjoy its highly fragrant, spring flowers. It is native to the hills and mountains of Japan and the mountains and low-lying areas of Korea. This plant has naturalized and established itself in the Southeastern United States where it grows in fields, at the edges of forests, in disturbed woods, and on floodplains.

Lonicera x heckrottii 'Gold Flame'

Gold Flame Honeysuckle
Vines and climbers

summer, the plant produces creamy white, fragrant blooms that turn yellow as they mature and send a heavenly scent throughout the garden. The flowers attract bees, hummingbirds, and butterflies. It likes full sun or partial shade. This vine also prefers regular irrigation, especially during the spring and summer, when it is most actively growing. The honeysuckle can also take some drought conditions and is hardy to fifteen to twenty degrees Fahrenheit. This plant handles most soils, as long as they are well draining. The vine may become invasive with its rampant growth and often looks scraggly during the winter. Prune back after flowering to maintain its size and growth. Also, watch for possible infestations of aphids during early spring through the summer and treat them as needed.

The twining, woody, deciduous to semideciduous, climber grows vigorously to twelve to fifteen feet tall and spreads to ten feet. It has shiny, oval, bluish green foliage with reddish stems that provide ornamental interest. The vine develops showy clusters of tubular, fragrant blossoms in coral, pink, and magenta on the outside of the flower and an orange-yellow on the inside of the bloom. It flowers throughout the warm season producing magnificent color and attracts hummingbirds and butterflies. In the fall, it produces inedible red berries. This honeysuckle likes full sun and regular irrigation. Irrigate it more often during the first season after planting to establish a deep root system. Do not overwater this plant

Lonicera x heckrottii 'Gold Flame'
Gold Flame Honeysuckle

Lonicera x heckrottii 'Gold Flame'
Gold Flame Honeysuckle

Pandorea jasminoides
Bower Vine
Vines and climbers

Pandorea jasminoides
Bower Vine

and give it rich, well draining, acidic to neutral soil. It is hardy into the low twenties Fahrenheit and is dormant during the winter. Prune it heavily in late winter to train its growth habit and control its size during the growing season. Watch for aphids in the spring as well as powdery mildew in hot, humid locations, and treat it as needed. Use it as a showy, color plant on arbors, trellises, and fences or as an espalier near porches and patios for its amazing twining and trailing growth habit. This plant can also be grown in containers. The gold flame honeysuckle is believed to be a cross between two Lonicera species, Lonicera x americana and Lonicera sempervirens.

The sprawling evergreen with twining stems climbs to twenty feet with pointed, dark glossy green foliage with divided leaves and woody stems. A variegated form has green leaves with white edges. In the spring and continuing through the first frost, large, beautiful, slightly fragrant, whitish pink flowers appear. The varieties "Southern Belle," "Charisma" and "Rosea" have a distinctive reddish pink center. The varieties "Alba" and "Lady Di" have pure white flowers. After blooming, the plant produces large fruits that contain many seeds. It likes full sun or light shade and needs a moist, fertile, well-draining soil with regular irrigation. Water the bower vine sparingly during the winter months. This vine needs some training with a trellis or other supports when young. The plant is hardy to the mid-twenties Fahrenheit, and if frozen back, cut

Pandorea jasminoides
Bower Vine

Passiflora foetida
Passion Flower, Baja Passion

it to the ground. It will recover quickly in spring. Apply applications of ammonium phosphate fertilizer before blooming. Prune and shape this vine after flowering. Use this graceful looking vine in containers and to cover arbors, trellises and fences. It can also be used to train, cascade, or twine along a wall or post. The bower vine is native to Queensland and North South Wales, Australia.

*Passiflora foetida
Passion Flower, Baja Passion
Vines and climbers

The deciduous, fast-growing, creeping vine climbs twelve to fifteen feet with tendrils and thin stems that are covered with sticky, yellow hair. Its dark green foliage has three- to five-lobed leaves and produces an unpleasant aroma when crushed. The exquisite blooms are white, pink, and deep purple with colored bracts, and it blooms from late spring to early summer. While beautiful, the blossoms can also produce an unpleasant odor. This plant is a butterfly, bird, and bee attracter. The flower bracts of this plant also serve as an insect trap. Its blossoms open in the morning and close in the evening. After blooming, the plant produces a sweet, kumquat-sized, edible, yellowish orange fruit with black seeds. The fruits are eaten by birds, which disperse the seeds. There are some medicinal applications to the leaves, but some parts of this plant can be poisonous. The dry leaves of this plant have been used in a tea in Vietnamese

Passiflora foetida
Passion Flower, Baja Passion

Pyracantha coccinea
Firethorn, Scarlet Firethorn

folklore or as a medicine to relieve sleep problems and tension. As a landscape plant, it prefers moist conditions with well-draining soil. Do not overwater this vine. Plant it in full sun to partial shade. It is hardy to about thirty degrees Fahrenheit, and if frosted back, it recovers quickly in the spring. Use it for its amazing flowers to cover a wall or trellis, train on arbors, or use it in entryways and patios. It is native to tropical areas of Southern Europe, Northern South America, the West Indies, Vietnam, and Hawaii. It can be an invasive species in some areas.

Pyracantha coccinea
Firethorn, Scarlet Firethorn

*Pyracantha coccinea
Firethorn, Scarlet Firethorn
Vines and climbers

The evergreen, noted for its spectacular display of orange-red berries and shiny, brown bark, climbs to ten feet tall and about twelve to fifteen feet wide. It has small, rounded, dark glossy green foliage and has extremely sharp, spurlike thorns on its branches. In the spring, the firethorn produces small clusters of slightly fragrant, white flowers. In late fall, clusters of red or orange berries form, and by the dead of winter, they ripen to add color to any garden. The berries are eaten by birds or other animals. In colder climates, the berries and leaves are darker in color. It takes full sun and reflected heat and is not particular about soil types. The plant prefers infrequent irrigations and is hardy

Pyracantha coccinea
Firethorn, Scarlet Firethorn

to about ten degrees Fahrenheit. Firethorn needs a good amount of pruning throughout its growing season to keep its shape. It is highly susceptible to spider mites. If infected, treat it with a blast of water to wash off the mites or use a systemic insecticide. It may also suffer from iron chlorosis. If needed, treat with chelated iron fertilizer. This plant is a very fast grower, and there are many varieties available. Use it as an espalier or vine trained up against the wall or shaped on a wall. It can also be used as a bank cover on a slope or groomed as a shrub or hedge. The firethorn branches look great in flower arrangements and the berries add color to wreaths. The plant is native to Southeastern Europe and into Western Asia.

Rosa banksiae
Lady Banks Rose Vine
Vines and climbers

Rosa banksiae 'Alba Plena'
White Lady Banks Rose Vine

Rosa banksiae 'Lutea'
Yellow Lady Banks Rose Vine

The popular, scrambling evergreen to semi-evergreen has an arching growth habit reaching heights of twelve to twenty feet with long, glossy green leaves with three to five leaflets per leaf. Leaves will defoliate at lower temperatures. In early spring, the plant develops beautiful white

Rosa banksiae 'Lutea'
Yellow Lady Banks Rose Vine

or yellow clusters of single or double flowers, depending upon the variety. The blossoms are fragrant, and attract bees and butterflies. The variety "Lutea" has yellow flowers and no thorns. "Alba Plena" has white flowers and some thorns. The stems of this plant are usually thornless, slender, and sprawling. The Lady Bank's rose is hardy to about thirteen to fifteen degrees Fahrenheit. This vine does best in full sun with reflected heat. It needs supplemental irrigation once or twice per week, especially in hot weather. This fast-growing vine should be given plenty of room to grow and requires training and pruning to look good. The foliage may attract harvester ants during the summer monsoon. The insects strip the leaves to build their nests. If needed, apply Amdro insecticide around anthills to prevent damage to the plant. Locate the anthills in the early morning hours when the ants trail back to their nest. Use this vine in the landscape on trellises, walls, arbors, and fences, or train it to cascade over embankments. This is a great choice for erosion control on slopes and a beautiful, early spring color plant. The largest Lady Bank's rose vine is growing in Tombstone, Arizona. The plant was installed in 1885 and covers an entire square block. The species is a native to Central and

Western China, where it has been cultivated for hundreds of years.

Wisteria sinensis
Chinese Wisteria
Vines and climbers

Wisteria sinensis
Chinese Wisteria

The long-lived, deciduous twining vine grows fifteen to twenty feet and is admired for its gnarly growth habit. It produces amazing clusters of fragrant, cascading purple, white, and lilac flowers that bloom over a long period of time, beginning in spring. The Chinese wisteria has shiny, oblong green leaves with seven to thirteen individual leaflets. Its flowers are actually racemes that drape and hang down from the vine, giving the air a sweet grape scent. The flowers attract bees, butterflies, and birds. After the blooms are spent, the plant produces large, flat, velvety, brown seedpods that mature in the summer. The

Wisteria sinensis
Chinese Wisteria

pods open and disperse black seeds. Many varieties of this plant are available. All parts of the plant are toxic if ingested. The plant prefers full sun or partial shade but will bloom more prolifically in the sun. It is not particular to soil type but prefers a rich, moist, well-draining soil. The Chinese wisteria is highly susceptible to Texas root rot and should not be planted in soils where this disease may be present. When using it on a trellis, it requires training and pruning. Do not overfertilize it but treat with iron chelate fertilizer as needed. It is very hardy into the low twenties Fahrenheit. Use it in containers or as a specimen vine trained over a large arbor or espaliered on a building. It can also be trained to grow over rooftops, arbors and trellises or as a bonsai plant. This vine is native to China.

7 Low-Water-Use Accent Plants

for Southwest Landscapes

Low water use, accent plant are comprised of many different species of Agave, Aloe, Yucca and other drought resistant plant material. The plants covered in this chapter are all excellent choices to use in areas with dry climates and low rainfall. Many of these plants will add a dramatic accent to your desert landscape and need very little water to exist and look beautiful.

Agave Species

There are several hundred species of agaves native to semi-arid regions of the United States, Mexico, South America, Baja California, and parts of the Caribbean. The plants grow naturally in rocky hillsides, on dry, barren, desert grasslands or in rocky soils. Agave plants can be found in woodland and tropical areas or they are sometimes found growing at sea level. About forty species of agave are native to the Sonoran Desert, where they grow on well-draining, rocky slopes. Agaves can handle temperatures over a hundred degrees Fahrenheit and at the other extreme, temperatures into the low twenties. Their sensitivity to the cold and frost vary from species to species.

The plant was originally introduced by Spaniards and Portuguese in the seventeenth century. Agaves were cultivated for many centuries by Native Americans for food, drink, fiber, and medicine. Today, the species is highly popular in desert landscapes, adding a great deal of drama and accent with minimal irrigation.

The agave produces leaves in rosettes on short trunks enabling the plant to adapt to harsh, dry desert conditions. Its leaves are thick and full of juicy succulent tissue, and sharp spines exist on the leaf edges and tips. This allows the plant to capture large amounts of rain and deliver it to the root zone. The size and shape of the teeth vary between species, but are small, large, sharp, or curved. The leaves of the agave have fiber inside them to store food, moisture, and energy to ensure survival. Foliage ranges from blue, gray, yellow, white, and different shades of green. Some of the foliage is variegated in interesting patterns and colors, which adds accent and excitement to landscapes.

Agave in bloom

The agave is monocarpic, meaning it produces only one major flower bloom in its lifetime and then dies. However, there are a few species of this plant that may bloom more frequently. Generally, after many years, the mother plant produces a tall, single flower spike that grows upright from the plant. It takes from five to twenty years to produce a bloom stalk that reaches heights of four to thirty feet or more. The flower stalk forms an impressive flower above the plant. These flowers develop petals, or tepals, which are the outer part of the flower. The tepals come in spectacular, colors, including yellow, green, gold, creamy white, or reddish-purple. The blooms are pollinated by insects, bats, birds, hummingbirds, and moths. A fruity capsule forms and contains black colored seeds. Eventually, the flower spikes dries up and the plant dies.

Some agaves produce offsets or pups. Offsets are shoots that develop laterally at the base of the parent plant just below the soil surface often rooting to form a new plant that will reproduce and ensure survival of the species.

Agaves are highly adapted for pollination. The seeds are also dispersed by wind for reproduction. Each agave plant is distinguished from all others by its flower stalk. The branched varieties are pollinated by bats; the bats are attracted to the fragrant nectar produced by the flower. Night blooming agaves are pollinated by hawk moths and bees. Agaves that do not form a branching inflorescence are pollinated by insects and hummingbirds.

Agave americana mixed
with Lantana camera

One major problem that may cause early death to the agave plant is the agave snout weevil (Scyphophorus acupunctatus). This insect is most active in March. It lays eggs that hatch into larvae that feed on the fleshy core of the plant. This insect is black in color, and about one inch long. Snout weevils prefer the larger, broad-leaf agaves. Infested plants show leaf wilt, shriveling or drooping lower leaves, and a rapid collapse of the plant. If left untreated, the plant will eventually collapse and die. To treat, drench the soil around the agave with a systemic insecticide.

Agave angustifolia var. marginata
Caribbean Agave

Agave americana
Century Plant

Most agaves do not need supplemental fertilizer or irrigation. However, some varieties require supplemental irrigation during the hot, dry summer seasons. This plant provides interest and accent to most desert garden spaces. Their shallow root system and dramatic presentation make them an excellent choice for many landscape situations.

Agave americana
Century Plant

The century plant is a massive succulent with thick grayish blue leaves that grows to seven feet at maturity and can spread up to twelve feet wide. Its forms a single rosette of growth at the base of the plant with leaves growing into a downward curve. Mature plants can have rosettes with twenty to forty leaves. The underside of the leaf can sometimes have a variegation of patterns. Each leaf has sharp, inch-long, brownish black spines along the margins and tip. After ten years or more, the plant produces a tall flower stalk from its center with as many as fifteen to thirty branches and large, showy, greenish yellow flowers. After the flower stalk dries out, flat, disklike seeds form, enclosed inside a capsule. The flower

stalk and heart of this plant are very sweet and can be roasted or eaten. The dried flower seeds can be ground into flour to make bread. Century plants like full sun and reflected heat. They are extremely drought resistant but prefer occasional irrigation when young. Mature plants can get by on natural rainfall, but plants look better with supplemental water. Plant the century plant in well-draining, slightly acidic, sandy, or gravelly soil. This fast-growing agave is hardy to thirteen to fifteen degrees Fahrenheit. Over its lifetime, it produces many offsets that can be transplanted. Prune and remove lower leaves when they dry out. Watch for infestations of the agave snout weevil, especially if the agave is weakened or old. The sap from the plant may be a skin irritant to some people. With its immense size, this plant will dominate the landscape and should not be planted near sidewalks or pedestrian areas. Use it as a barrier or an ornamental plant in containers, rock gardens, cactus gardens. You can also plant it in masses or as a single accent plant. It works well in coastal areas and is tolerant of sea spray and salty conditions. The century plant is native to the Eastern Sierras from Monterrey, Mexico, growing south into the state of San Luis Potosi, Mexico. It is also common in warm Mediterranean regions of the world, including parts of Europe and into Northern Africa, India, and Australia.

*Agave americana 'Cornelius'
Agave Cornelius

Agave americana 'Cornelius'
Agave Cornelius

The agave cornelius is a low growing, colorful plant. It has thick, wavy blue green and yellow variegated foliage with wide leaves. This spectacular plant has sharp black teeth along its leaves and a sharp tip. It will grow about two feet wide and tall to form an attractive medium-sized rosette. This plant is very slow growing and will rarely produce offsets. The agave cornelius likes full sun and well-draining soils. It also prefers to completely dry out between watering cycles. If overwatered, the plant will quickly rot. This agave prefers drier conditions during the cooler seasons. It is very hardy and will take temperatures below seventeen degrees Fahrenheit. Plant this desert accent in showy containers, small rock gardens, and areas that do not receive regular irrigation. It can also be used as a winter inter-

est plant or in succulent and cactus gardens. This plant was discovered by the late Dr. Cornelius of California and has been passed around in collectors' nurseries of California. There is not a lot known about the origin of this agave.

*Agave americana var. marginata
Variegated Century Plant

Agave americana var. marginata
Variegated Century Plant

The plant forms a large rosette of twisted silvery green leaves and strips of bright yellow along its leaf margins, giving it the appearance of a striped ribbon. Its swordlike leaves stand upright to about four to six feet tall and wide, growing in a stiff rosette. The leaves are armed with small brown hooks, and it has a sharp, spiny tip on each leaf. Agave americana has many variegated forms that show differences in the leaves and names. Like most agaves, it produces a flower stalk only once in its lifetime, after ten to twenty years. The flower stalk grows to twenty feet or more, producing exotic, pale yellow blos-

Agave americana var. marginata
Variegated Century Plant

*Agave americana var. medio-picta f. alba

White Striped Century Plant

soms. After blooming, the mother plant dies. The plant likes full sun and reflected heat but can also take partial shade. It is drought resistant but will take light watering from either irrigation or natural rainfall during the hot, summer season. Variegated century plant produces offsets by underground rhizomes and tubers that can be easily propagated. The plant will grow in most soil but prefers natural soil without any amendments added. It is hardy to thirteen to fifteen degrees Fahrenheit. Watch for signs of the agave snout weevil and treat it if needed. Use it as a dramatic, ornamental, or specimen plant in desert landscapes for its outstanding features. It can also be used in xeriscape or tropical landscape settings, or planted in tubs or large containers. This strikingly beautiful desert accent makes a dramatic statement and focal point in any landscape. The variegated century plant is native to Mexico but has naturalized itself in Mediterranean and desert climates.

**Agave americana
var. medio-picta f. alba**
White Striped Century Plant

This striking agave with its creamy, whitish yellow, central leaf color and bluish gray margins grows three to four feet tall. It has short, thick leaves that arch downward to a sharp tip. The leaves have indentations along their edges with small, grayish red colored spines. This species is smaller than the other variegated agaves. The variety "Aureo marginata" has yellow margins on the leaves. The variety "Mediopicta aurea" has a broad, yellow band down the center of each leaf. After many years, this particular agave produces a tall, yellowish green flower stalk. It also

Agave americana
var. medio-picta f. alba
White Striped Century Plant

grows slower than the other varieties and produces fewer offsets. The plant is drought resistant and only needs occasional water. During the hot, dry summer, irrigate it every week or two. It likes full sun or light shade with reflected heat and is hardy to fifteen to twenty degrees Fahrenheit. When planting, give it plenty of room to grow. The plant is highly susceptible to white grub damage. Treat it twice a year with Dimethoate insecticide drench as a preventative measure. Use it as an accent, in containers on patios, in raised beds, in cactus gardens, or on hillsides. This agave can be used for its dramatic appearance and color. It is native to dry, desert locations in Mexico.

*Agave americana var. striata
Striped Century Plant

Agave americana var. striata
Striped Century Plant

This is one of the rarest and most beautiful of all the agaves. It foliage is blue-gray with creamy white markings and multiple, white stripes that run throughout the length of the leaves. The plant grows six to eight feet tall and wide. Like other agaves, it produces offsets, but these lose some variegation as they grow. Also each leaf is slightly different in the amount of variegation. Sometimes, the offsets may resemble the Agave americana var. medio-picta. Its flowers are yellowish green and grow upward, rising to twenty feet or more. The plant takes full sun or partial shade and tolerates drought but prefers occasional irrigation, especially during the hot, dry season. It is hardy into the low twenties Fahrenheit and should be planted in well-draining, rocky or sandy soil. Use this striking variegated plant in large open areas either as an accent or specimen. It can also be used in containers on patios and porches as a focal plant or mixed with other agave species and low-water-use plants.

The variegated varieties can be very inconsistent in their color patterns from one generation to the next. The striped century plant is native to Central to Southern Mexico.

*Agave angustifolia var. marginata
Caribbean Agave

Agave angustifolia var. marginata
Caribbean Agave

This agave forms a dense rosette of sword-shaped, greenish blue foliage reaching three to five feet tall and six feet wide. It has been cultivated for hundreds of years and was used for fiber and as a food crop. In the landscape, it grows from a short trunk and forms numerous leaves with sharp, small, curved teeth and a sharp tip. The leaves are variegated with mostly whitish cream colors on the outside margins of the plant. However, leaf color and variegation differs from plant to plant. Years after maturity, the plant develops a ten- to sixteen-foot high flower stalk in late winter through the summer, with greenish yellow flowers. Once the agave blooms, the mother plant will die but produces many offsets to continue its lifecycle. Plant the Caribbean agave in full sun to partial shade in a protected area. This agave is susceptible to freezing temperatures in the low to mid-twenties Fahrenheit. While drought tolerant, provide supplemental irrigation during the hot, dry summer. Make sure the soil dries out between irrigation cycles and reduce water during the dormant season. Avoid planting near sidewalks or high pedestrian areas due to its sharp spines on the

Agave angustifolia var. marginata
Caribbean Agave

tips of the leaves. The Caribbean agave is very easy to transplant and will quickly root into a new location. Apply an application of fertilizer once a year during its growing season. It is very tolerant of salty conditions. Use it in containers or as a specimen in desert or tropical landscape settings. This handsome-looking plant is native to Tamaulipas, Mexico and south to Guatemala, Costa Rica, and throughout the Caribbean, where it grows on open, rocky slopes.

*Agave attenuata
Foxtail Agave

Agave attenuata
Foxtail Agave

This graceful accent plant has light, bluish green, smooth, pliable foliage that forms a rosette of growth to five feet tall and wide. It has arching leaves and does not produce spines. The variety "Nova" is smaller with wider, bluish green leaves and an erect flower stalk. "Kara's Stripes" is a newer, hybridized plant with butter yellow foliage marked by narrow, green stripes; it requires more sunshine to produces its color. All the varieties bloom once after about ten years, with a seven- to fifteen-foot tall flower stalk that

has yellowish green blooms that arch downward. After the plant flowers, offsets will develop to help the plant reproduce. The foxtail agave should be planted in partial shade to avoid sunburning the foliage. While drought resistant and salt tolerant, it likes additional, weekly irrigation during the hot, dry season. It is frost sensitive below thirty degrees Fahrenheit, so protect it by covering during the coldest nights. The foxtail agave also tolerates most soils as long as they are well draining. Use it as a background plant or as an understory in the protected shade of a large canopy tree. It can also be planted in shaded entryways and large planters for tropical effects. Use it around fountains and pools, or where bold foliage is needed. This is a great background plant in annual and perennial color plants or as an accent in cactus and succulent gardens. It is a rare species and is native to mountain habitats in Central Mexico.

*Agave 'Blue Glow'
Blue Glow Agave

Blue Glow is a hybrid that produces a glow-like appearance in bright sunlight. It grows two feet tall and wide, forming a single rosette with a clumping growth habit. This agave is a cross between Agave ocahui and Agave attenuata. It gets its broad leaf structure and attractive green color from A. attenuata and its sharp terminal spine and size from A. ocahui. This unusual plant offers wide, soft, spineless, bluish green foliage with distinctive red margins and a short, red, terminal spine. The blue glow likes filtered shade and light protection from the sun, especially in the Southwest. It is hardy

Agave 'Blue Glow'
Blue Glow Agave

Agave 'Blue Glow'
Blue Glow Agave

to the mid-twenties Fahrenheit and is drought resistant. Give it additional irrigation when the temperatures warm up in the spring. This slow grower needs well-draining soil to look its best. This plant needs less water during the winter seasons. Use this attractive plant in groupings, as an accent plant, or amongst boulders in smaller planting spaces.

*Agave bovicornuta
Cow Horn Agave

Agave bovicornuta
Cow Horn Agave

The plant grows three feet tall and four to six feet wide and is recognized by its satinlike, darker green to yellowish green foliage that forms a rosette. Brownish red teeth run along the edges of the leaves. The younger leaves have a distinctive, smooth looking sheen. At the end of its life, anywhere between five and eighteen years, this agave develops a stalk about fifteen to twenty-two feet tall with greenish yellow flowers. It likes filtered sun to partial shade and well-draining soil. Avoid planting it in areas with reflected heat and keep this plant away from pedestrian traffic and sidewalks due to its sharp spines. It is a fast grower and is drought resistant but likes supplemental water during the warm months. It is hardy to the mid to low twenties Fahrenheit. Plant it in a frost protected area to avoid foliage damage. Use it as a specimen, bold accent plant in tropical settings, in large containers, or with other agave species for its interesting appearance. The plant is native to the rocky slopes in oak and pine wooded areas of Chihuahua and Northern Sinaloa, Mexico, where it can be found growing between 3,000 and 6,000 feet.

Agave bracteosa
Candelabrum Agave, Squid Agave

Agave bracteosa
Candelabrum Agave, Squid Agave

Agave bracteosa
Candelabrum Agave, Squid Agave

This low-growing agave with an irregular appearance reaches heights of about two feet tall and wide. It has an interesting clumping rosette of spineless, bright-green, candelabra-like leaves. The foliage emerges from the center of the plant and arches gracefully, resembling the arms of a squid moving through water. At maturity, this agave sends up a three- to five-foot spike of showy white to pale yellow flowers that form a dense cluster. Unlike other agaves, this species blooms many times during its life, during the warmer months. It also produces many offsets, which grow and mature around the mother plant. The squid agave likes full sun or filtered shade and should be planted in well-draining soil. This plant tolerates extreme heat and is drought resistant but prefers regular irrigation to grow faster. It is hardy to ten degrees Fahrenheit. This particular species also shows some resistance to the agave snout weevil and is usually ignored by rodents. Use it in gardens with cactus and other succulents, in containers, raised planters, and small planting spaces, or among boulders. Mix the squid agave into cactus and succulent gardens. The plant is native to the mountains of the Chihuahuan Desert in Northern Mexico, and the states of Coahuila and Nuevo Leon. It grows on steep, vertical cliffs in limestone canyons at elevations of 3,000 to 5,000 feet.

*Agave colorata
Blue Ice Agave

This agave is admired for its striking, broad, powder blue leaves with distinct impressions and spiny brown teeth along the margins. The plant grows in a tight rosette to heights of two to four feet tall and wide. After five to fifteen years, it produces six- to ten-foot tall flower stalks with reddish buds opening to reveal showy, yellow flowers. The flowering stalks signal the end of the life cycle of this plant. It produces many offsets at its base to ensure reproduction. There

Agave colorata
Blue Ice Agave

Agave colorata
Blue Ice Agave

are two forms of this species in cultivation. One grows smaller to two feet high and wide. Its leaves are broad and spoon shaped. The other form grows larger to four feet tall and wide, with larger foliage. Historically, the heart of this agave was roasted and eaten by Native Americans. Plant parts were also used to make a winelike beverage. The blue ice agave tolerates salty air, full sun, reflected heat, and some partial shade. However, it develops a nicer form and leaf color when planted in full sun. It is drought resistant but likes occasional, supplemental water during the hot, dry season. This agave will take any soil as long as it is well draining. It is hardy to fifteen to twenty degrees Fahrenheit. Use it as a bold accent plant in rock gardens, on banks and slopes, in containers or in smaller spaces where other agaves might grow too large. This agave is native to the canyons along the coast of Sonora, Mexico and in the isolated mountain ranges of Northern Sinaloa, Mexico.

*Agave decipiens
False Sisal

The false sisal is a dramatic plant that grows five feet tall and wide. It will get much larger to about ten feet in frost-free locations. This agave is known for its bright green, long foliage that forms a tight, symmetrical rosette. Its fleshy leaves spread from the center of the plant and have small teeth along the margins. This plant produces many offsets for reproduction and propagation. Once in its lifetime, in late fall or early winter, it develops a ten- to twelve-foot flower stalk with many branches that support greenish yellow flowers. Plant this agave in full sun to partial shade. When planted in the shade, it will grow larger and develop a deeper shade of green. It thrives in hot, humid locations and needs well-draining soil or it may rot. The false

Agave decipiens
False Sisal

Agave deserti
Desert Agave

sisal is hardy to twenty-five to thirty degrees Fahrenheit and is drought resistant. It grows best with supplemental irrigation during the hot, dry season, particularly when young. Use this exotic-looking agave in containers, raised planters or as an accent plant in protected locations or for tropical effects. It combines well when planted along with Agave geminiflora and Agave victoriae-reginae. This agave is native to Florida.

Agave deserti
Desert Agave

This clumping plant was an important food source for Native Americans and grows two feet tall and four to six feet wide. It forms numerous rosettes of grayish blue to green, thick, sword-like leaves. Fibers from the leaves were used to make clothing, rope, and other useful products. The flower stalks were roasted, and the hearts of the plants were eaten. Alcoholic drinks were also made from the sweet juices of the plant. Sharp teeth form along the edge of the leaves and the tip. The leaf size ranges from six to fifteen inches long and two to three inches wide and sometimes develops a noticeable band in the center. The agave produces many offsets over its lifetime. After ten to twenty years, it develops a flower stalk that grows ten feet tall with bright yellow, funnel-shaped blossoms with many branches. The flowers bloom for an extended period from May through July. After blooming, the flower stalk dries and noticeable seed capsules remain on the plant for many months. There are two distinct subspecies of this plant that are hard to distinguish from each other. Agave deserti subsp. pringlei is greener with a distinctive spine in the middle of the leaf. Agave deserti subsp. simplex does not produce many offsets. The plant needs full sun and tolerates reflected heat. It is drought resistant but prefers supplemental irrigation and well-draining soil. The desert agave is hardy to five degrees Fahrenheit. Use it in hot, dry desert gardens or mixed in with large boulders. It can also be mixed into low-water-use cactus and succulent gardens. This plant is native to rocky areas in the high deserts of Southern California where it grows in arroyos and western slopes of the San Bernardino Mountains. It also is endemic to areas of Arizona and Northern Baja, Mexico where it grows at 300 to 5,000 feet in elevation.

Agave desmettiana, Agave desmettiana 'Variegata'
Smooth Agave, Dwarf Century Plant, Variegated Smooth Agave

*Agave desmettiana, Agave desmettiana 'Variegata,'

Smooth Agave, Dwarf Century Plant, Variegated Smooth Agave

This upright plant forms a beautiful, symmetrical rosette shape with slightly arching leaves and grows three feet tall and wide. It has light, bluish green foliage with smooth edges and a sharp spine at its tip. Sometimes, it develops small brown teeth along its edges. The variegated variety offers bright green leaves with yellow variegated edges. After eight to ten years, the agave develops an eight- to ten-foot high branched stalk with pale, yellow blooms. The flower stalk appears at the end of its life cycle; however, the plant also produces an abundance of offsets for reproduction. It is a fast-growing agave that tolerates full sun with reflected heat but looks better with filtered shade. It also prefers a well-draining soil. Smooth agave is hardy to twenty-five degrees Fahrenheit or less and needs protection from frosty conditions. The plant tolerates drought conditions, and once it is established, it is relatively low maintenance and survives on little water. Use it as an accent, in containers, and in transitional landscapes and tropical settings for a bold statement. This is a great plant choice for low-water-use or xeriscape situations or as an accent plant. It has a beautiful form and combines well with other low growing agaves. The growth habit is some-

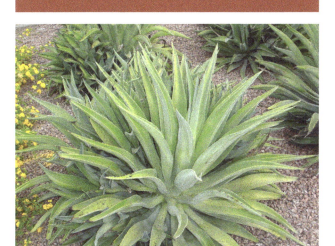

Agave desmettiana, Agave desmettiana
Smooth Agave, Dwarf Century Plant, Agave desmettiana

225

what similar to Agave weberi, but it is a much smaller plant. Smooth agave is only found in cultivation from a plant nursery, although it is believed that this agave originated in Sinaloa, Mexico. It is cultivated in Europe and in the Western United States.

Agave filifera subsp. schidigera
Thread-Leaf Agave

Agave filifera subsp. schidigera
Thread-Leaf Agave

This agave is admired for its decorative, dark-green to bronzy-green, swordlike, narrow foliage. The plant grows quickly to two feet tall and two to three feet wide. The foliage has white markings and fibers along the edges and a sharp point on the tip of the leaf. It is symmetrical in growth habit and well suited for containers. At maturity, in late summer, it produces a flower stalk that reaches eight feet or more with attractive purple blossoms that occur on the upper part of the stalk. The plant dies after blooming but can be repropagated by seed or by the removal of a rare offset. It is tolerant of most soil but needs adequate drainage. This agave is hardy to fifteen degrees Fahrenheit and is very drought resistant. It will respond to a fertilizer application during the monsoon season and likes supplemental irrigation during the hot, dry summer. Avoid watering it during the winter months. The plant prefers full sun or filtered shade conditions. Treat it several times each year with an insecticidal drench for possible infestations of agave snout weevil. Use it in masses or with other similar varieties, in tight spaces, patios, pots, or planted with other desert perennials. The variety "Durango Delight" is a trademark plant from Starr Nursery in Tucson, Arizona. It is an attractive, smaller and more compact cultivar. The plant is native to Chihuahua, Durango, Sinaloa, and Sonora, Mexico growing from 4,500 to 7,500 feet.

*Agave geminiflora
Twin-Flowered Agave

This agave has dense, symmetrical foliage that grows in a rosette producing about a hundred or more erect, narrow, dark green leaves. The slender foliage grows to two to three feet tall with sharp edges and smooth margins on a flat, gray terminal spine. Some plants have whitish

Agave geminiflora
Twin-Flowered Agave

fibers growing along the leaf edges while others are fiberless. Its flower stalk grows nine to twelve feet high with two flowering candelabra stems. The flowers are yellow with a reddish purple coloring at the base. After the plant produces its majestic bloom at about ten years or so, it dies. This plant is more solitary and does not produce offsets like the other agave species. It is hardy to about twenty degrees Fahrenheit or less and is adaptable to full sun or partial shade. When planted in the shade, its leaves will relax and bend to form a softer silhouette. Watch for signs of the agave snout weevil and treat it as needed. It also requires some protection from pack rats that chew on the foliage and which may cause substantial leaf damage. Use it in containers, in mass groupings or as a desert accent on the north side of a building. The twin-flowered agave can also be used as a foundation plant around pools and water features. Use this agave in a mini-oasis or tropical environment, where its amazing ornamental features can be viewed up close. It is native to the state of Nayarit, Mexico where it grows in oak woodlands at elevations of 3,000 to 4,000 feet.

Agave guiengola
Century Plant

Agave guiengola
Century plant

This medium-sized plant is an attractive ornamental that forms rosettes of broad, blue-gray leaves that are thick and succulent looking. It grows three to four feet tall and four to six feet wide. Its foliage is wide at the end and tapers off toward the tip of the plant. This agave has small, dark colored teeth along its edges and a small, brownish maroon spine. There are not many leaves on this plant, and its growth habit is somewhat open and flat to the ground. It does not produce many offsets, and if one develops, it remains close to the mother plant. In late winter to early spring, a five- to six-foot tall flower stalk appears with light yellow to yellowish white blooms. This agave prefers a shady location, and if planted in full sun, its foliage can sunburn. It is hardy to twenty-five degrees Fahrenheit and needs protection from long, hard freezes. The plant is drought resistant like most agaves, but it prefers supplemental irrigation during hot, dry periods before the summer monsoon arrives. Make sure it has plenty of good drainage or rot may occur during heavy monsoons. Plant it in succulent and low-water-use, xeriscape gardens for its attractive, striking blue color. Use it as an accent and specimen planting or in containers in lightly shaded locations or under the foliage or a large shrub or tree. The variegated variety, 'Creme Brulee', is a soft-leafed form with dark green leaves surrounded by a border of creamy white. The species is native to limestone cliffs in the Tehuacan Valley in Oaxaca, Mexico at elevations of 300 to 3,000 feet.

Agave havardiana
Havard's Century Plant

Agave havardiana
Havard's Century Plant

The striking plant has silvery blue to bluish gray, spiny, wide foliage, tapering to a tip. The teeth are larger toward the upper end of the leaf and are smaller toward the lower end. It grows to two to three feet tall and wide in a symmetrical dense rosette. This agave is more solitary and does not usually produce offsets. Once in its lifetime, in summer, at maturity, it will produces a seven- to fifteen-foot tall flower stalk with candelabra-like flowers in large yellowish green clusters. After flowering, the plant will die. It prefers full sun to light shade and well-draining soils. The heart of this agave was roasted and used by the Apache Indians as a food source. It is hardy to ten to fifteen degrees Fahrenheit or lower. While drought resistant, this plant benefits from intermittent summer irrigations. Keep it away from walkways and entryways and give it plenty of room to grow. Use it with hardy, ornamental grasses or as an accent plant with other species of agaves and yuccas to show off its interesting structure and form. Plant the Havard's century plant in masses, in rock gardens, and on slopes. Use this attractive agave in low-water-use, xeriscape gardens. The plant is native to Big Bend and the Trans-Pecos mountains of Central Texas, and in Chihuahua and Coahuila, Mexico. It grows at elevations of 4,000 to 6,000 feet.

*Agave isthmensis
Dwarf Butterfly Agave

This miniature, compact plant grows one foot tall and wide. It has powder blue leaves with prominent dark red teeth and a red, terminal spine. The leaves are narrow at the base and wider at the tips. At maturity, it develops a six- to seven-foot tall candelabra flower stalk with two-inch yellow blooms. This interesting agave produces many offsets that can be used to repropagate the plant. The offsets stay close to the mother plant. Plant it in filtered sun, where it receives morning sun or in full shade but avoid a location with hot, after-

Agave isthmensis
Dwarf Butterfly Agave

Agave lopantha
Thorncrest Agave

Agave lopantha quadricolor
Variegated Thorncrest Agave

noon sun. It is drought resistant but likes supplemental irrigation during the hot, dry season. The dwarf butterfly agave is hardy to twenty-five degrees Fahrenheit or lower and should be protected during frosty nights. It grows in most soils as long as it is well draining. Use it in small beds, cactus and succulent gardens, and rock gardens, or mixed into planters with other low-water-use, drought-resistant plants. Also, plant it as a contrast specimen near the golden barrel cactus. This agave looks nice in containers because of its small size and compact form. It will also grow well along the coast and is tolerant of salty air and soils. The dwarf butterfly agave is native to the Southern coast of Oaxaca, Mexico.

*Agave lopantha
Thorncrest Century Plant

This agave produces single or clumping rosettes reaching two feet high and four feet wide. It is admired for its numerous, dark rich-green to pale green, glossy leaves that have a whitish

yellow strip that runs along the midsection of the leaf. Sharp, curving gray teeth occur along the leaf margins as well as at the tip. Variations in leaf size and color will appear in different plants, and there are many hybrids available. At maturity, it produces a twelve-foot spike of greenish yellow flowers in early summer. The Thorncrest century plant also develops many offsets for reproduction throughout its life. It is an easy plant to propagate by carefully digging up its offsets and transplanting them to new locations. The plant prefers well-draining soil,

Agave lophantha
in bloom

along with full sun to partial shade conditions. It is hardy to about fifteen degrees Fahrenheit or lower and is adapted to drought conditions with occasional irrigation requirements. Extra water encourages faster growth. This agave is susceptible to the agave snout weevil, so treat it as needed with a systemic insecticide as a preventative measure. Use it in large decorative containers and raised beds or plant it in masses and groupings for desert gardens. It is a good choice for tropical effects or even in lush landscape environments. This agave is native to the Rio Grande Valley in southern Texas, where it grows on sandy hillsides. It also occurs south along the Eastern Mexico coast in the state of Veracruz, growing on cliffs and rocky outcrops growing at altitudes of 100 to 5,000 feet.

*Agave macroacantha
Black-Spine Agave

Agave lophantha
Thorncrest Century Plan

Agave macroacantha
Black-Spine Agave

Agave macrocantha
Black Spine Agave

This small agave forms clumps of short, tight rosettes growing one to two feet tall and two to four feet wide. It has a short stem and forms offsets at the base of the plant. Its foliage is bluish gray to powdery blue. The plant is heavily armed with prominent, brownish black, spiny teeth at its tips and has a long, black terminal spine. After fifteen years, this plant produces pinkish red buds that open to reveal striking, purplish green blossoms on a six-foot branched flower stalk. During the later part of its lifespan, it produces many offsets to allow for its reproduction. In cooler climates, the plant tolerates full sun but does best with some afternoon shade in the low desert. It prefers well-draining soil and is drought resistant. Provide supplemental irrigation during the hot, dry summer. This agave is hardy to twenty-five degrees Fahrenheit and should be protected in low-lying areas. Its sharp spines could be a problem if planted in high traffic areas. Use this ornamental looking agave in containers, planters, small spaces, and confined beds where it can be viewed up close. Also use it as a des-

ert accent in small cactus or succulent gardens, or plant it in the foreground of darker colored plants. The black-spine agave is native to dry, barren, sedimentary slopes and rocky grounds of Central Mexico near Oaxaca and Puebla.

Agave multifilifera
Shaggy Head Agave

Agave multifilifera
Shaggy Head Agave

The striking agave grows in a single, dense rosette reaching three feet tall with a four to five foot spread. It has a short, terminal spine and numerous, medium-green leaves with many fibers growing along the leaf margins, creating a shaggy appearance. There are white colorations along the sides of the leaves, and the bottom portion is slightly convex, with a sharp, black spine at the end. The plant does not produce many offsets and once in its lifetime, it sends up a flower stalk sixteen feet high with waxy, green buds and dense, lavender blossoms. After the blooms start to decline, the mother plant will die. The shaggy head agave is hardy to twenty to twenty-five degrees Fahrenheit. It is very drought resistant, needing supplemental irrigation occasionally during hot, dry weather. This plant tolerates most soil conditions as long as it is well draining. It also likes full sun locations or partial to filtered shade. Use this slower growing agave in low-water-use and xeriscape situations. Mix it into cactus and succulent gardens or plant it in containers or raised planters. The shaggy head agave can be found growing natively at elevations of 4,500 to 6,500 feet in mountainous regions, where it grows among pines and oaks on rocky cliffs and shaded areas of Durango, Sinaloa, and Chihuahua, Mexico.

*Agave murpheyi 'Variegata'

Variegated Hohokam Agave, Variegated Murphey's Agave

This dramatic, versatile, slow grower reaches three feet tall and two to three feet wide with light gray to bluish green foliage that has yellow stripes along the margins. It also has sharp, serrated, brownish gray teeth along its leaves. When this plant starts to bloom after many years, it forms a flower stalk that will grow up to thirteen feet tall in the spring. Its beautiful blossoms are pale green to greenish yellow and have reddish purple colored flower petals along the margins. The plant resembles the variegated form of Agave americana, except it is much smaller. Agave murpheyi has the same cultural requirements and is grayish blue in color without the variegated stripes. Historically, this agave was a major food source in Hohokam culture. The sugary heart of the plant was harvested during the bloom cycle and was considered a major delicacy. Plant the variegated Hohokam agave in full sun with reflected heat or in open shade. It is drought resistant, requiring irrigation during periods of hot, dry weather. Younger plants need additional irrigation but be very careful not to overwater. It handles any soil as long as it is well-draining and is hardy to twenty-four degrees Fahrenheit. This agave will produce offsets for regeneration. Do not plant it near sidewalks or heavily used pedestrian areas due to its sharp, terminal spines. Use it in combination with other drought resistant and low-water-use agaves, in containers, raised beds or as a specimen. It is native to rocky slopes of Central Arizona and Sonora, Mexico from 1,500 to 3,000 feet.

Agave murpheyi 'Variegata'
Variegated Hohokam Agave,
Variegated Murphey's Agave

Agave neomexicana,

New Mexico Century Plant

Agave neomexicana
New Mexico Century Plant

*Agave nickelsiae x scabra 'Sharkskin'

Sharkskin Agave

Agave nickelsiae x scabra 'Sharkskin'
Sharkskin Agave

This showy, low-growing agave grows two feet tall and two to three feet wide, forming a tight rosette. Its powdery blue leaves are broad with black or burgundy colored, heavily armed spines along the side of its foliage that grow from a central base. The handsome plant will produce many offsets over its lifetime. A cultivated variety "Sunspot" has greenish yellow variegation on its foliate with distinctive black spines along the leaf margins. In late spring through summer, at the end of its lifetime, it will produce an eleven-foot, pinkish red flower spike. The flowers open to form a golden yellow bloom that attracts hummingbirds. This agave prefers full afternoon sun and can take plenty of reflected heat. The plant is extremely drought resistant, preferring occasional water during the hot, dry summer season. It also likes well-draining, sandy soils. New Mexico century plant is very cold hardy to below zero degrees Fahrenheit or lower and will also take extreme hot conditions. This low-maintenance agave is resistant to deer and rabbits. Use it as a focal plant in large, decorative containers where it can be viewed up close. It can also be used in rock garden, as a mass planting or with other showy cacti and succulents. The New Mexico century plant is native to Southeastern New Mexico and Western Texas.

This elegant fast grower is named for its uniformly spaced, leathery leaves that have the texture of shark skin. It is an admired agave growing from two to three feet tall and three to four feet wide. The sharkskin agave develops a rosette of thick, smooth, triangular-shaped, olive green leaves with a blue cast. It forms an attractive architectural clump and its leaves have a strong terminal spine, smooth edges, and tips that give it an interesting appearance. This agave likes full sun with plenty of reflected heat and is drought resistant. Water the plant periodically through the hot months. It is hardy to about twenty to twenty-five degrees Fahrenheit. The

Agave nickelsiae x scabra 'Sharkskin'
Sharkskin Agave

agave produces offsets for reproduction later in its lifetime. However, it does not set seed and its flowers are sterile. Use this fast-growing specimen in cactus and succulent rock gardens for its interesting appearance and symmetrical shape. It can also be used in masses and groupings with other agave plants for interest in the landscape. This plant is a cross between Agave x ferdinand-regis and a subspecies of Agave scabra. It was discovered growing at the Ruth Bancroft Garden in Walnut Creek, California. This plant is sometimes referred to as Agave "Ruth Bancroft" and was given the name of sharkskin due to its texture and color.

*Agave ocahui
Ocahui Agave

This agave, which was used for its strong fibers, grows two to three feet tall and three feet wide. It has a dense rosette of dark green, narrow, yuccalike leaves. Its foliage is stiff and flat at the top with straight, smooth margins that are toothless and lined with a narrow reddish brown border. The name *ocahui* is the Indian word for

Agave ocahui
Ocahui Agave

cord or fiber. When the leaves are crushed, they can be used as a scouring brush. The plant has a sharp, terminal spine and does not produce offsets. This agave develops an impressive flower spike only once in its life at the end of its growing cycle. The stalk grows eight feet or taller with small, bright yellow blossoms. It prefers full sun with reflected heat but tolerates shade. The plant is drought resistant, requiring supplemental irrigation during the hot, dry weather. It does not like to be overwatered. This agave is easy to grow and is an incredibly tough plant that does not need much maintenance. The ocahui agave tolerates most soil types, including rocky conditions and is hardy to about fifteen degrees Fahrenheit. Use it in containers, in rock gardens, as a mass planting with boulders or as a contrast when planted with other blue or gray colored plants. It also looks great when planted in tropical settings or with other low-water-use perennials. This agave is native to the rocky slopes of Sonora, Mexico from 1,500 to 4,500 feet.

*Agave ovatifolia
Whale's Tongue Agave

Agave ovatifolia
Whale's Tongue Agave

The striking agave is admired for its light blue to powdery, whitish blue and slightly cupped foliage. It grows three to five feet tall and three to six feet wide, forming a dense rosette of short, wide distinctive leaves. Its foliage is similar to Agave parryi. Along the edges of the leaves, it develops sharp, grayish black spines and a long, sharp, brownish red leaf tip. At the end of its lifetime, it produces a ten- to fourteen-foot tall flower stalk with many branches that are densely clustered with large, yellowish green flowers. In its native habitat in Mexico, the flowers are sometimes harvested for cattle food. This agave does not produce offsets. The whale's tongue agave should be planted in full sun or lightly filtered shade. It is hardy to just below ten degrees Fahrenheit and is tolerant of most soils as long as they are well draining. This plant is also drought resistant but grows faster with supplemental irrigation. Use it in containers, in low planters, as an accent, near boulders, in groupings with other agave species or low-water-use plants, or under the light shade

of a tree. This agave was introduced in the United States, where it was recognized as a new species and renamed early in this decade. It is native to the Sierra de Lampazos Mountains of Nuevo Leon in Northeastern Mexico where it grows from 3,700 to 7,000 feet.

Agave palmeri
Palmer's Agave

Agave palmeri
Palmer's Agave

The plant is recognized by its banana-like fruit and dramatic flower stalks that reach ten to fifteen feet, producing a panicle of blooms in green and pale pink. It grows to four feet tall and four to five feet wide, forming a dense, symmetrical rosette. The Palmer's agave has long, thin, bluish green to light green or grayish green foliage. It has a needlelike spine and sharp, curved, brownish red teeth on the leaves. The plant produces a pale yellow to green flower stalk with dark red tips in late spring or early summer, just before the end of its life, after five to fifteen years. After the flowers bloom, a green fruit appears that is filled with sweet nectar and resembles a small banana. The fruit from this plant attracts bees, butterflies, hummingbirds, bats, and moths that help pollinate the plant. This agave was used in the production of mescal in Northeastern Mexico as well as a beneficial food source. The leaves were made into fiber. The plant seldom produces offsets. It grows best in full sun with reflected heat. This agave needs very little water; however, it benefits from supplemental irrigation during the hot, dry season. It is hardy to ten to fifteen degrees Fahrenheit. Plant it in areas where it has plenty of room to grow. Use this fast-growing plant in desert landscapes as a specimen or mix it with other agaves for interest. It is native to Southeastern Arizona, Southern New Mexico, and Northern Mexico where it grows in the mountains, oak woodlands, and dry rocky, limestone slopes between 3,000 and 6,000 feet.

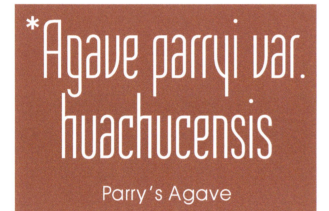

*Agave parryi var. huachucensis

Parry's Agave

Agave parryi var. huachucensis
Parry's Agave

This slow-growing, clumping plant with a tight, symmetrical rosette of broad, dense leaves grows to two feet tall and two to three feet wide. The leaves are grayish green to a steel blue-green and vary in size and shape. It has sharp, black margins with sharp teeth and brown, terminal spines on the leaf tip. The Parry's agave can be solitary or produce offsets. In late summer, it produces a tall, heavily branched flower stalk from ten to twenty feet tall revealing bright yellow flowers with red or pink colorations. It likes full sun but tolerates partial shade. This plant needs minimal irrigation once established. It handles most soils as long as they are well draining and is hardy to zero degrees Fahrenheit or below. This cold hardy plant is low maintenance and easy to grow. The Parry's agave is tolerant of salty conditions.

Agave parryi var. huachucensis
Parry's Agave

Use it as a specimen or accent plant for confined spaces, rock gardens, coastal gardens, desert gardens or in patios planters. Combine with golden barrel cactus, wildflowers, or other striking, compact plants in perennial gardens. It is native to Southwestern Arizona in Cochise County as well as in New Mexico and Northern Mexico, where it grows in oak and pine woodlands from 5,000 to 9,000 feet.

*Agave parryi var. truncata
Artichoke Agave

Agave parryi var. truncata
Artichoke Agave

Agave parryi var. truncata
Artichoke Agave

This slow-growing, clumping agave has short blue-gray leaves and grows two to three feet tall and two to four feet wide, resembling an artichoke, as its common name implies. It has dark reddish brown teeth along its margins and a terminal spine. The variety truncata is more compact than Agave parryi var. huachucensis. It produces a tall, bold fifteen- to twenty-foot high flower spike in the summer. The flowers start out pink or red and then turn a golden yellow. After blooming, the mother plant dies, but the plant develops offsets that continue to grow. It tolerates most

soil as long as it is well draining. The artichoke agave enjoys full sun and reflected heat but can also grow in partial shade. The plant is drought resistant but likes supplemental irrigation during the hot summer and will rot if overwatered. It is also hardy to fifteen degrees Fahrenheit or lower. The plant is susceptible to the agave snout weevil, so treat it as needed. Use it in containers and rock gardens, as an accent plant or in masses or groupings with other desert natives. It is native to Southern Chihuahua and Northern Durango in Mexico.

Agave pelona
Mescal Pelon

This beautiful and rare species forms a dense rosette of narrow, toothless, glossy green leaves with a white margin and prominent red spine. It grows four to six feet tall and wide and does not produce offsets. The mescal pelon must be propagated by seed. Once in its lifetime, it produces a six- to ten-foot spike with a reddish purple, bell-shaped flower. The blooms appear in early spring through summer. This agave is heat tolerant and can be planted in full sun or partial shade. It is

Agave pelona
Mescal Pelon

Agave phillipsiana
Grand Canyon century plant

also drought resistant, requiring deep, infrequent irrigation during hot, dry weather. Its foliage turns yellow if it becomes drought stressed. The plant is hardy to twenty-one to twenty-five degrees Fahrenheit and does not tolerate long periods of cold weather without protection. Historically, the plant parts were used for fiber, and the heart of the plant was roasted and eaten. It was also used to produce mescal. The Agave pelona is similar in size and coloration to Agave ocahui. This species has a bell shaped, wine colored bloom and Agave ocahui has a yellow bloom and a more flexible terminal spine with green leaves and no red cast. Use this attractive species in containers, as a spectacular ornamental, and to compliment other interesting succulents and cacti. It is native to the mountains located southwest of Caborca, Mexico, where it grows on steep limestone slopes.

This bluish green to deep green agave grows to three feet high and wide with serrated teeth along its edges and looks similar to Agave americana. It sometimes produces offsets for reproduction. This agave develops a ten-foot-high flower stalk once in its life and then dies after producing seeds. The flower stalk creates a panicle of greenish white, tubular blooms in early summer. It likes full sun and will take plenty of reflected heat. This agave is very drought resistant but prefers supplemental water during the hot, dry season. The Grand Canyon century plant is hardy to about thirteen to fifteen degrees Fahrenheit. Use with smaller-sized agaves as a specimen, accent plant in low-water-use gardens or in masses and groupings. It can also be used as an interest plant with its attractive foliage. Native Americans used this agave for food, fiber, beverages, and medicine. It is native to rocky slopes and terraces, and along waterways in Northern Arizona and in Grand Canyon National Park, as its common name implies. This plant can be found growing natively in pre-Columbian habitat sites and is a very ancient cultivar of agave.

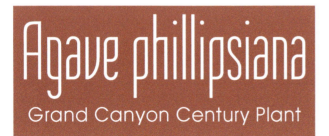

Agave phillipsiana
Grand Canyon Century Plant

*Agave potatorum
Butterfly Agave

Agave potatorum
Butterfly Agave

The short-growing plant forms an interesting symmetrical rosette and well-defined leaves reaching one to two feet tall and two feet wide. It is usually stemless and solitary in its growth habit. Butterfly agave has small, attractive, silvery blue leaves with reddish spines along the edges and a terminal spine. The species offers variations in its leaf shape, size, and color. After about ten years, in fall or winter months, it produces a ten- to fifteen-foot tall flower spike with a panicle of light green flowers tinged with red bracts. The plant enjoys full sun, hot conditions, reflected heat, and well-draining soil. Though it is drought resistant, provide it with supplemental irrigation during the hot, dry summer. It is hardy to about twenty-five to thirty degrees Fahrenheit and needs some protection from frost. Use it in containers, rock gardens, low planters, and raised beds. The smaller agave looks nice when planted in groupings with other agaves species and in succulent gardens. The plant was used by the Nahuatl-speaking tribes in Central Mexico to make an alcoholic beverage. It is native to the semiarid Mexican states of Puebla and Oaxaca, growing from 4,500 to 7,500 feet.

Agave salmiana
Maguey De Pulque

Agave salmiana
Maguey De Pulque

This magnificent agave has huge, graceful, greenish gray, curving leaves with a large leaf base. It grows five to six feet tall and spreads to ten feet. The leaves are ten to fifteen inches long with thick, sharp, brownish gray teeth along the leaf margins and sharp points at the end of each leaf. This agave usually produces a massive rosette of twenty-five to thirty leaves, and there are many forms and varieties of the plant. After fifteen years or more, the plant develops a flower stalk fifteen to twenty-five feet tall or more with many candelabra-like branches. Its flowers are yellow and tinged with reddish buds, but when the flowers open, they are somewhat inconspicuous. The mother plant dies after flowering, and offsets form to grow into a new plant. The agave produces a sweet sap, which when fermented is used to make an alcoholic drink called pulque. Its foliage has been used for livestock feed, and the leaves produce a strong fiber that can be woven into cloth, cord, or netting. It likes full sun to partial shade and is cold hardy into the mid-twenties Fahrenheit or lower. Some forms are more frost tolerant than others. It is drought resistant but likes supplemental water during the hottest months of the summer and requires less water in winter. Use it in large, open locations as a focal plant or under the light shade of a mesquite or palo verde tree as an accent. Avoid planting it near walkways or pedestrian traffic due to its sharp spines and enormous size. The plant is native to areas of Mexico and is commonly grown along the roadways around Mexico City.

Agave shawii
Coastal Century Plant, Shaw's Century Plant

Agave shawii
Coastal Century Plant, Shaw's Century Plant

The plant has attractive, fleshy, dark-green, leaves with sharp, serrated, brown teeth along its edges and a dark reddish brown terminal spine. It forms a tight rosette and grows three feet tall and four to five feet wide. After ten years or more, it produces a tall, branching flower stalk that is seven to twelve feet tall or more and resembles an asparagus. The flowering stem creates a greenish bloom with purple bracts in late summer through fall.

This agave produces many offsets in its lifetime. It is drought tolerant and likes full sun but prefers partial shade, especially in our hot desert climate. This agave prefers minimal irrigation, especially during the winter months but responds to supplemental irrigation during the hot, dry summer. The coastal century plant is susceptible to root rot if overwatered. It is also tolerant of salty soils and salty air. This agave requires adequate drainage and is hardy to twenty-five degrees Fahrenheit. It thrives in the heat and is low maintenance. Use this interesting ornamental in containers, in raised planters, in masses, on a slope, or in areas where a showy mass of green succulent color is needed. Its attractive deep green foliage makes a nice contrast when combined with gray-colored plants. It is native to volcanic soils of Southern California and Baja California, Mexico and is recognized as an endangered species.

Agave stricta
Rabo de Leon, Hedgehog Agave

Agave stricta
Rabo de Leon, Hedgehog Agave

The Mexican native agave grows two to three feet tall and wide, creating a spherical rosette of elongated, dark greenish yellow, lightly serrated, and lightly curved leaves. The pencil-like leaves are thicker at the base, tapering toward the tip with a thick leaf margin and a gray terminal spine. Its stems are thickly branched, and it will form offsets to create many colonies of new rosettes. This agave forms a crooked flower spike five to eight feet tall with purplish red blooms that open in late summer. Native Americans used the plant for rope, food and soap. Other products were made from its fiber and pulp. It enjoys full sun to shade conditions but prefers some shade in the low desert. The plant is extremely drought tolerant and does not like to be overwatered, especially in the winter months. It is also very hardy to twenty to twenty-three degrees. This agave is tolerant to extreme heat and neglect. Propagate it by suckers and offsets. Use it in dry, rugged, rocky locations to cover hills or slopes, in containers mixed in with softer looking plants, and in low-water-use rock gardens. Its attractive, deep green foliage makes a nice contrast when combined with other plantings. The agave is native to the Tehuacan Valley in Southern Puebla and Northern Oaxaca, Mexico, where it grows on dry hills and in limestone foundations in the open desert.

*Agave victoriae-reginae
Queen Victoria Agave

This rare, striking agave named for Queen Victoria in England forms a small, symmetrical, rosette of dark green foliage with white markings on the side of its toothless leaves.

Agave victoriae-reginae
Queen Victoria Agave

A sharp spine is apparent on the end of each leaf. It grows slowly to one to two feet tall and spreads eighteen inches wide. After many years of growth, it produces a dense, ten- to fifteen-foot flower spike. The blooms are green to creamy white and tinged with a red or purple. Flowers appear on the upper half of its flower stalk, and the plant will die after flowering. Some varieties of this agave do not produce offsets while other varieties develop profuse ones. The plant is hardy to twelve degrees Fahrenheit and likes full sun and reflected heat. It is extremely drought resistant but prefers monthly irrigation and well-draining soil. The Queen Victoria agave develops a tighter form when watered sparingly. Avoid watering during the winter seasons. Use this versatile plant in containers and raised planters or as a small accent plant in rock gardens along with other exotic cacti and succulents. Also use it as a small specimen or accent plant among large boulders. Do not plant it close to larger shrubs or they may take over and hide the beautiful simplicity of this plant. It is native to Coahuila, Durango, and Nuevo Leon, Mexico where it is recognized as an endangered species.

Agave vilmoriniana
Octopus Agave

Agave vilmoriniana
Octopus Agave

Agave vilmoriniana
Octopus Agave

The thick-leafed plant with its curved, twisted, pointed, bluish green leaves resembles an octopus. It reaches heights of four feet with a six-foot spread. At the end of its life, in springtime, usually within seven to ten years, it produces a ten- to sixteen-foot tall spike of yellowish white blossoms. These appear on a bulblet, which is a small or secondary bulb capable of producing a new plant when broken off and propagated. This agave does not produce the usual offshoots. After blooming, the mother plant will die. This species was widely used as a cleanser in its native habitat. The mature leaves were dried and then pounded to form a brush. When the leaves are wet, they release a sudsy compound and were used to clean clothes and other items. The plant tolerates full sun or partial shade but is intolerant of reflected heat, and the foliage may turn yellow if exposed to too much heat. Irrigate it occasionally during the hot, dry season to hasten its growth. It handles most soil as long as it is well draining. The octopus agave is hardy to the mid to low twenties Fahrenheit and shows frost damage at lower temperatures. When frosted, the plant is slow to recover. Use it in tropical settings around pools, ponds, and water features or in masses. It is native to rocky cliffs and the deserts of Southern Sonora, Sinaloa, Durango, and Jalisco, Mexico, growing from 2,000 to 5,000 feet.

Agave vilmoriniana
Octopus Agave in Bloom

*Agave weberi
Weber Agave

Agave weberi
Weber Agave

Agave weberi
in Bloom

This bold agave grows moderately to five to six feet tall with an equal spread, offering grayish green to shiny, bluish green, long, fleshy leaves and a sharp spine. The foliage is five to seven inches wide, with fine teeth along the top of the leaf. The foliage produces a large rosette with upright growth. At maturity, this plant creates a twenty- to twenty-six-foot high, branched, flower stalk with clusters of yellow blossoms. It also produces many offsets that help to further propagate the plant. The Weber agave enjoys full sun to partial shade but looks better when grown in full sun. This specimen plant is drought tolerant but likes monthly irrigation to look its best. During the summer months, provide it with frequent irrigation or the leaves will turn yellow due to heat stress. This agave is hardy to ten to fifteen degrees Fahrenheit and requires minimal maintenance. It also tolerates most soil but prefers amended, well-draining soil. The Weber agave is susceptible to the agave snout weevil and should be treated to prevent infestations. Use it as a focal or accent plant in large, open spaces or tropical settings around water features and ponds. This specimen agave also looks nice when mixed with ornamental grasses and perennials. A cultivated form of this plant can be found growing in the arid regions of Eastern and Central Mexico at elevations of 2,000 to 5,500 feet.

Agave weberi
Weber Agave

243

Agave zebra
Zebra agave

Agave zebra
Zebra agave

The relatively fast-growing, medium-sized plant reaches three to four feet in height and width and offers interesting bands of pale, grayish blue, whorled leaves. The bands are more significant in full sun than in the shade. Its foliage is heavily edged in brown or black with sharp, prominent teeth, which describes its common name. The strong, stiff leaves will bend or fold inward, creating an interesting look. Its flower stalk grows about twenty to twenty-six feet high above the plant with many branches, producing yellow blooms in the top part of the stalk, in late summer. This agave is mainly solitary and usually does not produce offsets. It is drought tolerant and hardy to about fifteen to twenty degrees Fahrenheit. Avoid overwatering it, especially during the winter. It also likes well-draining soils and full sun with plenty of reflected heat. Use it in containers with other desert accent plants, in rock gardens mixed with different species of agaves and other succulents. Also use it in raised planters and entryways where a medium size, drought-resistant plant is needed. Do not plant it close to walkways with heavy traffic since this plant has lethal spines. It is native to dry, rocky slopes and limestone soil in a limited area of Northwestern Sonora, Mexico, growing from 1,500 to 4,500 feet.

Aloe Species

More than thirty species of aloes are recognized, and many of these produce thick, fleshy foliage that consists of 95 percent water. The plants store moisture in their leaves as well as their root systems. They are either stemless or have branched or un-branched stems. Many aloes produce a rosette of thick, fleshy foliage and leaves with spines or teeth along their margins. The foliage will vary in colors of grays to greens and can be striped, mottled, or variegated. Unlike the agave species, the aloe does not die after blooming. Annual flowers appear in shades of yellow, orange, or red. The blooms are usually tubular and grow on stalks about two to four feet high above the plant and attract hummingbirds. In general, aloes prefer shade, but also grow in full sun with reflected heat. Aloes are very susceptible to cold weather. This plant is extremely drought-resistant, but it likes occasional irrigation during the hot part of the year, as well as well-draining soil. Let the soil completely dry out between irrigation cycles. They require minimal water during the winter season, when they usually go dormant.

Like the agave, aloes are propagated by offsets that are produced at the base of mature plants. They can also be propagated by seeds. The species has a gel-like sap inside their foliage and they are smaller in size and scale than agaves. Most aloes have some medicinal or commercial value, recorded since biblical times. They are used for many ailments, including burns, cuts, and for skin care. Extracted aloe vera juice is used to treat a variety of digestive disorders. The dried latex from the inner lining of the leaf has been used as an oral laxative.

In the landscape, aloes are valued as decorative specimens. Larger varieties can be used as accents, in masses around boulders and in low-water-use gardens, or in containers and raised planters. The aloe is native to Africa along South Africa's Cape Province and in the mountain regions. It is

also indigenous to the Arabian Peninsula and in Madagascar, growing on slopes and ridges.

Aloe arborescens
Candelabra Aloe, Torch Aloe

*Aloe arborescens

Candelabra Aloe, Torch Aloe

This decorative aloe is armed with many sharp, dense teeth along its margins. It is an upright plant with dark green foliage growing four to six feet tall with an equal spread. This aloe can be kept as a low rambler or trained to grow taller. The plant produces a bright, orangey red bloom on an unbranched stem in late winter or early spring and then again from late spring through early summer. Historically, in parts of Northern Africa, natives used the dry leaves to create a powder. The substance was used as protection against storms, during childbirth, or for stomach ailments. In parts of South Africa, this plant is still used as a living fence to secure domestic animals. It is hardy to the mid-twenties Fahrenheit. If frosted back, it recovers quickly in the spring. The candela-

Aloe arborescens
Candelabra Aloe, Torch Aloe

bra aloe is easy to grow in full sun or partial shade and is drought resistant. It likes supplemental irrigation during the hot, dry summer. This plant also needs well-draining soil and is propagated from cuttings or stems. Use it as an ornamental in low-water-use gardens or mix with other drought-resistant aloe species as a desert accent. Also plant it in containers and raised planters with other succulents or use it as a bank cover in warmer, protected areas. This plant grows natively along cliffs and ridges along the Cape Peninsula in parts of Northern Africa from sea level to mountain peaks as well as in dense bush.

Aloe 'Blue Elf'
Blue Elf Aloe

but prefers occasional, supplemental irrigation during the hot, dry season. It is hardy to twenty to twenty-five degrees Fahrenheit and prefers gravelly or sandy, well-draining soil to look its best. Since this aloe is low-growing and clumping in form, use it in containers and rock gardens or with cacti and succulents. Also use it in bird and hummingbird gardens, in masses with other low-water plants, or along ponds, fountains, or swimming pools. The plant is a hybrid, but the natural form is believed to be native to North Africa in the Canary and Cape Verde Islands.

Aloe 'Blue Elf'
Blue Elf Aloe

Aloe 'Blue Elf'
Blue Elf Aloe

This tight-clumping, dwarf aloe offers a dense rosette and grows to eighteen inches tall and two feet wide. It is mainly stemless with narrow, silvery bluish gray leaves that grow upright. There are small, sharp teeth along the margins that are reddish brown in color. The plant explodes with showy spikes of orangey red blooms in late winter through early spring. This is a long-blooming aloe with lots of vibrant color, and the flowers attract hummingbirds. It also produces many offsets that can be used for propagation. The plant likes full sun to partial shade and is drought resistant

Aloe brevifolia
Shortleaf Aloe

The low-growing, clumping aloe is stemless and grows eighteen inches tall and nine to twelve inches wide. It forms small, tight rosettes of deep, blue-green, triangular, fleshy leaves with white spots and white teeth along its serrated edges. The leaves are flat on the

Aloe brevifolia
Short Leaf Aloe

Aloe dawei
Dawe's Aloe

Aloe dawei
Dawe's Aloe

top and concave on the underside of the plant. Young leaves have a reddish tint. The plant produces many offsets that can be used for propagation. In spring, it sends up a dense, one- to two-inch, orange-scarlet flower spike. This aloe prefers filtered shade with morning sun and may sunburn in full sun. While drought resistant, provide additional irrigation throughout the year. Giving it extra water during the summer months will help produce a fat, plump appearance. Plant it in well-draining soil, mixed with amendments. It is hardy from twenty-five to thirty degrees Fahrenheit and needs some protection on cold nights. Use it as a groundcover in low-water-use gardens or in containers, small spaces and planters for its interesting and charming appearance. It can also be used as a foundation planting or as an edging plant around rocks or small boulders. It is native to South Africa where it grows along the Western Cape Province close to the coast and in high rainfall areas.

This evergreen jewel has clumping, upright clusters of elongated succulent stems and green, fleshy leaves with dark serrated teeth along the edges. It grows two to three feet tall and eighteen inches to three feet wide forming many offsets. In mid to late winter, it sends up a tall, brilliant orangey red flower stalk from the center of the plant. It is hardy from twenty-five to thirty-two degrees, and like most aloes, it is very drought resistant. While tolerant of heat

Aloe dawei
Dawe's Aloe

Aloe dorotheae
Sunset Aloe

Aloe dorotheae
Sunset Aloe

and sun, provide some shade protection during the summer and irrigate infrequently during the hot, dry seasons. The Dawe's aloe requires minimal maintenance and does well in most soil types. Use it for its colorful flower display during the winter in containers and planters. This low-growing accent works well as an understory plant, in the shade of larger shrubs and trees. Also, mix it in masses with other aloes, succulents, and low-water-use plants. The Dawe's aloe is native to the mountains of Eastern and Central Africa, as well as Uganda, the Congo, and Rwanda, where it grows at elevations up to 3,200 feet.

This low-growing aloe with stiff, shiny leaves grows two to three feet tall and twenty inches wide, producing many offsets. It forms a clump of rosettes or spirals on very short stems that stay low to the ground. Its leaves are yellowish green to bright orange-red with sharp whitish gray teeth that grow along the margins. In late winter to early spring, it produces a flower stalk that grows two feet high with dark red flowers and greenish yellow petals. The plant likes full sun to light shade, but its leaf color becomes redder in full sun. Sunset aloe is drought resistant but prefers supplemental water during hot seasons. It does not like to be overwatered and is hardy to twenty-five to twenty-eight degrees Fahrenheit. The plant tolerates most soil types as long as they are well draining. This whimsical aloe thrives in hot weather with little maintenance. Use it in rock gardens with other showy aloes and succulents, in containers and raised planters in protected locations, or where a splash of color is needed in a desert gardens. It is native to Eastern Africa and Tanzania.

*Aloe ferox
Cape Aloe

Aloe ferox
Cape Aloe

Aloe ferox
Cape Aloe

Aloe ferox
Cape Aloe

This common tree-type aloe is an impressive desert accent plant noted for its medicinal qualities and reaches heights of ten feet or more, with a three- to four-foot spread. It forms a dense clump of bluish green, fleshy, succulent leaves. The foliage is pointed at the tip and edged with sharp teeth along the margins. The fast-growing plant develops whorls of new foliage from its center. Older leaves dry and may leave a petticoat of growth on the stem. In late winter to early spring, it produces a large, candelabra-like, exquisite flower head. Each spike holds colorful orange to red or yellow blossoms. The blooms attract birds, bees, and butterflies. The bitter, yellow juice found below the skin of the aloe has been harvested in parts of South Africa for hundreds of years. Historically, the aloe juice from this species has been used as a laxative and for treating arthritis. The gel-like flesh from the leaves is used in cosmetics and also has healing properties. This is an excellent specimen and accent plant that is adaptable to many conditions. The plant likes full sun but tolerates shade. It is drought resistant and requires only supplemental irrigation during the hot, dry summer. Plant it in amended, well-draining soil. It is hardy to twenty-four degrees Fahrenheit and displays leaf damage in colder temperatures. Use it as a specimen or accent plant around boulders or in rock gardens with other succulents and low-water accent plants. This plant is a great choice where something bold is needed or to make a statement in a prominent place in the landscape. It is native of South Africa where it grows in a broad range of habitats form the South and Western Capes through Southern KwaZulu-Natal. This plant grows in the bush and along rocky slopes in large numbers, where it creates an amazing winter display of color when in bloom.

Aloe lineata
South African Aloe

Aloe lineata
South African Aloe

This compact, tropical, medium-sized aloe grows two to six feet tall and two to three feet wide, forming many clusters as it matures. It produces small rosettes of yellowish, dark green to lime green, smooth foliage with reddish brown teeth along its margins. Flowers bloom in early winter through late spring. Tight, fleshy bracts appear

Aloe lineata
South African Aloe

and hide the flowers until they emerge. The tubular-shaped blossoms are orangey salmon and emerge on multiple stalks above the plant. The blooms attract bees, butterflies, and birds. Plant this showy aloe in full sun or partial shade. It is drought resistant but does best with additional irrigation during the hot, dry summer. The South African aloe is hardy to twenty-two to twenty-five degrees Fahrenheit. Use this tropical plant in combination with low light, foliage plants around ponds and fountains for a green, lush appearance. It can be used in attractive containers and planters mixed with cacti and succulents. This plant is native to South Africa, growing along the Eastern and Western Capes.

Aloe maculata
African or Tiger Aloe

This fast, low-growing aloe produces short, stemless rosettes and many offshoots that grow in low clumps. This plant will grow rapidly to twelve inches or more, producing many offsets over its lifetime. It has thick, succulent, pale green foliage with distinctive white speckles. Sharp, brown teeth are visible along its leaf margins. The sap

Aloe maculata
African or Tiger Aloe

Aloe marlothii
Flat-Flowered Aloe

from the leaves can be used to produce sudsy foam when mixed with water, and the plant has been used as a soap product. The species is sometimes called the "soap aloe." However, the sap can also be a skin irritant. In late spring or summer, it produces a purple flower stalk that is two feet tall with yellow, orange, or red tubular blossoms. The flowers attract hummingbirds. The plant likes to grow in sandy or gravelly soils and needs good drainage. It takes full sun but does better in partial shade. It is salt- and drought tolerant but requires occasional irrigation during the hot, dry summer. African aloe is hardy to twenty-eight degrees Fahrenheit and if frosted back, recovers quickly in the spring. Use it in rock and cactus gardens, in colorful containers, or as an understory plant beneath a tree or large shrub. This desert accent is a good choice for seaside gardens because of its salt tolerance. It is native to arid regions of South Africa, Botswana, and Zimbabwe.

Aloe marlothii
Flat-Flowered Aloe

*Aloe marlothii
Flat-Flowered Aloe

The large, impressive, single-stem aloe grows to ten feet or more. The plant has a broad base and

tapers as it grows upward. Older foliage forms a dry skirt around the plant. Its new foliage is broad, heavy, and grayish green with reddish brown teeth that form along the margins and randomly occur along its orange leaf tips. This plant has thorns along the stems that help protect it from browsing animals that might eat the foliage. It produces striking flowers in colors of orange, yellow, or red form on branched candelabra-like stalks in early spring. They are somewhat slanted or flat, giving this plant its common name. The flowers are very rich in nectar and attract hummingbirds. After the flowers bloom, dry, papery-thin seeds appear and are dispersed by winds. The plant grows best in full sun and well-draining soil. It is able to withstand long periods of drought because of its ability to store moisture in its leaves and stems. Well-established plants can survive without water for a few months before showing signs of drought stress. It is hardy to twenty-five degrees Fahrenheit but will need protection during prolonged periods of frost. The flat-flowered aloe requires minimum maintenance to look good. Use it as a specimen in low-water-use gardens or plant it next to large boulders and tall walls as a silhouette or accent plant. It is native to mountainous areas, rocky terrains, and warm slopes of the Northwest Province, Swaziland, Zimbabwe, Botswana, and Mozambique and in KwaZulu-Natal, north of Durban in South Africa.

Aloe striata
Coral Aloe

Aloe striata
Coral Aloe

Aloe striata
Coral Aloe

The plant has attractive, broad, bluish green, smooth leaves and coral red blossoms. It grows two to three feet tall and two feet wide. Unlike other aloes with serrated leaves or a spine, it has a smooth, pink margin. This aloe will grow in large, solitary clumps and has a nice appearance even when it is not in bloom. When grown in full sun, the leaves turn red. When grown in the shade, the leaves are a bluish green. It flowers during the winter months, producing a coral red blossom in upright inflorescences. The nectar from its blooms attracts many insects and hummingbirds during the cooler season, when most flower food is not available. It prefers full sun or partial shade and well-draining soil. Protect it from reflected heat during the hot, dry summer. Coral aloe is drought resistant and can withstand long periods without water, but it prefers supplemental irrigation, especially during the hot season—it will grow more rapidly, and its foliage will be plumper. It is hardy from twenty-five to thirty degrees Fahrenheit and should be planted in protected areas in cold locations since it can freeze easily. When frosted back, it is slow to recover. Use it as an accent plant for its bold, textured foliage or in containers for its winter color. Mix it with other aloe species in masses. It is native to the Eastern and Western Capes in South Africa, where it grows on rocky hills and along the coast and dry inland areas.

Aloe tomentosa
Hairy green aloe

Aloe vanbalenii
Van Balen's Aloe

Aloe tomentosa
Hairy green aloe

This aloe gets its name from its unique greenish white flowers that are covered in thick wool. Its species name, tomentosa, means dense wool. The plant forms a large, solitary rosette to two feet tall and about four feet wide. It is a stemless plant with thick, fleshy, pale green foliage, tapering from a wide base with pointed tips. Sap from the leaves has been used for skin problems and to treat wounds, fevers, headaches, and inflammation of the eyes. In late spring through early summer, it develops its tall, branching, unique flower stalk with the wooly flowers. The plant likes full sun and reflected heat. It is drought tolerant but likes some supplemental irrigation during the warmer seasons. The hairy green aloe grows best in well-draining soils and is hardy to about twenty-eight degrees Fahrenheit. Use this plant in low-water-use gardens with other aloe species or plant it in large containers and raised planters. Also use it in rock gardens and among large boulders as an interest plant. It is very easy to grow and maintain. This aloe is native to the mountains around Yemen, Saudi Arabia, and tropics along the African peninsula.

Aloe vanbalenii
Van Balen's Aloe

This low-growing aloe forms many tight, dense rosettes reaching two feet tall and three to four feet wide. It develops many offsets with long, twisting, coppery brown foliage in sunny exposed areas, and greener when grown in the shade. This plant has fine teeth along its leaf margins. In late winter through early spring, it produces multiple, orangey yellow flowers on ten feet tall spikes. The plant likes full sun to light shade and regular irrigation during the hot season. Keep it on the dry side during the winter months and the foliage will look healthier. It tends to grow rapidly during the summer monsoons. When planted in full sun with little water, the foliage turns a deep red near the end of the tips. The plant likes well-draining soil and is hardy to twenty-five to thirty degrees Fahrenheit. Plant the Van Balen's aloe in protected areas where freezes are common. Since this plant will form many clumps, give it room to grow. Use it in raised planters, small entryway beds or containers for its attractive foliage and form. Combine it with other aloe species in rock and desert gardens. This plant can also be used for tropical effects and looks nice when mixed with plants the have yellow flowers. It is native to KwaZulu-Natal and Southeastern Mpumalanga in South Africa, where it grows on dry, rocky hills and mountains in exposed areas and among bushes and brush. The species was named after J. C. Van Balen, who first collected and named the plant.

*Aloe variegata
Partridge Breast Aloe

Aloe variegata
Partridge Breast Aloe

Aloe variegata
Partridge Breast Aloe

This dwarf aloe with spotted white and green leaves resembles the breast of a partridge, as its common name implies. It grows in a clump and stays low to the ground, usually below one foot tall. It is one of the most distinctive and well known of the South African aloes. Plants may be solitary but generally form dense rosettes with many offsets and spread through underground rhizomes. Its smooth, thick leaves are triangular in shape with ridges along their surface. The spotted foliage does not produce any spines but has a soft surface with white edges. The blooms appear in late spring on hanging spikes in pink, red, or yellow. After flowering, a capsulelike fruit appears, that splits into three parts, with winglike seeds. While there are no known medicinal uses for this species, indigenous people would hang the plant upside down inside the huts of young women. If the plant flowered, then the woman was considered to be fertile and would have many children. This aloe was also planted on graves in the belief that the dead would enjoy a long, eternal afterlife. Plant the partridge breast aloe in full sun to partial shade and in well-draining soil. This plant likes infrequent irrigation. It is hardy to eighteen degrees Fahrenheit. Use it in small spaces, as filler in containers or raised planters or in tight beds. Also use it along walkways and in foundation plantings. The species is native to hard, rocky, or sandy soils throughout arid and semiarid regions of South Africa, in Namibia, and in Southern and Central parts of the Western Cape and Namaqualand.

Aloe vera
Medicinal Aloe

Aloe vera
Medicinal Aloe

This is probably the most common aloe grown in the southwest desert and reaches eighteen inches to two feet tall and six feet wide. It has clumping, thick, fleshy leaves and produces many offsets over a period of time. The plant is noted for its light to medium green, speckled, succulent, fleshy leaves, armed with whitish red teeth along its margins. Its one-inch blooms appear in spring and grow high above the plant with yellow spikes in tubular clusters. Hybrids of this species may bloom in an orangey red color. The blossoms attract humming-birds. This plant likes full sun and reflected heat but also takes shade and is tolerant of drought. It prefers occasional irrigation, especially during the hot, dry season. The aloe vera is drought tolerant

but looks better with supplemental irrigation and should be planted in well-draining soil. The plant is hardy to about twenty-five degrees Fahrenheit. Propagate it from cuttings, seed, or division of its offsets. The sap from the fleshy part of the leaves is commonly used to treat burns and some skin problems. Use it as an understory plant, an accent or specimen planting in low-water-use, desert landscapes. It can also be planted in combination with cactus and other succulents in rock gardens, containers and planters. This is a great choice to use in medians and along roadways. It is native to islands in the Mediterranean, as well as the West Indies and Africa.

*Aloe x nobilis
Gold Tooth Aloe

Aloe x nobilis
Gold Tooth Aloe

The low-growing, clumping aloe reaches about one foot tall and wide with many clustering off-sets. It has thick, succulent, short, green leaves that grow in rosettes with large, yellow, toothed edges along the margins of the plant. The gold tooth aloe produces tall, striking orangey red blooms in late spring through midsummer on two feet tall stalks that grow above the plant. It has a long blooming cycle. The flowers attract bees, butterflies, and birds. The plant likes full sun to light shade and is hardy to about twenty degrees Fahrenheit. It is drought resistant but like most aloes, grows best with supplemental irrigation during the hot, dry summer. Do not overwater this species, as it is susceptible to root rot. Use it in containers and raised planters. Mix this stunning aloe with other drought-resistant cacti and succulents in rock gardens or with boulders. Use it as an accent, in edging gardens, along small, entry beds, and in masses. This aloe is believed to be a hybrid and does not occur naturally.

Other Low-water-use Accent Plants

*Beaucarnea recurvata
Ponytail Palm

Ponytail palm is a grasslike evergreen with a large, bulbous base, long, swollen trunk, and palmlike features. It grows to heights of thirty feet or more and twelve feet wide. With age, the trunk may develop a few branches. In the Southwest deserts, it grows much smaller. The ponytail palm produces

Beaucarnea recurvata
Ponytail Palm

narrow, bright green, slender leaves that grow in dense, moplike, long, showy clusters, forming a tight rosette. After many years of growth, it can develop large, upright clusters of creamy white flowers, but only female plants produce seed. It stores moisture in its large base and is drought resistant. Do not overwater this plant or let water sit around its roots. It also prefers well-draining, dry, sandy soils and full sun to partial shade conditions. Ponytail palm is a low-maintenance plant and a slow to moderate grower. This plant is hardy to the low to mid-twenties Fahrenheit, and if hit by a hard freeze, it recovers slowly in the spring. Use this interesting specimen in large containers, as a showy accent, in tropical or in transitional landscapes, in pool areas, or around fountains, ponds, or courtyards. The ponytail palm is a unique specimen planting that can be integrated into many landscape or xeriscape situations. It is native to the Mexican states of Tamaulipas, Veracruz, and San Luis Potosi.

Beaucarnea recurvata
Ponytail Palm

Dasylirion acrotrichum
Green Desert Spoon

Dasylirion acrotrichum

Green Desert Spoon, Green sotol

This fast-growing evergreen is known for its long, slender, bright green, arching foliage and wisp of distinctive leaf fibers. It reaches five to six feet in height and resembles the common desert spoon, except for its leaf color and narrower leaves. The green desert spoon has spines along its leaf margins that can be extremely sharp and wisps of fiber along the tips of the plant. This plant produces a seven- to fifteen-foot tall flower spike with small, greenish, creamy white flowers that appear like a plume. It likes full sun, reflected heat, is drought resistant and needs little water once it is established. However, giving it additional irrigation during the dry, hot summer will help its appearance. It will take any soil as long as it is well draining. This desert accent is hardy to ten to fifteen degrees Fahrenheit. Give it plenty of room to grow and avoid planting it near walkways or pedestrian traffic since its spiny leaf margins are sharp and it can quickly take over a narrow space. The plant makes a nice accent when combined in masses with Dasylirion wheeleri, the common desert spoon. Use it for tropical effects or in desert gardens as a bold accent plant. This attractive desert accent can also be used for ornamental effects. It is native to the dry mountains of Central and Northeastern, Mexico. It also grows in the states of Durango, Jalisco, and Tamaulipas.

*Dasylirion quadrangulatum

Toothless Desert Spoon, Mexican Grass Tree

Dasylirion quadrangulatum
Toothless Desert Spoon, Mexican Grass Tree

Dasylirion quadrangulatum
Toothless Desert Spoon, Mexican Grass Tree

This mounding grasslike shrub grows six to nine feet tall with an equal spread. It produces long, flat, narrow, leathery, green leaves that emerge from the center basal portion of this symmetrical growing plant. It does not have any sharp spines along its margins like the other Dasylirion species. After many years of growth, it develops an insignificant, whitish green flower stalk that reaches heights of ten to twelve feet tall. This plant is dioecious, bearing female and male flowers on different plants. The flowers attract birds, bees, and butterflies. The toothless desert spoon grows best in full sun with reflected heat. It does not

look very attractive when grown in the shade. While drought resistant, it prefers occasional irrigation, especially during the hot, dry summer months and when it is very young. It also prefers well-draining soil and is hardy from sixteen to twenty degrees Fahrenheit. Use it as an attractive desert accent plant in arid or tropical gardens. It can be combined with palms or plant it in large, decorative containers for a tropical, whimsical effect. Use the toothless desert spoon around fountains and ponds. Give this plant plenty of room to grow and mature. It is native to Northeast Mexico in the states of Nuevo Leon and Tamaulipas, where it grows along hillsides and dry riverbeds.

Dasylirion wheeleri
Desert Spoon

Dasylirion wheeleri
Desert Spoon

This grasslike evergreen shrub grows four to six feet tall and three to four feet wide to form a whorl of silvery green to gray, slender, serrated leaves that create a shaggy skirt around the plant. From a distance, the plant resembles a large, gray clump of coarse grass. The leaf margins have sharp, yellowish white teeth along the edges and are frayed at the tips. The base of each leaf, if removed from the plant, looks like a spoon. Leaves from the plant are used to make woven ornaments in Mexico. The fibers in the leaves were used by native people to make mats, thatch for roofs, and cords. The young stalks were roasted and eaten. Today, in Northern Mexico, a rough form of liquor called sotol is still being produced. Desert spoon produces an insignificant greenish white flower cluster from the center of the plant in late spring. The flower stalk may be as tall as fifteen feet above the plant. It prefers full sun with plenty of reflected heat and will tolerate partial shade. This plant is extremely drought resistant and will get by on natural rainfall once established, but additional irrigation helps it to grow faster and maintain its appearance. It will take any soil as long as it is well draining. This plant is hardy to five degrees Fahrenheit. Use it as an accent with other drought-resistant plants for its interesting silhouette. Do not plant it near walkways or busy pedestrian areas. The desert spoon grows naturally on dry, rocky slopes and grasslands of Southern Arizona, Southern New Mexico, Western Texas, and Northern Chihuahua, Mexico from 3,000 to 5,000 feet.

*Fouquieria columnaris

Boojum Tree

Fouquieria columnaris
Boojum Tree

Fouquieria columnaris
Boojum Tree

Fouquieria columnaris
Boojum Tree

The distinguished, rare, and slow-growing tree has an unusual growth habit and appearance with its tall and upright stature. It grows to fifty feet tall and ten to fifteen feet wide. This desert accent plant produces no branches, is wide at the base, and tapers upward as it grows, resembling an upside-down carrot. The trunk is very woody with many short, twiggy stubs. At the very top of the plant is a cluster of leafy growth. Boojum tree is usually deciduous or leafless during the summer. Foliage appears during the winter rainy season. The bark is greenish yellow, and it produces yellowish green, sharp thorns at the base of each leaf cluster. Twiggy spikes occur along the entire trunk of this specimen, all the way to the top. After the plant is six years old, in late summer to early fall, it develops fragrant, tubular, creamy yellow blossoms toward the top of the plant, followed by a light brown fruit capsule. The flowers attract bees, beetles, ants, and butterflies. Larger insects feed on the open

flower petals to extract nectar. It likes full sun with reflected heat or partial shade. The boojum tree grows naturally in volcanic, rocky, desert soils and needs extremely good drainage to survive. This plant is drought resistant but looks more attractive with supplemental irrigation when its growth is more active. It is hardy to about thirty-two degrees Fahrenheit and can be damaged by high winds. Use it as a focal point in desert landscapes. Plant it in protected areas where it can be viewed and has plenty of room to grow and mature. The boojum is native to the forests of Central Baja California and along a small portion of the Sonora, Mexico coastline. It is a heavily protected specimen in its native habitat.

Fouquieria macdougalii
Mexican Tree Ocotillo, Candlewood Tree

The interesting and rare semi-evergreen is admired for its intertwined, spiny green branches. It grows upright and slowly to twenty feet tall and about four feet wide, but most specimens reach only six to eight feet tall in the Southwest desert. This plant has brownish green bark when young, which turns yellowish green with age. Small, green leaves appear when water is present and fall off the plant in drought situations. In late spring through summer, it produces showy, red, tubular flowers that appear in clusters near the tops of the branches. The flowers are a major source of food for hummingbirds. After the blossoms fade, it produces light-brown seed capsules. The plant likes well-draining soil, full sun to

Fouquieria macdougalii
Mexican Tree Ocotillo, Candlewood Tree

Fouquieria macdougalii
Mexican Tree Ocotillo, Candlewood Tree

Fouquieria splendens
Ocotillo

Fouquieria splendens
Ocotillo

partial shade, and plenty of reflected heat. It is drought resistant but produces abundant foliage with supplemental, monthly irrigation. This plant is hardy to twenty-three degrees Fahrenheit and is low maintenance. Use it as a desert accent, in masses, as a screen, barrier planting or focal point in an attractive container. Also use this plant as an interesting, showy silhouette against a wall. It is native to the rocky hillsides of Sonora, Mexico and just North of Sinaloa, growing from 500 to 2,500 feet.

This tall, graceful deciduous shrub with long canes grows slowly to twenty feet tall with a fifteen-foot spread. It has spiny, sharp, pole-like stems and light to dark green, oval, two-inch leaflets. The ocotillo grows upright and has few branches. The plant produces showy, dense spikes of orangey red tubular blossoms on the ends of its branches that hang like tassels. In lower elevations, the blossoms appear in February or as late as May in higher elevations. The blooms last about a month with flower clusters up to one foot long. When in bloom, this plant attracts hummingbirds, bees, and butterflies. The long tubes on the flowers form an excellent food source for the hummingbirds to obtain nectar, using their beaks to reach the bottom part of the flower. Antelope and ground squirrels climb onto the branches to feed on flowers and seeds from this plant. The blossoms can also be soaked in cold water to make a refreshing drink. The cut stems can be used for fencing or as a barrier planting and for ramadas since the canes are long lived. This plant likes full sun and reflected heat and needs little water once established. A newly planted ocotillo requires water once per week during the hot, dry summer and can take monthly irrigation during the cooler months. The ocotillo prefers rocky, well-draining soil and is hardy to ten degrees Fahrenheit or lower. It has a shallow root system, so when planting bare-rooted specimens from the nursery, water the canes by spraying them with a hose. Dig the planting hole twice the size of the root ball. It may take several months for a transplanted shrub to develop leaves, since the plant is generally leafless for most of the year. Large, bare-rooted plants are slow to establish new roots and it may take two years or more for leaves and root to grow. When the summer monsoons arrive, the plant develops new foliage. Use it as an accent or specimen for its magnificent silhouette or as a specimen plant against large walls for its exquisite shape and form. This is a great choice for desert landscapes. It is native to the Sonoran and Chihuahuan deserts, the Southern Mohave Desert, Central Mexico, and Central Texas, growing at elevations below 6,000 feet. At higher elevations, the plant grows in limestone and rock, while at lower elevations it grows in granite and sandy soil.

*Hesperaloe funifera
Giant Hesperaloe

Hesperaloe funifera
Giant Hesperaloe

This excellent, slow-growing evergreen has an erect, bold, striking growth habit. It produces stiff, narrow green leaves that form a massive clump of upright growth and reaches six feet tall and wide. Its leaf margins have white, stringy fibers that peel away as the plant matures. In summer, it develops a creamy, greenish white flower stalk that shoots out of its center. The flowers are nocturnal and pollinated by bats and hummingbirds. Its blossoms are not extremely showy and produce woody capsules with flat, black seeds after blooming. The plant is hardy to about five degrees Fahrenheit or lower. It is drought tolerant when established and can go for a long time without supplemental irrigation. The giant hesperaloe likes well-draining soils and prefers the soil to be somewhat rocky. The plant also enjoys full sun with plenty of reflected heat. This very low-maintenance accent is relatively easy to grow. Newly planted shrubs should be protected with chicken wire since rabbits love to eat the foliage. Use it for its bold foliage as a desert or accent plant around pools and ponds or in an attractive pot along a large wall or open space. Also use it in medians or as a streetscape shrub in a mass planting for a bold effect. It is native to the Chihuahuan Desert in Northeastern Mexico and parts of Southern Texas, growing at elevations up to 7,500 feet.

Hesperaloe parviflora
Red Yucca

Hesperaloe parviflora

Red Yucca, Yellow Yucca

The medium-sized, evergreen produces stiff, dense clumps of leathery, gray-green leaves that when blooming, grow three feet high and wide in a tight rosette. Its upright growth habit has arching foliage that forms a dense whorl of growth. In the spring, it produces tall, upright, tubular, pinkish coral or red flowers that attract hummingbirds, birds, and insects. The showy, flower stalks grow three to six feet tall and last for a long time. An attractive yellow flowering variety is also available. After flowering, woody tan-brown seedpods appear. Mixing different varieties of the red and yellow yucca plants

Hesperaloe parviflora
Yellow Yucca

together produce a showy color combination in spring. It is a tough plant that thrives in full sun with reflected heat but can also take light shade.

This accent prefers well-draining soil and is hardy to minus twenty degrees Fahrenheit. It is a great choice for low-lying washes and colder locations. While drought resistant, this plant does best with occasional irrigation during dry, hot weather. Supplemental irrigation helps stimulate growth and flower blooms. The plant is low maintenance and easy to grow, but young plants need some protection from javelina and rabbits that may feed on the fleshy roots and leaves. Place chicken wire around the plants as needed. Use it as an accent or specimen, in mass plantings, in rock gardens, raised beds, or containers, and in streetscapes, medians, or low-water-use landscapes. It also works well around pool areas, ponds, or water features, or mixed into perennial and succulent gardens and hot areas of the landscape. The red yucca is native to the Rio Grande area of Texas, growing into Northern Mexico.

Manfreda maculosa
Rattlesnake Agave

Manfreda maculosa

Rattlesnake Agave

The dramatic succulent grows to eighteen inches tall and one to two feet wide to form a tight, clumping rosette of fleshy, sword-shaped, smooth-textured leaves. The foliage is green and mottled with purplish red, irregular spots. It produces a six-foot tall spike of slightly fragrant creamy white blooms in spring that turns a rosy pink it ages. Hummingbirds are attracted to the tubular blossoms. Historically, the roots of this plant were crushed and pounded, and then water was added to create a soapy substance. The plant prefers full sun or light shade. It is drought tolerant but likes supple-

mental water during the hot, dry season. Let it completely dry out between watering cycles. The plant is hardy to ten degrees Fahrenheit. In winter, the foliage will sometimes burn or dry out, but new fleshy leaves soon reappear in the spring. Protect it from possible infestations of rabbits or pack rats by using chicken wire around newly installed plants. This desert accent grows by underground rhizomes and needs a well-draining, rocky or clay soil. Use it in masses or groupings for its interesting variegated foliage and visual effects. It can be used in containers, rock gardens, tight spaces, raised planters, or areas of the landscape with limited water available. Its striking foliage blends well with other agaves and yuccas in succulent gardens. The rattlesnake agave is native to Southern Texas and Northern Mexico.

Nolina matapensis
Tree Bear Grass

Nolina matapensis
Tree Bear Grass

Nolina matapensis
Tree Bear Grass

This lush-looking, treelike specimen grows from nine to fifteen feet tall and about six feet wide. It produces a trunk with a large head of unarmed, three- to four-foot long, flat, straplike, glossy green leaves that hang downward. The old foliage will turn brown and dry out with age, hiding the bark and trunk. It can be removed or left on the plant to form a thick thatch. Once established, the plant may develop multiple trunks that branch at the top and become wider at the base of the plant. The desert accent grows about three inches a year and needs plenty of room to spread. In late spring through summer, it produces a tall, erect six- to fourteen-foot bloom with small, creamy-tan blossoms that attract bees. After flowering, it develops a seed with a papery fruit inside. Plant the tree bear grass in full sun, reflected heat or partial shade locations. Avoid planting it near pedestrian walkways as its leaves have sharp edges. This plant is drought resistant but responds to infrequent irrigation during the hot, dry summer. Keep it dry in the winter. Tree bear grass grows in most native soil as long as they are well draining. It is hardy to fifteen degrees Fahrenheit and is low maintenance. Use it in groupings or masses, as an accent plant, or border or informal barrier. The foliage has been used for making baskets in Mexico. It looks interesting if planted with variegated or other interesting agave varieties. Tree bear grass is native to the Sonoran and Chihuahuan deserts of Mexico, growing below 4,800 feet.

Nolina microcarpa
Bear Grass

Nolina microcarpa
Bear Grass

Nolina microcarpa
Bear Grass

The evergreen accent plant is a great choice for desert and transitional gardens, forming a bold, grassy clump to about five feet tall and seven feet wide. The ends of its leathery, coarse, green leaves will fray to form a white, curling, ornamental look. Its leaves grow from underground stems. In late spring through early summer, the plant produces a three-foot-high stalk of greenish creamy flowers that extend out from the center of the plant. After flowering, in early summer, it produces papery seeds. Native Americans used the foliage to weave baskets, brooms, and mats. They ate the flowers and boiled or roasted the roots. The plant is hardy to ten degrees Fahrenheit or lower. It takes full sun to part shade and likes well-draining soil. Bear grass is drought resistant but prefers supplemental irrigation during hot, dry summers. It grows at a moderate rate with minimal maintenance needs. When needed, prune the dried foliage and dig out old clumps to rejuvenate older plants. Use it as a grassy accent around ponds and pools, in planters, on banks and medians, and in rock gardens. This plant also works as a soil stabilizer on hillsides with its fibrous root system. It is native to Arizona, New Mexico, Western Texas, and Southern Nevada, as well as Northern Sonora, Mexico, where it grows on rocky or grassy hillsides from 3,000 to 6,000 feet.

*Nolina nelsonii

Blue Nolina

Nolina nelsonii
Blue Nolina

The stunning, architectural beauty resembles the yucca species, developing a ten- to twelve-foot trunk and large rosette of foliage. It is one of the larger plants found in the Nolina genus. As the plant matures, it may develop multiple heads and older leaves can form a shaggy look along the trunk if not removed. It produces two- to three-inch-long, bluish green leaves with tiny serrations along the margins. The older, mature foliage is less flexible than the juvenile leaves. In summer, mature plants send up a four-foot flower spike that is densely packed with many tiny, whitish tan flowers. The plant enjoys full sun

Nolina nelsonii
Blue Nolina

with plenty of reflected heat or light shade. It is drought resistant during the winter months but prefers supplemental irrigation during the hot, dry summer. Only lightly water it during the winter months and avoid overwatering. It is hardy to ten degrees Fahrenheit and needs well-draining soil to look its best. Use caution when working around this plant. Its tiny teeth along the leaves can inflict cuts. Use it as a focal point around ponds, fountains, and water features for a tropical or bold appearance. It is native to the Mexican state of Tamaulipas.

Yucca Species

Yuccas are a remarkable group of flowering plants with more than eighty species to choose from. Some are tropical while others appear succulent. Most have rosettes of stiff, sword-shaped leaves coming from the ground level or the center of the plant. Some are treelike with distinct trunks and limbs. The size and shape of the leaves varies from plant to plant. Their leaf color can be grayish green, blue, glossy green, and their texture can be smooth or serrated with sharp tips at the ends. Most yuccas are covered with strong leaf fibers that have been used to make rope and cords. Native Americans combined the bleached, sun-dried leaf fibers with other plant fibers to make beautiful woven baskets.

The yucca produces waxy, white, bell-shaped flowers that rise out of the plant as showy clusters in late spring. The blossoms are arranged high on the flower stalk or midway up the stalk. Flowers range from creamy white to greenish white with streaks of purple, red, brown, and maroon. Some flowers and fruits are edible when they are fresh or dried. Yuccas are very unique in their method of pollination. The yucca moth is vital for the survival of the plant, and pollinates the flowers during the night, laying its eggs on the plant. When the eggs hatch and the flowers start to fade, the larva feed on the yucca fruit, leaving seeds to regenerate. After blooming, half of the species produces a woody capsule while other yuccas develop a large, fleshy fruit. The fruits are contained in small, black seed capsules and take many months to develop.

The roots of the yucca are strong and fibrous. Chemicals in the roots of some species are used to produce soaps. Yuccas love full sun, reflected heat, are drought resistant and cold hardy. They prefer well-draining soil, but some tolerate clay and rocky soil. While generally low-maintenance plants, some species require treatment for white grubs that may feed on the roots. Treat grub worm infestations with a systemic insecticide when needed.

The species makes an amazing desert accent plant with its distinctive foliage and silhouette. Yuccas can be used in desert landscapes or for

Yucca bloom

tropical accents, as a focal point, or mixed in with boulders. This plant is versatile in the landscape and combines well with non-desert species. The thick, leathery leaves blend in with tropical foliage, grasses, and wildflower gardens. Yuccas are native to the United States, Mexico, Guatemala, and the Caribbean islands, where they prefer arid and semiarid areas—anywhere temperatures are humid or dry and the soils are gravelly and sandy.

*Yucca aloifolia

Spanish Bayonet

The erect, upright plant grows ten to twenty feet tall with a five-foot or greater spread and is admired for its showy, creamy white flowers and thick, dark-green, elongated leaves. An attractive variegated

Yucca aloifolia
Spanish Bayonet

Yucca aloifolia
Variegated Spanish Bayonet

Yucca aloifolia
Variegated Spanish Bayonet

will take occasional irrigation when it is young or during the hot, dry summer season. It is hardy to zero degrees Fahrenheit or lower. Use it as an accent plant behind beds and borders, as a silhouette against white or light-colored walls or in large containers as a showy accent. It works well in coastal situations and can take salty air and soils. This plant is native to coastal areas, growing from the Southeastern United States to the Caribbean and into Yucatan, Mexico.

Yucca baccata
Banana Yucca

Yucca baccata
Banana Yucca

form has medium green, bayonet-like foliage and margins of light green, edged in creamy yellow. If the plant gets too tall it can become top heavy and topple over. The Spanish bayonet spreads by underground runners to produce offsets that form new plants. Its sword-shaped leaves have sharp, pointed edges that can be dangerous if you brush against them. The older leaves turn brown and dry out, forming a skirt around the plant. Its fibrous leaves were used to make rope and string. The blooms appear in the spring or summer on tall, erect flower stalks. The flowers are two to six inches long. Fleshy fruits are produced after the blooms fade. Birds usually eat the fruit, and the flowers can be used in salads. This plant likes full sun, reflected heat, and light, sandy, well-draining soils. The Spanish bayonet is drought tolerant and

This yucca was named for its edible, banana-shaped fruit that was a historic food source for

271

Native Americans. The plant grows slowly to three to five feet tall and wide with large, strap-like, dark-green foliage that is stiff, erect, sharply pointed, and arranged spirally at the base of its stem. This plant also produces white fibers along its leaf margins that tend to curl on the plant. The fibers from its leaves can be soaked and used to make string or rope. In spring, the plant sends up tall flower stalks that come from a center whorl of leaves. The flowers are creamy white, bell-shaped and appear in thick clusters. Its young flowers are also edible and taste like asparagus. After flowering, the plant produces banana-like fruit that contains flat, black seeds. When the fruit is baked, it has a flavor similar to potatoes. This tough, durable plant is hardy to seventeen degrees Fahrenheit or below. It likes full sun, reflected heat but also grows in partial shade. It is drought resistant but likes well-draining soils. Give it supplemental irrigation during the hot, summer months. Use it as a low-growing accent plant in desert landscapes or as a specimen planting. It can also be used as a focal plant in front of tall walls and foundations because of its picturesque form and growth habit. The banana yucca also looks good in large containers in front of walls, entryways, or pillars. It is native to Arizona, California, New Mexico, Colorado, Texas, Utah, and parts of Mexico, where it grows at elevations of 2,500 to 8,500 feet. The banana yucca grows amongst piñon pines, junipers, and ponderosa pines in its native habitat.

Yucca brevifolia
Joshua Tree

Yucca brevifolia

Joshua Tree

This magnificent, slow-growing plant is the largest of all the yucca species, reaching thirty feet or more in height with a fifteen-foot spread. The species is an important wildlife plant in its natural environment. Native Americans used the leaves to weave baskets and sandals and harvested the seeds and

Yucca brevifolia
Joshua Tree

flower buds for many food products. The canopy of the Joshua tree will tilt to the south, which makes it a good indicator of the sun's location at all times. Joshua trees are unique in their growth habit, and usually no two plants look the same. Many species of birds use the Joshua tree as their nesting site. It has short, sharp, spiny-tipped, grayish green leaf blades, and bark that is rough and grayish brown in color. The leaves are six to fourteen inches long and form dense clusters at the end of the branches. A thick thatch of dried leaves forms a dry skirt around the trunk of the plant. Waxy, bell-shaped, greenish white blooms appear in early spring and are densely arranged. The blossoms have tough, leathery petals and produce a slightly unpleasant fragrance. The species flowering cycle is controlled by rain and climate changes. After flowers die, an egg-shaped, fleshy fruit appears. When the fruit dries, it falls to the ground revealing many flat seeds. The Joshua tree prefers a sunny location with fast-draining soils. It is drought tolerant but needs additional watering once or twice during the hot season. However, overwatering of this plant will kill it. It is hardy to thirteen to fifteen degrees Fahrenheit and does not like to be transplanted after it is established. It is extremely long lived and can exist for a few hundred years. Use it as a large accent plant with its strong, vertical silhouette and form, or where a large specimen is needed. It is native to mostly desert flats and slopes of Southern and Southwestern Nevada, Northwestern Arizona, and Southeastern California, where it grows in dense numbers in the Mojave Desert. This plant is found growing on desert flats and slopes at 1,500 to 6,000 feet in elevation. Joshua Tree National Park in Southeastern California is named for the forest of Joshua trees native to the park.

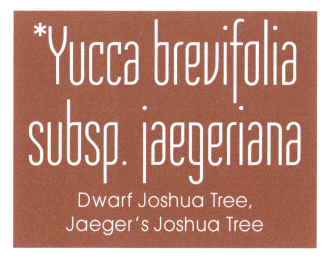

*Yucca brevifolia subsp. jaegeriana
Dwarf Joshua Tree, Jaeger's Joshua Tree

Yucca brevifolia subsp. jaegeriana
Dwarf Joshua Tree, Jaeger's Joshua Tree

This dramatic evergreen has a smaller, stouter trunk than Yucca brevifolia, growing six to twelve feet tall with a denser, more compact branching pattern. It produces multiple stems that start branching two to three feet above the ground. This yucca also has shorter, narrow leaves that appear in tight, terminal rosettes. In spring, the plant develops beautiful, ivory white, bell-shaped blossoms but does not always flower annually. When the plant does produce blossoms, they are followed by elliptical, greenish brown, fleshy fruit with black seeds. This plant enjoys full sun, reflected heat and is drought resistant. It is hardy from about sixteen to twenty-two degrees Fahrenheit. This yucca is easy to grow but does not like to be transplanted once established. Keep this desert accent away from walkways and pedestrian traffic because of its sharp, pointed leaves. Use it along tall walls and foundations for its amazing silhouette and graceful appearance. It can also be used in hot, dry, low-water-use situations because it is extremely drought resistant and very heat tolerant. This plant is native to Northeastern California, Northeastern Nevada, Utah, and Arizona, where it grows on rocky slopes, hillsides, and plains in very dry locations at elevations of 3,500 to 6,500 feet.

*Yucca elata

Soaptree Yucca

This historic yucca grows six to twenty feet tall or more with an erect, upright trunk and spreads eight feet wide. Its showy, white, bell-shaped flowers are the state flower of New Mexico. The plant was named for the substances in its roots and trunks used by Native Americans as a substitute for soap. The coarse fibers of the leaves were used to weave beautiful baskets, sandals, mats, cords, and other useful items. In times of drought, ranchers used this plant as an emergency food for cattle. The buds, flowers, and stalks can be eaten raw or cooked. The yucca has long, slender, pale green, flexible leaves with sharp points and threads along their margins. As older foliage dies, it bends downward to form an attractive thatch coat around the trunk. Flowers emerge on tall stalks from the central portion of each branch and grow four to six feet above the plant. The flowers are loose spikes of white, bell-shaped blooms that appear in the spring and are lovely in dried flower arrangements. Tan fruits in brown pods appear after blooming, revealing many small, black seeds. This slow-grower is hardy to zero degrees Fahrenheit and likes full sun and reflected heat. It is drought tolerant and survives on natural rainfall. However, supplemental water increases its growth rate. Use it for its graceful form and silhouette as an accent plant, focal point, or specimen along tall walls or at the entrance to a property. It is native to grasslands and dry, sandy plains, mesas, and desert washes in Arizona, Texas, New Mexico, and the

Yucca elata
Soaptree Yucca

Yucca elata
Soaptree Yucca

Sonoran and Chihuahuan deserts, where it grows up to 6,000 feet in elevation.

*Yucca faxoniana
Faxon Yucca

Yucca faxoniana
Faxon Yucca

This slow-growing yucca reaches fifteen feet tall with a ten-foot spread to form an upright, attractive trunk and distinctive rosette with sword-shaped leaves. It can sometimes branch out, forming two heads. Branched heads are uncommon but impressive. The old, dried foliage bends downward along the trunk to form a thick, attractive thatch. The thatch buildup helps protect the plant from sun and cold. Its dark-green leaves are sharp and pointed with reddish or black margins. They have curly threads along their edges and grow three feet long. In the spring, the plant produces a three- to four-foot flower talk with a showy display of creamy white, bell-shaped blossoms that emerge from the center of the plant. A red fruit pod develops after the flowers die. Grow it in well-draining soils, full sun, and somewhere with reflected heat. The plant is drought resistant and can take extremely hot, dry conditions. Provide supplemental irrigation during the summer months. This plant is hardy to ten degrees Fahrenheit or lower and is extremely slow growing. Use this low-maintenance yucca in large commercial or residential landscapes where it has plenty of room to grow as a showy accent or specimen planting. Keep it away from sidewalks or pedestrian areas because of its immense size. It is native to rocky slopes of Western Texas and into the Chihuahuan Desert in Northern Mexico, growing at 2,700 to 6,500 feet.

Yucca filifera
Palma China, St. Peter's Palm

The dramatic, fasting-growing landscape specimen with a massive base towers to heights of fifteen to twenty feet. It has sharp, pointed, short, rigid leaves that are dark to olive green with filaments growing along the margins. The plant can form multiple, spherical heads with many green leaves. Its leaves end in a sharp terminal spine. In late spring, it develops an interesting four- to six-foot flower stalk with creamy white, bell-shaped blossoms. The large blooms hang downward instead of standing upright and tall. Plant it in full sun to light shade and in well-draining soil. It is drought tolerant but likes supplemental water during warm weather. It is hardy to fifteen go twenty degrees Fahrenheit and does not like long periods of frosty tem-

Yucca filifera
Palma China, St. Peter's Palm

Yucca gloriosa
Spanish Dagger

Yucca gloriosa
Spanish Dagger

peratures. Use this spectacular specimen where it has plenty of room to grow and spread as a striking accent or plant it against a tall wall for its amazing silhouette and form. It is native to Northeast Mexico from Chihuahua to Nuevo Leon and south to Hidalgo.

*Yucca gloriosa
Spanish Dagger

The fast-growing, tropical-looking yucca grows ten feet tall and eight feet wide and can form single or multiple trunks. It has sword-like foliage that originates from the center of the plant. The leaves are bluish green with smooth margins and pointed tips, but there are also variegated forms available. The foliage bends from the middle and arches in a down-

276

Yucca gloriosa
Spanish Dagger

Yucca recurvifolia
Pendulous Yucca, Weeping Yucca

Yucca recurvifolia
Pendulous Yucca, Weeping Yucca

ward direction. The plant is noted for its showy spikes of fragrant, white flowers with purplish edges that appear in the late spring and early summer. It likes sandy, well-draining soils and full sun but tolerates partial shade. Provide supplemental water every few weeks to keep its nice appearance. This species is hardy to twenty-two degrees Fahrenheit. Use it for its exotic, bold green foliage in tropical settings, or around a pool or water feature. The Spanish dagger can also be used as an accent, foundation, background, or sculptural plant. It works well in mixed borders or in rock, cactus or succulent gardens. Use it in attractive containers on patios and porches. The Spanish dagger can also be used in coastal settings. It is native to the Southeastern United States from North Carolina to Northeastern Florida, where it grows in sand dunes and along coastal barrier islands.

This single-stem or sometimes multiple-stem plant grows to six feet and is recognized by bluish green, pendulous leaves that have a sharp point at the tip. There are also beautiful, variegated forms available. In late spring through early summer, the plant produces a showy, two-foot flower stalk. Creamy white, bell-shaped clusters appear, followed by a seedpod. After the bloom dies, a dried seedpod forms and will eventually need to be pruned from the plant. This attractive yucca likes full sun or light shade conditions. It pre-

Yucca recurvifolia
Pendulous Yucca, Weeping Yucca

fers well-draining soils and occasional irrigation. This plant does not like to be overwatered. The pendulous yucca is highly susceptible to root rot and white grub damage. Treat it with a systemic insecticide in the spring as a preventative measure against insect damage. It is hardy to about fifteen degrees or lower. Use this plant for tropical effects around pools, fountains, and ponds. It works well in raised planters, and as a foundation or entry plant. This species also look good when used in small groupings or as an accent. It is native to the Southeastern United States, growing in sandy soils in Louisiana, Georgia, and Mississippi.

*Yucca rigida
Blue Yucca

Yucca rigida
Blue Yucca

This yucca is a valued plant for desert gardens because of its stiff, flat, powdery blue leaves. It is a tall plant that grows moderately to twelve feet with an eight-foot spread. As the plant matures, the trunk may develop a thatch skirt. It has attractive, long, bluish gray, swordlike foliage with a sharp tip and yellow margins. A creamy white cluster of bell-like flowers appears from the center of the plant in the late spring or summer. The

Yucca rigida
Blue Yucca

Yucca rigida
Blue Yucca

blooms grow on five- to six-foot stalks above the plant, adding a nice color show in contrast to its blue foliage. After flowering, it produces small, black seeds that are contained in two-inch long seed capsules. It is hardy to five degrees or lower. The blue yucca likes full sun, reflected heat, and grows best in rocky, desert soils that are well draining. It is drought resistant and needs very little supplemental irrigation except during hot, dry summers. Plant this dramatic looking yucca where it has ample room to grow and away from high traffic areas. The sharp points on its leaves

are extremely dangerous. Use it as a silhouette or focal point in the landscape and combine this showy plant with other shrubs and groundcovers to create a striking effect. The blue yucca also looks very attractive when planted with other dark green vegetation. This plant is native to the Mexican states of Chihuahua, Coahuila, Durango, and Zacatecas.

*Yucca rostrata
Beaked Yucca

Yucca rostrata
Beaked Yucca

The spectacular bloomer grows ten to fifteen feet tall, forming an attractive, thatched trunk and branching toward the top of the plant as it matures. It has narrow, slightly waxy, greenish blue leaves with a thin, yellowish edge and

Yucca rostrata
Beaked Yucca

a sharp, terminal spine. In late spring or early summer, the plant produces dramatic clusters of white flowers that rise from its center. Following the bloom cycle, it produces seeds that resemble a bird's beak. The species name, rostrata, means beak. This yucca is extremely hardy to minus twenty degrees Fahrenheit. It enjoys full sun or partial shade and is drought resistant. The beaked yucca grows quicker with supplemental irrigation and prefers rocky well-draining soils. This plant can also be easily transplanted. Watch for infestations of grubs or desert beetles, and treat them as needed. Use this moderate- to slow-growing plant for dramatic focal points, in mass groupings or as an accent in low-water-use landscapes or colder locations. It is native to the deserts of Southwest Texas and areas of the Chihuahuan Desert in Northern Mexico.

*Yucca thompsoniana
Thompson Yucca

Yucca thompsoniana
Thompson Yucca

This amazing, slow-growing plant resembles Yucca rostrata but is somewhat smaller, reaching six to twelve feet tall and six feet wide. It has symmetrical, columnar rosettes of stiff, thin leaves, and its foliage is greenish blue in color with fine teeth along the edges. The older foliage hangs down neatly like a coat around the trunk. The Thompson yucca produces small, yellow lines and teeth along its leaf margins with a sharp terminal spine at its tip. In April through May, it produces three- to five-foot flower stalks with dramatic, creamy white blossoms. This plant likes full sun and reflected heat. It grows in any soil, including rocky slopes that are dry and exposed, but it prefers well-draining soil. This species will transplant and root easily in a container or in the ground. The plant is drought resistant and hardy to ten degrees Fahrenheit or lower. Use it against tall walls and buildings for its amazing silhouette and form. Combine with low-growing agaves and golden barrel cactus. This yucca is native to limestone hills, rocky slopes and plains in Southwestern Texas, Southeastern New Mexico, and parts of Northern Mexico.

Yucca torreyi
Torrey's Yucca

Yucca torreyi

Torrey's Yucca

This picturesque plant, which is one of the most common yuccas found in Western Texas, reaches eighteen to twenty feet tall at maturity, eventually producing multiple trunks. It forms a symmetrical rosette with stiff, bluish green leaves that grow three to five feet long and are sharply pointed. The bark is grayish brown and forms a dense thatch as the plant matures. In its native habitat, it sometimes grows into an asymmetrical, untidy-looking plant and has been given the nickname "old shag." In spring, it produces beautiful, fragrant, bell-shaped, white blooms that reach heights of four feet. However, this plant may not produce blossoms each year. After it does bloom, in late summer, greenish brown, fleshy fruits appear, becoming leathery as they mature. The plant likes full sun to light shade. It is hardy to ten degrees and is drought tolerant, but it grows quickly if given supplemental irrigation. Use it as a specimen or plant it in front of a tall wall for its interesting silhouette and growth habit. Mix it with low-water-use agaves and other succulents. It grows natively in Edwards Plateau through Trans-Pecos, Texas, as well as into New Mexico and south into Northern Mexico.

8 Penstemon
for Southwest Landscapes

Penstemon belongs to a large genus of herbaceous perennials native to North and Central America from Alaska to Guatemala and coast to coast. In the Southwest desert, Penstemon grows natively between 4,500 and 6,000 feet. There are more than 275 different species of this plant. The common name for Penstemon is "beard tongue".

Penstemon and Desert Marigolds
in Oro Valley, Arizona

Penstemon and Desert Marigolds
in Oro Valley, Arizona

The plants form dense rosettes of long, green foliage that hug the ground and blend into the landscape. For most of the year, the plant goes unnoticed until the late winter or early spring when it produces a tall flower spike that emerges in colors of violet, pink, magenta or red, depending on the species.

The height and spread of the flowers also differs among species. The flowers are pollinated by bees, wasps, moths, butterflies, and hummingbirds. This plant prefers full sun, but some species can take partial shade conditions. Provide monthly irrigation, well-draining, sandy or gravelly soil, and avoid overwatering it. In the low desert, this plant may rot out during summer. Penstemon is easily propagated by seeds or cuttings. After a few years, they need to be thinned out and pruned heavily in winter. When new volunteers emerge in early spring, they tend to outgrow and take over older plants. These plants are hardy to fifteen to twenty degrees or lower. Use penstemon in rock gardens with other perennials, in borders, along a garden path, in an entry courtyard, around ponds and other water features, in street medians or as a colorful display for spring and early summer color.

Penstemon baccharifolius

Baccharisleaf Penstemon
Rock Penstemon

Penstemon baccharifolius
Baccharisleaf Penstemon

Penstemon baccharifolius
Baccharisleaf Penstemon

This small, compact evergreen grows one to two feet tall and wide with thick, fleshy leaves that are dark green and round with a slightly serrated edge. Throughout the summer, it produces tubu-

lar, scarlet flower spikes on the tips of branches attracting hummingbirds. When setting out young plants, protect them from rabbits with netting or chicken wire fences. Plant it in well-draining soil and be careful not to overwater this plant. It is hardy to about twenty degrees Fahrenheit and may die back to the ground during the colder winter months. Prune it back in late winter to encourage new spring growth. Use this plant in full sun to partial shade. This penstemon remains compact, making it a great choice for containers, narrow entries, street medians, parking lots, or patio settings. It is native to Western Texas and Northeast Mexico, where it can be found growing on rocky slopes at elevations of 2,000 to 4,000 feet.

Penstemon eatonii

Firecracker Penstemon

This showy penstemon has lush, pointed, dark-green foliage that grows into a mounded shape to one to two feet tall and two to three feet wide. In late winter through the spring, it develops two feet tall clusters of tubular, bright red flowers that

Penstemon eatonii
Firecracker Penstemon

Penstemon eatonii
Firecracker Penstemon

Penstemon parryi
Parry's Penstemon

Penstemon parryi
Parry's Penstemon

attract hummingbirds and butterflies. It is hardy to zero degrees Fahrenheit and is also drought resistant. After blooming, it spreads seeds that propagate into new plants. This plant is relatively low-maintenance but will need to be cut to the ground every few years. Collect seed from spent seed stalks yearly to sow in the ground and create new plants. Plant it in full sun where there is good drainage. Provide protection from rabbits when setting out new plants. Use it in wildflower gardens and desert landscapes with other flowering and perennial plants. It can also be used in butterfly, bird, and hummingbird gardens. This penstemon is native to the rocky slopes of Arizona, Utah, Colorado, New Mexico, and Mexico, growing at 2,000 to 7,000 feet in elevation.

The spectacular plant reaches three to four feet tall and three feet wide when in bloom. It has dark green foliage that is broad at the tip and thin toward the base of the leaf. This species is noted for its spectacular flowers that bloom in February through April. Blooms can be either light pink, dark pink, or white. Flower stalks die back after seed formation, but the plant produces more stalks the following season. Scatter dry seed after flowers mature to repropagate. This penstemon likes full sun to partial shade conditions. The species is hardy to about fifteen to eighteen degrees Fahrenheit. It is drought resistant but likes supplemental irrigation during the fall, winter, and spring. Protect it from rabbits with chicken wire when the plant is young since they like to eat emerging flower shoots. Use it in xeriscape and low-water-use gardens for a splash of spring color and accent. The plant also looks nice when mixed into wildflower and perennial gardens. This penstemon is native to washes, slopes, and canyons of the Sonoran and Mojave

Penstemon parryi
Parry's Penstemon

deserts, where it grows at elevations of 2,000 to 4,000 feet.

Penstemon pseudospectabilis
Canyon Penstemon

Penstemon pseudospectabilis

Canyon Penstemon
Desert Penstemon

This magnificent, easy-to-grow penstemon reaches three to four feet tall with triangular, fleshy, bluish green serrated leaves. In spring,

it produces three-foot spikes of funnel-shaped, pinkish purple blooms. Its showy flowers attract bees, butterflies, and birds, and are a nice contrast against its large leaves. The canyon penstemon loves the heat and prefers well-draining sandy soils. Water every week or two during the hot, dry summer when monsoons are not present. Prune spent flowers after the blooming cycle. The plant is hardy to about ten degrees Fahrenheit. This moderate-to-fast grower can be planted in full sun or partial shade. Use it low-water gardens for a splash of spring color and accent or mix into wildflower and perennial gardens. This penstemon is extremely easy to grow and works well in our hot, dry climate. It is native to canyons and washes in Arizona, New Mexico and California, ranging in elevations of 2,000 to 4,500 feet.

Penstemon superbus
Coral Penstemon

Penstemon superbus
Coral Penstemon

Penstemon superbus
Coral Penstemon

This showy but short-lived plant grows three to four feet tall and two feet wide. It has grayish green to blue-green, pointed leaves that are nar-

row at their base and broaden near the tip. From spring through early summer, it develops three-foot, spiked, dark-coral to scarlet colored flowers that attract hummingbirds. The flowers produce seed that can be scattered in early fall to hasten reproduction of the plant. Remove the dried flower stems after the seeds ripen. This penstemon is hardy to five degrees Fahrenheit. It prefers well-draining soil and full sun to filtered shade. Overwatering can shorten this plant's lifespan. Provide protection from rabbits, which eat its new, emerging shoots. Use it along walls, in borders, or among other spring wildflowers. It is native to washes and rocky canyons in Southeastern Arizona and Chihuahua, Mexico from 3,500 to 5,000 feet.

Penstemon triflorus
Scarlet Penstemon
Hill Country Penstemon

Penstemon triflorus
Scarlet Penstemon

This hummingbird magnet has a long blooming period from early spring to summer. The plant

Penstemon triflorus
Scarlet Penstemon

Penstemon wrightii

Wright's penstemon
Texas rose

Penstemon wrightii
Wright's Penstemon

is usually one of the first of the penstemon to bloom in the spring. It has glossy, deep green leaves, and has a bushy, upright growth habit to two feet tall and wide. The plant produces large spikes of funnel shaped, deep pink or magenta flowers. This moderate grower likes amended, well-draining soil. Be very careful not to over-water this plant, as it will rot out quickly. After it blooms, allow the flower stalks to dry out, then cut them off the plant and sprinkle the seeds to increase the chances of new plant germination. It is hardy to about ten degrees Fahrenheit and prefers full sun to shade. This penstemon will naturalize quickly in a shady area of your garden and makes a great foundation or edging plant. Use it in perennial borders, rock gardens, and mixed in with wildflowers for attractive, spring color. It is native to the rocky, limestone soils and plateaus of Texas.

This fast-growing plant resembles the coral penstemon but is more compact in its growth habit. It also has egg-shaped, light green, shiny foliage and is larger than most of the other penstemon species, reaching about three feet in height. In late spring, it produces beautiful, coral to pink, bell-shaped blooms that stand out in the landscape when in color. It grows in full sun to light shade and has very low water needs but requires well-draining soil. After it blooms, reduce the amount of water to avoid rotting. It is hardy to ten degrees, or lower. Remove spent flowers and scatter the seeds for regeneration of the plant when the stalks dry out in the summer. Use it as a background or border plant in raised planters or in wildflower gardens. It can also be used as an accent with other colorful peren-

Penstemon wrightii
Wright's Penstemon

nials. This penstemon is native to mountainous areas and rocky soils of the Trans-Pecos area of Texas.

 Cacti and Succulents
for Southwest Landscapes

Cacti and succulents are important landscape plants in the Southwest desert. Generally, they are low-maintenance and require minimal water to thrive. Basically, all cacti are succulents, but many succulents are not cacti. These special desert plants retain water in their leaves, stems and roots, giving the plants a fleshy, swollen appearance. Succulents and cacti have many water-saving features built into their systems. For instance, they have stems instead of leaves. Cactus and succulents have ribs that increase their plant volume and size, but decrease the surface that is exposed to the sun. They usually have waxy, hairy, or spiny outer surfaces that help reduce water loss from the plant. If you forget to water them on a regular basis, their foliage does not wilt or drop.

plants are also found naturally along coastlines and in salty soils that are high in minerals. They are highly adaptive to the climates of the desert and semi-desert regions, making them an excellent plant choice for our gardens.

These unique plants are usually slow growers and can be kept in the same area or container for many years without needing much attention. There are so many species and varieties available to experiment with in your garden. Most cacti and succulents originated in areas of the tropics and subtropics, ranging from hot, desert conditions to rainforests, and are adaptable to extreme temperature changes. They can survive in high temperatures with little water or in conditions that are wet, cold and covered with snow. These

Most cacti and succulents are active during the spring and summer months, when they require irrigation and fertilizer to help them grow. They need minimal irrigation during the cooler, winter months. If you are fertilizing them to stimulate new growth, use a low-nitrogen* fertilizer at about half of the recommended rate for other plants. Succulents need plenty of light, but sometimes prefer partial shade. In the wild, they are typically tucked or buried under a large shrub or tree, so plant them in areas of your garden that have filtered light. They also prefer soils that allow nutrients, water, and air to get to the roots.

Try growing cacti and succulents in containers, as accents, or in groupings in the garden. They have interesting shapes, textures, and colors. Remember, smaller-sized cactus and succulent plants can be transplanted and shifted throughout your garden to add interest to your landscape

with very little effort. For best success, when shopping for these plants in the nursery, purchase them in smaller containers. This allows some experimentation with different species. Before installing, prepare the planting hole with soil amendments to ensure a well-draining soil. Mix bagged potting soil or compost into your garden area. It helps to lightly moisten the soil before planting, making it easier to work with.

Be careful to avoid damaging their stems or roots when planting or transplanting succulents and tender cacti. After setting plants in the planting hole, cover the plant base with additional soil and irrigate lightly.

A Hummingbird feeding on
a Lady Slipper Plant

Austrocylindropuntia subulata

Eve's Needle, Eve's Pin Cactus

Austrocylindropuntia subulata
Eve's Needle, Eve's Pin Cactus

The branching, treelike specimen grows to thirteen feet tall and about ten feet wide with cylindrical deep green leaves. New growth does not have many spines, but as the plant matures, yellowish red spines develop on its tip. The Eve's needle will rarely bloom in cultivation, but when it does, it produces long, coppery red, showy blooms. Its fruit is oblong with small spines. This plant is fast growing once established and requires minimal care. It is hardy from twenty-five to thirty degrees Fahrenheit. If it is damaged by winter frost, cut frozen areas to live wood, and it will recover in the spring and summer months. The Eve's needle needs full sun to light shade and well-draining soil. The plant prefers more water than most cacti but do not water it as much during the winter months. It can be easily propagated from seeds and cuttings. Use it in attractive containers, raised beds, and cactus gardens, as a showy specimen in atriums or as an understory plant. This exquisite cactus is native to the higher elevations of Peru, Ecuador, Argentina, and Bolivia, where it is used and cultivated as a living fence.

Carnegiea gigantea

Saguaro Cactus

This giant monarch cactus grows to fifty feet or more with a large spread, depending on how many arms it produces in its lifetime. It is slow growing-only one inch a year-with a thick, massive, columnar trunk and waxlike skin that helps it retain moisture. The saguaro can produce many branches or arms but usually only produces one to five. Its trunk and branches have large ribs with straight spines growing out of each rib. When the saguaro receives water by rainfall, the outer pulp expands like an accordion. In May, the plant produces three-inch-wide, creamy white blossoms with yellow stamens that grow in clusters on the southeast-

Carnegiea gigantea
Saguaro Cactus

Carnegiea gigantea
Saguaro Cactus

ern side of the stem tip. The blossoms open during the night and close again by the next day. Saguaro flowers are fertilized by birds, bats, and insects. After flowering, the plant produces a reddish green, three-inch, oval, edible fruit that opens in late June through July. The fruit, which has red pulp and black seeds, can be eaten or made into jams and jellies. When the seeds disperse in the wild, the seedlings may germinate but stay very small for many years. This large cactus is an endangered species and a protected plant. While available at specialty plant nurseries, if the plant is dug in the wild, it must have a protected tag, especially when salvaged as a result of road construction or new subdivisions. The saguaro blossom is the state flower of Arizona. This plant is hardy to about

Carnegiea gigantea
Dried Out Ribs of The Saguaro Cactus

fourteen degrees Fahrenheit and likes full sun with reflected heat. It is drought resistant and mainly gets its moisture from summer monsoons and winter rains. The saguaro is susceptible to a disease called bacterial necrosis. If it becomes infected, the plant eventually dies. Heavy rains may topple large plants to the ground if the soil becomes too saturated. Use it as a large, dramatic accent against tall buildings or in large, open spaces. The hardwood and ribs from a dead, decomposed saguaro can be used for fences, ramadas, and ceilings. It is native to the Sonoran Desert of Arizona and Mexico as well as in an extremely small area of California.

Cephalocereus senilis

Old Man Cactus

Cephalocereus senilis
Old Man Cactus

The slow-growing cactus reaches about twenty feet or more in its native habitat, producing many columnar stems that are usually unbranched. Its species name, senilis, comes from the Latin word meaning old man. As the name implies, it has grayish white, distinctive, long, wooly hairs that look like a beard. The hairs cover the plant to protect it from scorching summer temperatures and to provide warmth in the winter. Its shaggy coat of hair conceals many tiny, sharp, yellow spines. In springtime, it produces two-inch-long, whitish pink flowers that open at night. At maturity, following the blooms, the plant develops pinkish red fruit that is covered with yellowish hair. It enjoys well-draining soil and full sun but prefers light afternoon shade. Bright sun-

Cephalocereus senilis
Old Man Cactus

light encourages the growth of hair. Provide minimal to moderate water in the hot, summer months and almost no water at all during the winter months. It is hardy to minus ten degrees Fahrenheit. Use it as an accent plant or in masses along with other cacti in rock gardens and raised planters. Use the old man cactus as a foundation plant against a white or colored wall. It is native to Guanajuato and Hidalgo in Eastern Mexico.

Cereus repandus, Cereus repandus f. monsrose

Peruvian Apple

Cereus repandus
Peruvian Apple

The cactus is admired for its knobby branches, flowers that open at night and red, applelike fruit. It is a moderate grower, reaching heights of ten to twenty feet with a spread of fifteen feet or more. However, the variety "Monstrose" is a slower grower and is smaller in height. The plant forms many offsets that eventually grow as tall as the mother plant. It also has ribbed and cylindrical-shaped, deep grayish green, upright branches. Spines, sharp edges, conspicuous bumps and knobs can be found along the branches. The name Cereus is from Greek and Latin, meaning large torch. During the warmer months, the plant produces large, white or reddish and slightly fragrant blossoms that bloom at night. The species is also distinguished by the red fruit that remains on the plant for a long time. Its fruit is large, hairless and contains

Cereus Repandus
Peruvian Apple

Cereus repandus f. Monrose
Peruvian Apple

Cereus repandus f. Monrose
Peruvian Apple

small, edible, crunchy seeds called pitaya. The plant grows in full sun to partial shade and does best in sandy soils that are well draining. It likes supplemental water every month or two and less water during the winter months. If planted in containers, it requires more water. The night-blooming Peruvian apple is hardy to eighteen degrees Fahrenheit and will freeze in the low teens. Cover the ends of the plant with Styrofoam cups or sheets to protect it as needed during periods of frost. Use it as a striking accent against tall buildings or large, open walls. It can also be used in containers with other cacti and succulents, around foundations, and in entrances or raised planters. The Cereus genus consists of many columnar cacti that grow natively through South America, Brazil, Argentina, and Peru.

*Cleistocactus strausii

Silver Torch Cactus

This striking cactus develops slender columns up to eight to ten feet tall. It is a vigorous grower that has interesting, silvery blue spines on hairy, bluish gray columns. The silver torch begins to flower when the columns reach about eighteen inches tall. The decorative flowers are deep red or burgundy and protrude from the sides of the columnar stems and along the tips. This showy plant grows quickly during the summer with supplemental irrigation but is generally drought resistant. The silver torch likes to be kept dry during the winter and will rot with too much water. It likes full sun or partial shade. The plant is hardy to about thirteen to fifteen degrees Fahrenheit but

Cleistocactus strausii
Silver Torch Cactus

Crassula ovata
Jade plant

Crassula ovata
Jade plant

Crassula ovata
Jade plant

can show signs of tip frost in the low twenties. Use it in combination with other columnar cacti and succulents in exotic cactus gardens. Plant the silver torch in foundations, raised planters, containers, courtyards, or narrow, confined spaces. It looks interesting when mixed with other columnar cacti along a tall wall with its striking silvery blue color. This cactus is native to high, mountainous regions in Bolivia and Argentina.

Jade plant is noted for its interesting green, oval-shaped succulent foliage that grows out from a multibranching trunk. The shrub can grow as tall as twelve feet in its native habitat of South Africa. However, in the Southwest desert, it usually reaches four to six feet tall and remains compact and rounded. Sometimes, the smooth leaf is tinged with a reddish strip along its edge. In warmer locations, during the winter, it produces clusters of star-shaped, fragrant, ivory white to pinkish white blossoms. The flowers attract bees, flies, beetles, and butterflies. African tribes used the roots as a food product. Historically, the leaves were boiled and used medicinally to treat diarrhea and other stomach ailments. The jade plant grows best in filtered sun to partial shade and may sunburn if planted in reflected sun. It is drought tolerant but requires occasional irrigation and does not like to be overwatered. It is hardy to about thirty-two degrees Fahrenheit and thrives in most soils. The plant is low-maintenance and easy to grow. For best results, fertilize it once per year with a high-nitrogen fertilizer. Use it in attractive containers, raised planters, and rock and cactus gardens. It can also be used as an accent plant on porches and covered patios. The jade plant is native to the Eastern Cape and KwaZulu-Natal valleys of South Africa, where it grows among aloes, euphorbia, and other succulent plants.

*Echinocactus grusonii
Golden Barrel Cactus

The golden barrel cactus has a globelike appearance and is recognized by its magnificent color that comes from vertical yellow ribs that line its edges. The spines of the golden barrel cactus will light up any landscape with its magnificent color. This architectural beauty is a signature cactus of the Southwest desert.

Echinocactus grusonii
Golden Barrel Cactus

The golden barrel is considered a rare and endangered species. It grows slowly to three feet high and spreads two feet wide. At maturity, yellow blossoms appear at the top of the plant in spring, followed by fruit. This cactus is drought resistant, so water it once per month during the warm, dry season. It does not need any irrigation during the winter months. Too much water can cause this cactus to rot. Plant the golden barrel in well-draining soil. It prefers full sun or filtered shade locations and is hardy to thirteen to fifteen degrees Fahrenheit. Use this showy accent in containers with other desert plants. It can also be planted in groupings, as a mass planting with boulders in rock gardens, or to create a striking statement in the landscape. The golden barrel cactus can add significant texture and accent to the landscape. This plant is native to Central Mexico from San Luis Potosi to Hidalgo.

Echinocereus ennecanthus

Pitaya, Strawberry Cactus Cob Cactus

Echinocereus ennecanthus
Pitaya, Strawberry Cactus
Cob Cactus

This exotic-looking cactus noted for its strawberry-like fruit, prolific flowers, and bright green, wrinkled appearance grows two to three feet high. During prolonged periods of drought, the plant often becomes shriveled. It has seven to twelve prominent ribs on each stem and curved needle-like, grayish brown spines. In the spring, the plant produces colorful blooms in varying shades of pinkish red to magenta. The blooms cover the plant in an amazing display. After blooming, this cactus produces an edible, yellowish green fruit about one inch in diameter that tastes like a strawberry. It prefers full sun, is tolerant of reflected heat and drought, and needs good drainage to avoid rotting. During the hot, dry summer, it requires supplemental irrigation. However, in winter, it prefers dry conditions. This cactus is hardy into the mid-twenties Fahrenheit. Use it in cactus gardens, raised planters, and containers nestled among rocks and boulders with other low-water-use plants and succulents. Also, use this interesting cactus in an area where its showy spring flowers can make a statement and be seen up close. The pitaya is native to dry desert, scrubby flats in New Mexico, Texas, and Northeastern Mexico.

Echinocereus stramineus

Spiny Strawberry Hedgehog, Straw-Colored Hedgehog

Echinocereus stramineus
Spiny Strawberry Hedgehog,
Straw-Colored Hedgehog

This clumping cactus forms multiple clusters of mounding stems that reach two feet tall with a one- to two-foot spread. Each individual mound has sharp, grayish tan radial spines that are about three feet long. Its common name comes from the fact that the plant resembles a pile of straw until it flowers. In spring, a large, showy display of pinkish magenta blooms appear and last for a long time. After flowering, large, dark red, edible fruits develop that taste like a strawberry. The fruit is one of the largest produced by this genus. This plant looks best when grown in full sun and reflected heat. It is drought resistant and needs minimal water to survive but prefers monthly irrigation and well-draining, rocky soil. Do not water this cactus during the winter. It prefers dry conditions during the cold season. Spiny strawberry hedgehog is hardy into the mid teens Fahrenheit. Use it in cactus and succulent gardens for its incredible spring flower show. Mix it into containers with other low-water-use plants. It is native to Southeastern Texas and New Mexico. This cactus is also found in Chihuahua, Coahuila, and Nuevo Leon, Mexico where it grows on rocky, limestone slopes, small hills and in desert scrublands at elevations of 2,000 to 5,000 feet.

Echinocereus triglochidiatus
Claret Cup Hedgehog

Echinocereus triglochidiatus

Claret Cup Hedgehog

Echinocereus triglochidiatus
Claret Cup Hedgehog

This cactus belongs to a diverse family of plants, and the species is widespread. It forms large, rounded mounds with many individual, clumping stems and dense spines to about one foot tall and six inches in diameter. *Echino* is the Greek word for hedgehog. The plant is leafless, but its stems contain chlorophyll and are tightly packed together. In spring, it forms attractive, orangey scarlet, funnel-shaped flowers that produce an amazing show of color. The blossoms attract hummingbirds, stay open at night, and last for two to three days. After blooming, this cactus develops a juicy red, edible fruit. Historically, Native Americans used the flower stems as a food source. The plant likes full sun or light shade, prefers supplemental irrigation during the hot, dry season, as well as cooler and dry conditions during the winter. Plant the claret cup hedgehog in rocky, gravelly, or sandy desert soils. It is hardy to fifteen degrees Fahrenheit. Use this cactus in containers, raised planters, or rock and cactus gardens. It is native to Sonora, Mexico, Arizona, California, Southwestern Texas, New Mexico, and Utah, where it grows in a variety of habitats, including rocky slopes, low, desert scrublands and mountain woodlands.

Echinopsis species

There are many different species and a great deal of variation in this plant. They range in size and shape from small, spherical or globular plants to treelike giants. The name Echinopsis comes from *echinos*, which means hedgehog or sea urchin, and *opsis*, which is a reference to the dense spines that cover the plant. The main thing that ties these plants together is their magnificent and showy flower blooms. The flowers are all similar in their funnel-like shapes and hairy, round fruit that is filled with a mushy pulp. The flowers usually last only one day or more and may bloom at night, depending on the species.

The Echinopsis is very easy to hybridize and has resulted in numerous, beautiful hybrids. These hybrids are easy to grow and produce tremendous flower blooms in a variety of colors. The plants of this genus are native and widespread throughout South America. They grow in a wide range of climates and habitats.

Echinopsis candicans
Argentine Giant

The columnar, clumping cactus grows three feet tall and four feet wide or more with multiple stems. As it grows, it tends to lean sideways, forming many offsets. It is composed of many stems that originate from the base of the plant, and it produces a large crown at maturity. The main stem is greenish yellow with white spines along its sides. It late spring, the plant devel-

Echinopsis candicans
Argentine Giant

Echinopsis hybrids
Easter Lily Cactus

Echinopsis hybrids
Easter Lily Cactus

ops beautiful, three-inch wide, funnel-shaped blossoms that open at night. The highly fragrant flowers are pinkish white on the outside with a yellow center. Its blooms close up the next the morning, and the same flower opens again over a few nights. The flowers attract moths and bats as pollinators. Following the bloom, a purple fruit with red pulp emerges. This genus is distinguished from other cacti by the length of its flower tube and the size of its stem. The plant grows in full sun to partial shade, is drought resistant, and needs minimal water to survive. Supplemental irrigation can be applied during the hot, dry season. Do not overwater this plant, especially during the winter months. It likes well-draining soil and is hardy to fifteen to twenty degrees Fahrenheit. Use this slow-growing plant in cactus gardens, raised planters, containers, and rock gardens. It is native to Northern Argentina, where the plants are widely adaptable to a range of exposures.

Echinopsis hybrids
Easter Lily Cactus

This fast-growing group of cacti varies in size, from small, low-growing globular plants to large, branching, columnar specimens. Some of the hybrids within the species have thin, trailing stems and produce many offsets, while others are

Echinopsis hybrids
Easter Lily Cactus

Echinopsis hybrids
Easter Lily Cactus

solitary. The hybrids are known for their spectacular fragrant blossoms that produce white, pink, or yellow flowers, as well as many multicolored varieties. They are grown mainly for their exquisite flowers, which are nocturnal and close up during daylight. The flowers last a day or two before drying up.

They bloom in the springtime, around Easter, as their common name implies. The Easter lily cactus can take up to four years to produce flowers if planted from seed. The flowers are so large that they sometimes dwarf the plant. Generally, these cacti are easy to grow and are hardy to fifteen to twenty degrees Fahrenheit. Plant this cactus in well-draining soil, in full sun or partial shade. The species is drought resistant and requires minimal irrigation during the hot summer season. Use it in cactus and rock gardens, along pathways, as an understory plant with filtered shade or in containers. The Easter lily cactus is an extraordinary plant that should be used in an area of the landscape for its spring color show. The species is native to Mexico and South America.

*Echinopsis pachanoi
San Pedro Cactus

The night-blooming, columnar plant has many branched stems and reaches twenty feet tall with a six-foot spread. It is dark green with six to eight rounded, vertical ribs, a broad base and small, whitish gray spines that protrude from individual areoles. In summer, it produces large, fragrant, showy, white flowers that open at night. After blooming, it develops a dark-green, oblong fruit that is covered with scales and black, curly hairs. The plant grows best in full sun to partial shade and likes well-draining soil. It is drought tolerant and prefers supplemental irrigation during the hot, dry season. Do not overwater and give it less water during the winter months. The San Pedro cactus is hardy to fifteen degrees Fahrenheit and withstands much lower temperatures than most cacti. Use it in narrow spaces for its vertical height and attractive green color. It can also be used in large containers and raised planters or mixed with other cacti and low-water-use

Echinopsis pachanoi
San Pedro

Echinopsis pachanoi
San Pedro

plants. Also use it along a wall or building as a foundation plant where a low-water-use plant is needed. It is sometimes confused with its close relative, Echinopsis peruviana, the Peruvian torch cactus. The San Pedro cactus is native to the Andes Mountains of Peru, Ecuador, Bolivia, and Northern Argentina. It is also found growing in other South American countries in tropical locations. It grows naturally in higher altitudes, where it can withstand low temperatures.

Echinopsis peruviana

San Pedro Macho, Peruvian Torch Cactus

This species is closely related to Echinopsis pachanoi and the two are sometimes confused with each other. The columnar Echinopsis peruviana is a branching, treelike specimen that reaches fifteen feet tall. San Pedro macho grows much quicker than Echinopsis pachanoi and will grow one to two feet per year in height. It has erect branches with cylindrical, stout stems and an arching habit. The cactus develops bluish green foliage with more long, reddish brown spines than Echinopsis pachanoi. It also produces fragrant, white, showy, nocturnal blooms that are nine to ten inches wide and only open for one night and then die. The plant likes full sun to partial shade and is drought resistant. It prefers occasional water during the hot, dry season and well-draining soil. The San Pedro macho is hardy to about twenty-five degrees Fahrenheit. Use this attractive cactus in large containers as a specimen or accent plant. Mix it with other tall cactus species in narrow beds along walls and founda-

Echinopsis peruviana
San Pedro Macho, Peruvian Torch Cactus

tions for its vertical form. It is native to the western slopes of the Andes Mountains in Peru.

Echinopsis spachiana
Golden Torch

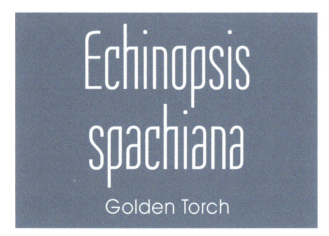

Echinopsis spachiana

Golden Torch

Echinopsis spachiana
Golden Torch Cactus in Bloom

The golden torch is a beautiful, multistem, columnar cactus that produces many upright branches and grows five to seven feet tall. It is lime green with long, radial, yellowish white spines that turn gray as the plant ages. It produces large, white, nocturnal flowers that are six to eight inches in diameter. The blossoms appear in late spring and are showy and fragrant. The flowers open during the evening and last until noon the following day. This plant needs moderate water during hot dry summers but is drought tolerant and should not be overwatered. Plant it in full sun to partial shade, and in sandy, well-draining soil. It is hardy to about twenty-five degrees Fahrenheit and does not like long periods of frost. The golden torch cactus needs some protection on cold nights. Use it as a desert accent plant in rock gardens, in groupings surrounded by boulders, and in raised planters or containers. This vertical accent also looks good in small, confined spaces or against a tall wall or foundation of a building. It works well mixed with other interesting and exotic cacti. The golden torch is native to Western Argentina and Bolivia.

Echinopsis terscheckii
Cardon Grande

Echinopsis terscheckii

Cardon Grande

One of the largest of the Echinopsis species, this fast-growing, attractive, columnar cactus reaches heights of twenty-five feet or more. Mature plants will develop branches or side arms that are ten inches in diameter and have eight to fourteen deep ribs with yellow spines. In late spring, it produces showy, white, nocturnal blossoms that are eight inches long with dark red to green outer segments. The cardon grande grows best in full sun with reflected heat and thrives in hot, dry climates. It is drought resistant and does not like to be watered during the winter season. The cactus prefers most soil types as long as they are well

Echinopsis terscheckii
Cardon Grande

draining and have good aeration. It is hardy to eighteen degrees Fahrenheit and is low maintenance and easy to grow. Use it as a substitute or in combination with the saguaro cactus, where a strong, vertical accent plant is needed. Plant the cardon in wide-open spaces where it has plenty of room to grow and mature. This large cactus can also be used as an exotic plant in xeriscape gardens. The cardon is native to Northern Argentina.

Euphorbia species

Euphorbias comprise over two thousand species of plants. The genus is extremely diverse with a great deal of variation in plant growth, from low-growing spurges to large, cactus-like giants and trees. Euphorbias are recognized by a milky, poisonous, latex sap found under their skin. Additionally, they have unusual, colorful flowers and tuberous or fleshy roots. Some species are more succulent or offer lush foliage, while others are armed with thorns or spines. The euphorbia can either be evergreen or deciduous with leaves that grow in whorls and drop when temperatures decrease in the winter months. The flowers are unisexual and most of the species are monoecious, where male and female flowers grow on the same plant. The true flowers of the euphorbia are small and surrounded by brilliant red or yellow bracts. Flowers last for many weeks on some species.

When the stems are cut or bruised they emit a milky white sap that can be an irritant to skin or eyes. After exposure to the air for several minutes, the sap congeals and eventually will dry. Wear protective clothing and gloves when working around this species to avoid an allergic reaction, especially if you have sensitive skin.

The euphorbia thrives in full sun or partial shade, and likes well-draining, fertile soil that is lightly amended with nutrients. Most euphorbias are drought-resistant, so avoid overwatering them. They need supplemental irrigation during periods of dry, hot weather. This diverse succulent has a hardiness range into the low to mid twenties Fahrenheit. However, some euphorbias are only hardy into the low thirties. The species is easily propagated by leaf cuttings and is considered low-maintenance. After flowering, lightly prune off dead flowers.

The growth habit of euphorbias is wide-ranging. Larger specimens can be used as a focal point in the landscape, while smaller species work well as a groundcover or accent in rock and succulent gardens. Euphorbia pulcherrima, the Christmas poinsettia, is an icon plant that is grown primarily for the winter holiday season. Most euphorbias originate from tropical and subtropical regions of Madagascar and Africa, but are also native to temperate regions of the world, including the Hawaiian Islands. Euphorbia was named after a Greek surgeon, Euphorbus, who used the milky substance from these plants as an ingredient in medicinal potions.

Euphorbia antisyphilitica
Candelilla

Euphorbia antisyphilitica
Candelilla

The low-growing shrub has clusters of thin, upright, bluish green, pencil-like stems that grow in clumps to about three feet. The flowers are small, pinkish white and occur in clusters on mostly leafless stems in spring through early summer. The common name of this plant means "little candle" because the stems are covered with a waxy substance. It is a moderate grower that takes full sun with plenty of reflected heat. This succulent needs little water once established, but benefits from occasional irrigation during the hot, dry summer. It is hardy into the low twenties Fahrenheit and grows in most soil types. The plant is also easy to propagate by spitting its roots apart and dividing them into separate clumps. Prune it heavily to the ground if the plant becomes scraggly and to hasten new growth. This succulent produces a sap that may be a skin

Euphorbia antisyphilitica
Candelilla

irritant to some people. Use it in raised planters, narrow planting strips, and small rock gardens. It can be planted with other low-water plants and succulents as an accent. The candelilla makes a nice focal point in a small garden or as a nice potted specimen with its pale color and columnar shape. It is native to the Trans-Pecos area of Southwestern Texas and the Chihuahuan Desert in Mexico, growing in Durango, Chihuahua, and Coahuila.

Euphorbia canariensis
Canary Island Spurge

Euphorbia canariensis
Canary Island Spurge

Canary Island spurge is a tall, striking, succulent plant with a quadrangular trunk that reaches heights of ten to fifteen feet with a ten-foot spread. It has a branching habit and grows upward with columnar stems. Short, grayish black spines form in perfect regular rows along the four corners of each plant column. It produces a pistil flower that is scarlet to dark red and blooms in late winter to early spring. Canary Island spurge likes full sun to light shade and is extremely heat tolerant. It is also very drought resistant, requiring minimal irrigation except during the hot, dry season. Keep it on the dry side during the winter months rather than overwater it. This plant is hardy to the mid to high twenties Fahrenheit. Like most euphorbias, it emits a poisonous sap and is considered to be one of the more poisonous spurges. It is a moderate grower and can become a large landscape specimen in three to five years. Use it in protected locations for its strong vertical appearance or in containers or raised beds. This vertical accent can be used with other attractive, low-water-use plants for its exquisite appearance and interesting growth habit. It is native to the Canary Islands off the coast of Africa, where it grows in a narrow coastal belt just above sea level.

Euphorbia coerulescens
Sweet Noor

This columnar, branching succulent grows four to six feet tall and spreads two to three feet. It develops numerous underground stems that spread to form new plants. The plant is dark green and creates a thicket of dense growth. It has

Euphorbia coerulescens
Sweet Noor

Euphorbia coerulescens
Sweet Noor

valley basins. After the plant dries out, animals may feed on it in its native habitat.

large, gnarly, brown spines that grow along its columns. As this succulent matures, it develops a branching, shrubby, irregular shape. Bright yellow flowers appear in the spring along its thorny ridges. This fast-growing plant likes full sun to light shade. It is drought resistant but prefers additional irrigation during the hot, dry seasons. Do not overwater it as it can very easily rot. The sweet noor also likes well-draining, rich, sandy soil. It is hardy into the low thirties Fahrenheit and freezes if temperatures stay below freezing for a period of time. Use it in protected areas or cover it during the coldest nights to protect it from winter frosts. Parts of this herbaceous plant are poisonous if ingested. It can be easily propagated from young tender cuttings. Use it in containers, raised planters, and cactus and succulent gardens. Sweet noor can also be used as an interest plant for its unique appearance and growth habit. The sweet noor is native to the Cape Province in South Africa where it grows in dry areas and hot

Euphorbia horrida
African Milk Barrel

The spiny, succulent with irregular, clumping, grayish green stems grows upright to three feet with prominent ribs and red spines. There are many different varieties and forms. It also develops small, yellow flowers in late spring or early summer. African milk barrel is an easy plant to grow and maintain and will produce many offsets for propagation. It prefers well-draining soil and light shade to full sun but does not like a lot of reflected heat. This plant is hardy into the low twenties Fahrenheit. Provide supplemental water during the hot summer but do not give it

Euphorbia horrida
African Milk Barrel

a lot of water during the winter months since it can rot. Like many plants in this genus, it emits a thick, white sap known as latex. The liquid is poisonous and could irritate the skin or cause an allergic reaction. Use it as a showy succulent with other interesting plants in rock gardens or in large, glazed containers. This succulent can also be used in xeriscape situations and mixed in with attractive, taller cacti and succulents as an accent. African milk barrel is a native of South Africa, growing along the Cape Province.

Euphorbia mauritanica
Pencil Milk Bush

Euphorbia mauritanica
Pencil Milk Bush

The pencil milk bush is a pencil-like, branching plant with upright, bright green, cylindrical stems that sprout in the shape of a small shrub. Its small leaves will grow along the grayish green stem. The clumping, low-growing plant grows eighteen to twenty-four inches tall. In warmer climates, in late winter, it produces a yellow flower at the end of each young branch. It is heat and drought tolerant but likes additional water during the hot summer. Do not overwater this succulent because it will rot. Plant it in full sun to partial shade. It is hardy into to the mid to high twenties Fahrenheit. When the plant stems are broken or pruned, it produces milky-white latex that may cause an allergic reaction if it comes in contact with skin. This succulent is extremely brittle and can break easily. Handle it with care when planting or transplanting. Use the pencil milk bush in colorful containers and raised planters or as a foundation plant. It can also be used in groups or rock gardens mixed with other cacti and low-water-use plants. When planting it in masses, space it four to six feet apart. It is native to the Northern, Western, and Eastern Capes and KwaZulu-Natal in South Africa, where it grows extensively in dry valleys and along hillsides.

Euphorbia milii
Crown of thorns

Euphorbia milii
Crown of Thorns

Euphorbia milii
Crown of Thorns

Euphorbia milii
Crown of Thorns

The bushy, spiny succulent develops shoots that can reach up to three to four feet in height with a two-foot spread. It has half-inch thorns that adorn its branches and stems. The tough, leathery foliage grows on slender, young stems. Its leaves may defoliate if moisture stressed or with extreme temperature changes. The plant blooms intermittently throughout the year, but flowers are more prolific in the spring. Small flowers are surrounded by attractive bright red or pink bracts. Hybrids are also available with yellow or white blooms. The plant produces a poisonous latex sap that may cause skin irritations. It likes full sun or filtered shade. The crown of thorns is a slow-growing plant that needs well-draining, sandy soil. It is salt tolerant and drought resistant but likes regular irrigation, especially during the summer months to prevent leaf drop. This attractive succulent is hardy into the high twenties to low thirties Fahrenheit. Protect it from frost during freezing temperatures. Apply a light application of fertilizer once per year in the spring to boost vegetative growth and flower production. Use it in containers, low planters, rock gardens, sunny borders, and succulent gardens. It can also be used along foundations or in small, tight spaces. This tropical-looking plant works well as a houseplant in sunny locations. It is native to Madagascar.

Euphorbia officinarum
Spurge Euphorbia

Euphorbia officinarum
Spurge Euphorbia

The herbaceous succulent is decorated with long, white spines, has dark green coloring, and a reddish brown crown. It grows from eighteen to twenty-four inches tall and two to three feet wide. It is a cylindrical, clumping plant with deep margins. In late summer through fall, it develops a rusty red flower with a yellow-colored inflorescence. The spurge euphorbia, like most of the plants in this genus, emits a latex substance when broken or cut. This euphorbia likes full sun or light, filtered shade. It is drought resistant and needs minimal irrigation to survive. Supplemental water can be applied during the hot, dry season but do not over-water it. This plant is hardy to twenty-five degrees Fahrenheit and prefers well-draining soil. It is easily propagated from stem cuttings but needs to calloused over before planting. Use this interesting plant in succulent, cactus, or rock gardens and xeriscape situations. It can be used with other low-water-use plants in containers and raised planters as an accent plant. The spurge euphorbia can be used in small tight spaces but be careful of its spines. It is native to Morocco in Northern Africa.

*Euphorbia resinifera
Resin Spurge, Moroccan Mound

Euphorbia resinifera
Resin Spurge, Moroccan Mound

This low-growing succulent has erect, thick, bluish green to lime green, four-sided stems with

Euphorbia resinifera
Resin Spurge, Moroccan Mound

Euphorbia rigida
Gopher Plant

small brown thorns, reaching one to two feet with a three- to four-foot spread. Historically, it is one of the oldest documented medicinal euphorbias. The resin spurge forms mounding clumps that look like pincushions with small columns and is leafless most of the time. Small green to yellow blooms appear in late winter to early spring along its stem margins. The plant is hardy to twenty-five degrees Fahrenheit. It likes full sun to partial shade and tolerates most soils as long as they are well draining. Resin spurge is very easy to grow, extremely trouble-free, and does not require any maintenance. All parts of this plant are poisonous if ingested. Provide occasional water during the hot, dry summer and less water in the winter. Plant it in groupings with other succulents in cactus gardens or containers. Also use it in areas with high animal and rodent populations. Animals will not touch it since it is highly toxic. The plant is native to Morocco, where it grows on rocky slopes in the Atlas Mountains. Resin spurge plant is one of the oldest documented medicinal plants of all the Euphorbia species.

Euphorbia rigida
Gopher Plant

*Euphorbia rigida
Gopher Plant

This mounding evergreen grows to about two feet tall with a three-foot spread and has attractive, narrow, pointed, blue-green, sharp leaves. It produces rounded clusters of papery chartreuse yellow flower bracts that appear at the end of each branch in early spring. The blooms turn a greenish tan as they age. This late winter to early spring bloomer adds a great deal of accent to the landscape and is easy to grow. After blooming, the main stems die back, and new growth appears from the center of the plant. The gopher plant is extremely hardy to zero degrees and is a moderate to fast grower. It performs best in full sun to partial shade. While drought resistant, it prefers supplemental irrigation during the warm weather. The gopher plant grows in any soil as long as it is well draining. Do not overwater it as it is susceptible to damping off and dying. After it flowers, the old, dry stems and blooms need to be heavily pruned. When pruned or broken, the plant produces a white sap that can be toxic if ingested. The gopher plant works well in containers as a specimen or a low foundation plant in combination with other desert natives. Also use it in perennial gardens and low planters or as a border or background planting. It reseeds naturally in desert landscapes after the summer monsoons. The gopher plant is a native of South Africa and the Mediterranean region.

*Euphorbia royleana
Churee

Euphorbia royleana
Churee

The attractive, fleshy succulent has deep green branches and ornamental, knobby bumps on its columns. It grows eight to ten feet tall and four to six feet wide. In warm weather, it produces a whorl of small, oval, short green leaves along its stems with a pair of spines at the base of each leaf. In the summer, yellow flowers appear in clusters along the branches. Plant the churee in well-draining soil in full sun to partial shade. It is hardy to twenty-five to thirty degrees Fahrenheit. Protect it from frost on the coldest nights. This plant is drought resistant but likes supplemental irrigation, especially when the weather warms up in spring and summer. It is an easy plant to grow and can be propagated by stem cuttings. The milky resin emitted from the plant may cause skin and eye irrigations, but parts of the plant are also used medicinally. A paste made from ground leaves can be used to treat wounds and cuts. The latex emitted from the plant can be warmed

Euphorbia royleana
Churee

over a fire and used for muscular swellings and sprains. Plant parts cut into pieces may be used as bait to catch fish. Use it as a showy succulent along walls for a vertical or upright silhouette. Also, plant it in filtered shade under the canopy of trees, in large containers or in raised planters. Use it for its green, lush, tropical appearance around a pool or pond. It is native to subtropical valleys and dry, rocky slopes of Nepal and throughout Bhutan and India.

*Euphorbia tircucali, Euphorbia tirulali 'Sticks On Fire'

Tree Euphorbia, Pencil Tree

Euphorbia tirucalli
Tree Euphorbia, Pencil Tree

This endangered species is recognized for its light green, pencil-thin, bushlike branches with miniature leaflets. It is fast-growing reaching heights of eight to ten feet or more in the southwest desert. In its native habitat, it can reach thirty feet with a ten-foot spread. The older branches are woody, and the young branches are green and cylindrical. This plant produces a group of petal-like bracts with yellow flowers that are mainly inconspicuous. Its flowers are propagated by butterflies, bees, and other insects. In warmer locations, a capsulelike, hairy, pale green fruit appears in late fall. The variety Euphorbia tirucalli "Sticks of Fire" is a form of Euphorbia tirucalli. This plant

Euphorbia tirucalli, 'Sticks On Fire'
Tree Euphorbia, Pencil Tree

317

does not have the chlorophyll of its parent plant and is a smaller sized plant and a much slower growing succulent. The branches on this variety are pencil thin with a reddish golden color. The color in its stems will fade to a greenish yellow as summer approaches. This plant becomes redder during the winter months and does best when grown in full sun. Plant it in well-draining soil and full sun with reflected heat or light shade. It is salt and drought tolerant and grows well in coastal areas. Provide supplemental irrigation during the hot, dry season. It is hardy into the low thirties Fahrenheit. The plant emits a milky sap when pruned or a stem is broken. The sap is toxic and may cause an allergic skin reaction in some people. The plant is easy to propagate from stem cuttings. Water your newly propagated plants occasionally to establish new roots. Use the pencil tree in raised planters, containers or as a tropical accent, specimen, focal point or background planting. It is native to Eastern and Southern Africa as well as parts of India, Indonesia, China, and the Philippines, where it grows on grassy hillsides and rocky outcrops and in open savannas.

Ferocactus emoryi subsp. rectispinus
Emory's Barrel Cactus

twenty prominent ribs above each areole. An areole is a modified branch that appears as a small, cushionlike structure with spines or barbed bristles. In summer, the plant produces pale yellow or red blossoms. After the flowers die, oblong, scaly, yellow fruit with black seeds emerges on top of the plant. This is a slow-growing cactus, and while drought resistant, it grows more rapidly with supplemental irrigation during warm weather. It likes well-draining soil and full sun. The plant is hardy to twenty-five degrees Fahrenheit. Use it in low-water-use landscapes, cactus gardens, as a specimen or in masses. Use it in rock gardens along with other interesting varieties of barrel cacti and succulents. The Emory's barrel cactus is native to Central Baja California and Mexico, in an area near the coast called Bahia de la Concepción, where it grows on high, coastal cliffs.

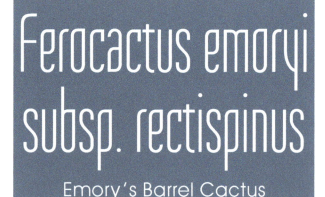

Ferocactus emoryi subsp. rectispinus
Emory's Barrel Cactus

This specimen is recognized by its long, brown, razor-sharp spines protruding from all over the cactus. This plant is a solitary barrel cactus and rarely produces offsets. It is globular when young and then forms a stout, cylinder shape at maturity, reaching a height of five feet and a spread of three feet. The Emory's barrel has fifteen to

Ferocactus glaucescens
Blue Barrel Cactus

Ferocactus glaucescens
Blue Barrel Cactus

This barrel cactus is about two feet tall and wide with a globular shape and a greenish blue skin. As the plant matures, it may produce multiple heads and forms a large mound. It has thick, whitish gray spines that are distributed evenly throughout the plant, along with deep ribs. Beginning in spring and through late summer, funnel shaped, yellow flowers emerge near the top of the plant. The flowers last for a long time with white, rounded fruit appearing after flowering. The plant is slow growing when young and is generally easy to grow and care for. It likes full sun to partial shade and well-draining soil. Blue barrel cactus is drought resistant but prefers additional irrigation during the hot, dry summer. It is hardy to the mid-twenties Fahrenheit. This cactus is easily propagated by seeds. Use it in rock gardens and raised planters with other low-water-use cacti and succulents for its colorful, long-blooming cycle. This interesting plant works well in masses with other barrel cactus and xeriscape plantings. It is native to limestone rock formations, boulders, and rocky hillsides in the state of Hidalgo, Mexico.

*Ferocactus pilosus

Mexican Fire Barrel

Ferocactus pilosus
Mexican Fire Barrel

The spectacular species grows six feet tall or more and is recognized by its thick, attractive, coral red to dark red spines. Some varieties may have fine, white hairs on the areoles that become more noticeable as the plant ages. The actual body of this cactus is green, but the spines can be so impressive that from a distance, only the thick, red spines are visible. It is a solitary plant, but some specimens may cluster from the base, producing multiple trunks. In the spring, the plant develops bright yellow or red blossoms. This round, clumping cactus is slow growing and likes full sun with reflected heat. It is drought resistant and needs little water once established. The Mexican fire barrel prefers well-draining soil and

Ferocactus pilosus
Mexican Fire Barrel

Ferocactus wislizeni
Fishhook Barrel Cactus

Ferocactus wislizeni
Fishhook Barrel Cactus

is hardy to twenty-five degrees Fahrenheit. It is easy to grow and can be propagated by seeds. Use it in desert landscapes, in medians, along roadways, and in areas where water is scarce or nonexistent. This cactus looks nice when combined with the golden barrel cactus and low-water-use agave species. It also works well when planted among rocks and boulders with its amazing red color. It is native to the Nuevo Leon region in North and Central Mexico. In its native habitat many specimens will produce multiple trunks that cluster from the base of the plant.

Ferocactus wislizeni

Fishhook Barrel Cactus

The fishhook barrel cactus is recognized by its curved and hooked central spine and by its large, ribbed, barrel-shaped body. This slow-growing desert native will reach heights of two to five feet or more. In rare instances, it can reach heights up to ten feet tall and has a width of up to thirty-three inches in diameter. Its life span has been reported up to 130 years old. This plant can produce twenty or more vertical ribs up its side with distinctive reddish to gray hooked spines that can be dangerous and sharp. It is commonly seen with only a single trunk, and on rare occasions, it may form a multiple trunk. The root system is shallow and confined to the upper soil levels. In late spring through early summer, it produces an attractive red or yellow bloom that creates a circle at the top of the plant. Birds, javelina, mule deer, and other wildlife will feed on the fleshy, yellow fruit that is prevalent during the summer months. This cactus prefers full sun to partial shady conditions. When transplanting or moving it from the nursery, mark the south side of the plant and maintain this natural orientation to prevent sunburn. This cactus does not need additional irrigation and will grow well with natural rainfall. The cactus is hardy to ten degrees Fahrenheit. It is very easy to grow and can be propagated by seeds. Use this plant in desert gardens and in areas where there is limited water since it is extremely drought resistant. Plant in areas for revegetation or in cactus and succulent gardens. It makes a great accent plant for anyone who loves blooming cacti. This cactus tolerates most native soils with good drainage, requiring little attention or special care. The fishhook barrel cactus is tolerant of extreme heat as well as cold. This plant relies on annual rainfall, making it a good choice for low-water-use landscapes. Native Americans also used this barrel cactus pulp for making jelly and cactus candy. It is native to Arizona, New Mexico, and Texas and in the states of Chihuahua, Sinaloa, and Sonora, Mexico.

Grusonia bradtiana
Organillo

Grusonia bradtiana

Organillo

The columnar cactus with dense thickets of trailing, spiny, bluish gray stems grows eighteen inches to two feet tall and two feet wide. The plant forms multiple, thick, segmented stems, and sometimes tends to lie over sideways as it grows. In this position, it reroots and propagates itself into the soil, forming new roots along its stems. The organillo has long, whitish gray, rigid spines that protrude from the plant. In the spring, it produces yellow to pale yellow blossoms. After flowering, a spiny fruit appears with a small amount of seed. This plant likes full sun to light shade. It is drought resistant, preferring supplemental irrigation during the hot, dry season. Let it dry out during the winter and do not overwater it. The organillo is hardy to twenty-five degrees Fahrenheit and needs well-draining, rocky or gravelly soil. Use it in rock, cactus, and succulent gardens, in low-water-use situations, and with other drought-resistant plants. This cactus also can be planted in masses and groupings for interest. It is stunning when planted with the golden barrel cactus or Mexican fire barrel cactus. This plant is native to the plains of Coahuila, Mexico, growing into North and Central Mexico in areas where rainfall barely exceeds eight inches a year.

Kalanchoe tetraphylla

Paddle Plant, Desert Cabbage

Kalanchoe tetraphylla
Paddle Plant, Desert Cabbage

This fleshy, fast-growing succulent is noted for its striking, oval, red-margined foliage that forms a large rosette, and grows eighteen inches to two feet with a one-foot spread. It produces a red color along its margins when it receives additional light. When grown in deep shade, the leaves turn a dark green color. As the plant matures, it produces many offsets for reproduction. In early spring, after two years or more, it sends out an unusual yellow, urn-shaped, tubular-like flower that is very fragrant. The flowers last for a long time and are pollinated by bees, ants, and other insects. When the flowers start the die, the plant begins to die back also. The paddle plant likes partial shade to filtered sun and can sunburn in full sun with reflected heat. This plant needs a rich, well-draining soil and likes weekly irrigation during the hot, dry season. Lightly water during the winter but do not overwater it. As the plant grows, its leaves usu-ally point upward toward the sun in order to minimize the surface area that is exposed, helping the plant conserve moisture. It is hardy to thirty-two degrees Fahrenheit. Use this attractive accent plant in atriums, shaded areas, containers, planters, rock gardens, and cactus beds for its unique color. It can also be mixed with other larger succulent or as a foreground plant in front of taller specimens. The paddle plant works well as a houseplant. It is native to Cape Province, South Africa, where it grows in grasslands and rocky areas.

Mammillaria bocasana

Powder-Puff, Pincushion Cactus

Mammillaria bocasana
Powder-Puff, Pincushion Cactus

This small, fuzzy, spherical, silvery blue cactus is known for its airy, hooked spines. It is a low grower, reaching six to twelve inches high and three to six inches wide. It has sharp spines and produces attractive pink to pinkish white blossoms in the spring. Some varieties have straw-col-

Mammillaria bocasana
Powder-Puff, Pincushion Cactus

Mammillaria compressa
Mother of Hundreds

ored flowers. After flowering, a long, thin, red seedpod may appear with reddish brown seeds. There are many varieties and forms available of this plant. It is easy to grow and likes full sun and will take some filtered shade during the hot, dry summer. This cactus is drought resistant but needs additional water during the summer and prefers well-draining soil. Powder-puff pincushion is hardy into the low twenty degrees Fahrenheit. Propagate by cuttings or seeds. Use it in attractive containers or raised planters with other showy cacti and succulents. Plant this cactus along pathways or mixed into rock gardens and mounded cactus gardens. Its attractive color looks interesting when planted with darker green colored plants. Use it as an accent planting in dry locations where water is not readily available. Powder-puff pincushion is native to the regions of San Luis Potosi, Zacatecas, and Queretaro of Central Mexico.

Mammillaria compressa
Mother of Hundreds

Mammillaria compressa
Mother of Hundreds

This low-growing, globular cactus produces multiple, golf ball-sized clumps up to six to ten inches tall and three inches wide. It is grayish green with small, pincushion-like balls that grow in tight clusters with white, stiff spines. The spines are wooly with thick grayish white, long hairs. In late winter through early spring, this vigorous plant produces small and beautiful, rosy-mauve blooms on the top of the plant. The flowers are rare in cultivation. After flowering, it may develop a brownish, club-shaped, glossy, red fruit. This cactus is drought resistant but likes supplemental irrigation during the hot, summer season and does not like to be overwatered. It also prefers well-draining sandy or gravelly soils. Plan this fast-growing cactus in filtered sun or partial shade. It is hardy into the mid-twenties Fahrenheit and can be propagated by cuttings or seeds. Use it in rock gardens, containers, and smaller, narrower beds where a small accent is needed or in areas where water is scarce. Plant this interesting cactus in raised beds with other showy, taller, low-water-use plants and succulents. This is a great low-water-plant choice and very easy to grow. It is native to Northeast and Central, Mexico in the states of Hidalgo, Queretaro, and San Luis Potosi, where it grows in sandy and gravelly soils.

*Myrtillocactus cochal

Candelabra cactus

Myrtillocactus cochal
Candelabra Cactus

The large, sprawling cactus is admired for its funnel-shaped, ivory flowers, and reaches heights of eight to ten feet tall and wide. It has multiple, dark green branches with a very woody trunk. The branches have six to eight ribs with a central spine along the middle and shorter radial spines on each areola. The plant produces stunning, white, cupped flowers in late spring through early summer. They open during the day and close at night. After flowering, edible, slightly acidic, globular, red fruit appear. Historically, the stems of this plant were used for firewood, and the fruit was eaten by the native inhabitants of the area. The cactus likes full sun and reflected heat and grows in rocky, fertile soils. It is drought resistant, although it prefers supplemental irrigation during the hot, dry summer. The candelabra cactus grows faster with additional water. It is hardy to twenty-five to thirty degrees Fahrenheit. Use it as a single specimen or grow it in containers for its showy, strong silhouette. This cactus can also be mixed with other succulents in rock gardens or raised planters. It is native to the northern hillside slopes of the Baja peninsula of Mexico growing in Todos Santos Bay, where it receives ample winter rainfall.

Myrtillocactus geometrizans

Blue Candle, Whortleberry Cactus

Myrtillocactus geometrizans
Blue Candle, Whortleberry Cactus

Myrtillocactus geometrizans
Blue Candle, Whortleberry Cactus

This columnar, architectural, treelike specimen grows to fifteen feet with a candelabra form. Its spiny green stems are thick and heavily ribbed. It has radial and central spines that fill each areole. When the plant is about two years old, it produces showy, greenish white flowers in early spring that eventually turn a darker red. The flowers are pollinated by moths and are edible. Following the bloom, the plant also develops edible, currantlike fruits called garambullos. The fruit is popular and can be purchased throughout Mexico and Guatemala either dried or fresh. The dried fruits resemble a raisin. This plant likes full sun and reflected heat. The blue candle is drought resistant but prefers occasional water. It is hardy to twenty-five degrees Fahrenheit and can show some unsightly damage on its branches if frosted. This cactus is easily propagated by cuttings that root in warm weather. Use it as specimen in cactus and succulent gardens, as a tall silhouette in front of a white wall or as accent plant in large containers. There are many clones of this cactus that make spectacular landscape specimens. It is native to Mexico from San Luis down to Oaxaca and into Baja California.

Neobuxbaumia polylopha

Mexican Gold Saguaro, Golden Saguaro

Neobuxbaumia polylopha
Mexican Gold Saguaro, Golden Saguaro

Neobuxbaumia polylopha
Mexican Gold Saguaro, Golden Saguaro

This columnar cactus resembles a saguaro and grows to thirty feet or more but rarely produces any branches. The species name, Polylopha, means having many ribs. It has deep, narrow ribs that are green with sharp, yellow spines. In mid to late summer, it produces dark red blossoms along the sides and near the top of the plant. The flower color is a rarity among columnar cacti, which usually produce only white blossoms. The flowers open during the day and are pollinated by insects. After flowering, it develops a purplish black, cylindrical fruit with white pulp that is eaten by birds and other animals. The fruit is sweet and resembles a plum. This plant is drought resistant and likes full sun and reflected heat. It will also take colder temperatures into the very low teens. The Mexican gold saguaro is propagated by seeds. The fruit need to be overripe before harvesting seed. Plant it in groupings of three or more for a dramatic effect in the landscape. Use this cactus as a silhouette against a tall wall. Plant the Mexican gold saguaro with groupings of agave species or dasylirion species mixed in with other desert accent plantings. Use it in drought resistant, low-water-use, or xeriscape gardens. It is native to the Mexico states of Hidalgo, Guanajuato, Queretaro, and San Luis Potosi, where it grows along canyon walls and limestone slopes.

Opuntia basilaris
Beavertail Cactus

This interesting, oval-shaped cactus grows two to three feet tall and four feet wide. It has short, greenish purple segments resembling the tail of a beaver. Brown, wooly looking, bristly spines grow along its edges, which are

Opuntia basilaris
Beavertail Cactus

Opuntia basilaris
Beavertail Cactus

soil. This plant needs minimal irrigation when established and only occasional water during the hot, dry season. It does not need any water during the winter months. This showy prickly pear can be used in attractive containers and rock or cactus garden beds with limited water. It is extremely drought resistant and suitable for xeriscape situations. The beavertail cactus is very showy and provides winter interest. It is a great plant for medians and roadsides planted with the golden barrel, Santa Rita prickly pear cactus, and other cacti or succulents. It is native to the southwest in Arizona, Nevada, Utah, and California, where it grows on dry, rocky desert slopes, and sandy flats, and along hillsides. The beavertail cactus is also native to Northwestern Mexico in Baja California and Northern Sonora, Mexico, growing at elevations of 2,000 to 3,000 feet.

Opuntia cochenillifera

Wooly Joint Prickly Pear, Nopales Cactus

spotted throughout the pads. In late spring, showy fuchsia colored to reddish purple flowers appear, followed by spineless, brown edible fruit. There are many subspecies and several different varieties of this cactus. Beavertail cactus likes full sun with reflected heat and is hardy from about nine to fifteen degrees. Plant the cactus in fast-draining, sandy or gravelly

This exotic-looking cactus has tiny spines with dark green, thick leaves, and grows eight to ten feet tall with four to six-foot spread. The plant has interesting, thin, narrow cactus pads that are pleasant to touch, especially when the leaves get hot, during the heat of the summer. The cactus pads can be eaten, either raw or cooked. The young pads are sold as nopales and are popular in Mexican dishes. The species name, cochenillifera, comes from the cochineal insect (Dactylopius coccus) that lives on this cactus. Red fluids that ooze from this insect are a major source of dye

Opuntia cochenillifera
Wooly Joint Prickly Pear, Nopales Cactus

or succulent gardens. This cactus will form a nice ornamental tree or shrub with its attractive, tall silhouette. It can also be used as a large accent plant on a colorful wall for its whimsical appearance. The wooly joint prickly pear is native to Southern Mexico and is a popular landscape plant in Hawaii and Costa Rica.

Opuntia ficus-indica
Indian Fig, Tuna Cactus

used to color clothes, garments, drinks, liquors, and food products. In late spring through early summer, the plant produces tubular, crimson red blossoms with many stamens coming out of the tube and pistil of the plant. Following the bloom cycle, rigid, red fruit emerges and is difficult to remove from the plant. The flowers and fruit attract butterflies, hummingbirds, and bats. The seeds from the fruit disperse easily, making it a good specimen to propagate. It can also be propagated from leaf cuttings that root easily into the soil. This cactus is easy to grow in full sun to partial shade. It is hardy to twenty-five degrees Fahrenheit and grows best in well-draining soil. The wooly joint prickly pear takes hot, dry conditions but also grows well in wet and humid locations. It is drought resistant but prefers infrequent irrigation and does not like to be overwatered. This cactus will take a lot of neglect and is a perfect plant for a laid-back gardener. Use it as a large screening plant in low-water-use, cactus,

Opuntia ficus-indica
Indian Fig, Tuna Cactus

This immense, branching cactus with a massive trunk grows to fifteen feet tall and ten feet wide.

Opuntia ficus-indica
Indian Fig, Tuna Cactus

Opuntia ficus-indica
Indian Fig, Tuna Cactus

is eaten by birds and animals and is also used to make jams, jellies, and alcoholic beverages. The Indian fig likes full sun and reflected heat. It also prefers well-draining soil and tolerates drought. During the hot, dry summer, the cactus pads shrivel up when stressed for water. Provide occasional irrigation during drought periods but do not overwater it. This plant is hardy to fifteen to nineteen degrees Fahrenheit. At maturity, it may get top heavy, so prune it back as needed to shape and thin it out. The Indian fig can be used as a screen, fence, or barrier plant. It can also be used as a large silhouette against a tall wall. Use this plant in attractive containers or as a specimen or backdrop. The origin of the India fig is unclear, but it has naturalized in warmer regions of the United States, including California and Arizona.

Opuntia macrocentra

Black-Spine Prickly Pear

Opuntia macrocentra
Black-Spine Prickly Pear

It produces large, oblong pads that are either spineless, or have a few spines. The cup-shaped blossoms appear in late spring to early summer in orange or yellow. Its flowers usually appear along the edge of the pads. After the flowering cycle, rounded, reddish purple, fleshy fruit appears. The fruit usually has sharp bristles and can be hard to handle, but it is attractive, edible, and delicious, resembling a strawberry. The fruit

This prickly pear is recognized by its beautiful flowers and large, black spines along its thick purplish green cactus pads. It grows three to four feet tall and spreads four to seven feet. The pads become a deeper purple during the winter and in the peak of summer. In spring, the cactus produces a magnificent color show with its bright yellow flowers and red centers that are two to three inches in diameter. A single plant may be covered with sixty-five to seventy large blossoms at one time. After flowering, it produces a dark, round, purplish red fruit. The black-spine prickly pear likes full sun and reflected heat. It also prefers hot, dry temperatures and well-draining soils. This cactus is drought resistant, preferring only supplemental irrigation during the hot, dry season. It is very hardy to ten degrees or less. Use this cactus for its attractive coloring as an accent or specimen. It can also be used in containers and raised planters or in rock and cactus gardens. Plant this whimsical cactus in masses with the golden barrel cactus in dry locations, where it thrives. This cactus is native to the desert uplands, oak woodlands, grasslands, sandy flats, rocky hills, and valleys of Texas, New Mexico, Eastern Arizona, and Northern Mexico.

Opuntia monacantha variegata
Joseph's Coat Prickly Pear, Irish Mittens

Opuntia monacantha variegata
Joseph's Coat Prickly Pear, Irish Mittens

This shrub or treelike cactus has long, flat pads on green and tan stems and grows upright in segmented trunks to four to six feet. Its showy pads are intertwined in dark and light greens forming an interesting, twisted shape. This attractive cactus produces more coloration when planted in full sun. The Joseph's coat prickly pear also produces an attractive yellow bloom in late spring through early summer. It thrives in hot, dry, sunny locations and is very drought tolerant. Provide supplemental irrigation during the summer but do not overwater it. It is hardy from twenty-five to thirty degrees Fahrenheit. Use caution when handling this cactus since it has many spines. The fruit should be very ripe before harvesting seeds for propagation. Use for its interesting foliage and silhouette as a foundation planting against a white or light colored wall. It can also be used in attractive containers as an accent planting in low-water-use, succulent, and cactus gardens. This cactus is native to parts of Brazil,

Opuntia monacantha variegata
Joseph's Coat Prickly Pear, Irish Mittens

Opuntia santa-rita
Santa Rita Prickly Pear, Purple Prickly Pear

Opuntia santa-rita
Santa Rita Prickly Pear, Purple Prickly Pear

Argentina, Paraguay, and Uruguay. It has naturalized in Australia and parts of South Africa, where it grows in low-lying forests and along sandy shores.

Opuntia santa-rita

Santa Rita Prickly Pear, Purple Prickly Pear

This low-growing prickly pear cactus forms large clumps and has a short trunk growing to heights of two to five feet with an equal spread. It produces flat, round, reddish purple pads that grow to eight inches. The color of the pads intensifies when the plant is stressed by cold weather or drought conditions. During the summer months, the pads are a softer bluish gray color. The pads will not always develop spines, but spines may be present along its perimeters and areoles. Its flowers are orange-red in color and appear in late spring. After flowering, the plant develops an oblong, purple, plump fruit. It is hardy to fifteen degrees Fahrenheit or lower. The Santa Rita prickly pear is drought resistant but needs supplemental, monthly irrigation during the hot, dry summer. It also likes full sun and well-draining soil. This cactus is susceptible to cochineal scale, which appears as a white, cottony tuft on the plant. Hose off infected plants with a hard stream of water or use an insecticide. The plant requires minimal maintenance and is easy to propagate by replanting individual pads. Use it as colorful accent in containers or as a silhouette against white or light colored walls. It provides great color in winter, when other plants are dormant. This cactus plant also looks interesting in attractive containers where water is sparse. This prickly pear is native to Arizona, Texas, New Mexico, and Sonora, Mexico at elevations of 2,000 to 4,000 feet.

Opuntia stenopetala

Tuna Colorada, Red Crawling Prickly Pear

Opuntia stenopetala
Tuna colorada, Red crawling prickly pear

This low-growing, sprawling shrubby cactus with creeping stems grows to four feet with a three- to four-foot spread. Its pads are round with green gray colorings, tinged in an attractive mottled purple color and covered in long whitish gray spines. In the spring, it produces a medium-sized, attractive, small, reddish orange blooms followed by a round edible fruit with or without spines. This prickly pear will take full sun with plenty of reflected heat and also partial shade conditions. It is very drought resistant, but it likes supplemental irrigation during the hot, dry seasons. This plant is hardy to twenty-five to thirty degrees Fahrenheit. Use the tuna colorada for its interesting foliage in cactus and succulent gardens. It can be used in containers or planters as a specimen plant. This prickly pear looks great as a low foundation plant, along walls or in rock gardens. This is a choice for xeriscape and low-water-use landscape situations and also works well as a winter interest plant. It grows in Northern and Central Mexico in the states and districts of Coahuila, Nuevo Leon, San Luis Potosi, Tamaulipas, Zacatecas, and Hidalgo.

Oreocereus celsianus

Old Man of the Andes

This exotic specimen grows slowly to ten feet and four to five feet in diameter. It has silvery white, fuzzy hairs along its spiny, ribbed, columnar trunk, and columnar stems. This plant is also recognized by sharp, yellowish white to reddish brown spines that are hidden beneath its abundant white hairs. The genus name, Oreocereus, comes from the Greek word for mountain cactus. In spring through midsummer, this cactus produces deep magenta to pinkish purple, tubular flowers on stems near the crown. The blossoms are about four inches long and open during the day. Only mature plants produce flowers. This plant is extremely low maintenance and is easy to grow. It likes full sun or filtered shade and is very drought

Oreocereus celsianus
Old Man of the Andes

Pachycereus marginatus
Mexican Fencepost, Mexican Organ Pipe

resistant but does not like to be overwatered. This cactus is hardy to ten degrees Fahrenheit and will also thrive in our hot climates. Use it in containers, raised beds, rock gardens, and dry, desert locations. This showy cactus can also be used as an interest plant or for visual effects in the landscape. It is native to the mountains of Bolivia, Southern Peru, and Northern Argentina.

*Pachycereus marginatus
Mexican Fencepost, Mexican Organ Pipe

This handsome cactus has tall, columnar trunks and reaches heights of twenty feet, or more. It produces clusters of stout, cylindrical stems that resemble a pipe organ. The plant develops many arms during its lifetime and grows quicker with supplemental irrigation. It is deep green with ribs that have minor spines. Its central spine is yellowish, and the smooth stems have five to seven ribs. The plant's common name is derived from the fact that in many villages and towns of Mexico, it is used to construct a living fence, mainly along roadways. In spring, the cactus produces tubular, pinkish red flowers that are very showy. Following the bloom cycle, it develops spiny, yellowish to red fruit with black seeds. Plant the Mexican fencepost in well-draining soil and full sun with reflected heat or partial shade. It is drought resistant but likes occasional water during the hot, dry months. Let the soil completely dry out between irrigations. It is hardy to about twenty-five degrees Fahrenheit. Protect the tips of the plant when temperatures dip below the low twenties by placing Styrofoam cups on the tips of the cactus. Use it as a desert accent or specimen; plant it against a tall wall, as a vertical accent, or create a living fence from cuttings of this plant. It also works well when used in desert or tropical settings and is relatively maintenance free. The Mexican fence post is native to the states of Hidalgo, Queretaro, and Guanajuato and is widely planted and naturalized throughout Mexico.

Pachycereus schottii

Senita Cactus

Pachycereus schottii
Senita Cactus

The columnar cactus grows fifteen feet tall and about ten feet wide, branching upward from its strong base at ground level to form thickets. Each stem produces about five to ten ribs and clusters of areolas with bristlelike gray spines. Hairy beards cover the ends of the spiny stems on some plants, reflecting its common name senita, which means "old one" in Spanish. In spring, it develops pale pink flowers on upper stems of the plant. The blossoms open during the night and then close when the sun starts to rise in the morning. The plant is pollinated by a small moth that lives its life solely on this cactus. After blooming, it produces a spineless, edible, red, oval, fleshy fruit with red pulp. This fruit was a vital food source for early inhabitants of Arizona and Mexico. The seeds were separated from the pulp and then ground into a nutritious meal. Native Americans believed that the senita cactus fruit was a powerful, spiritual plant. It is extremely drought resistant and usually survives on natural rainfall. The sen-

ita cactus is hardy to about seventeen degrees Fahrenheit but newly emerging tips should be protected on extremely cold nights. It likes full sun, reflected heat, and well-draining, rocky soils. Use it as a specimen against tall walls or buildings as a strong vertical accent. Also use it in containers, raised beds, or areas where water is not readily available. This plant is native to the Organ Pipe National Forest in the Sonoran Desert of Arizona and along the Gulf of California in Mexico growing 1,000 to 2,000 feet in elevation.

Pachycereus schottii f. monstrosus

Totem Pole Cactus

Pachycereus schottii f. monstrosus
Totem Pole Cactus

Pachycereus schottii f. monstrosus
Totem Pole Cactus

The slow-growing, smooth-skinned, columnar cactus grows ten to twelve feet with tall stems that branch at the base to form a short trunk. It is a slow-growing cactus with smooth skin and no visible spines. The totem pole has light to medium green coloring and small bumps or areoles along the entire length of its long columns, giving it the illusion of having multiple faces carved into the plant. Totem pole cactus is a night bloomer, and in late spring, it produces light pink blossoms that open at dusk and close up by midmorning. It also develops an edible, egg-shaped, red fruit with red pulp. Over time, this cactus forms multiple, upright arms. When a stem falls over in the wild, it will root along its side. The plant is hardy to twenty-five degrees Fahrenheit and should be protected against frost. It likes full sun with plenty of reflected heat, is drought resistant, and needs minimal irrigation. Plant this cactus in gravelly, well-draining soil. Use this cactus as a showy display in cactus gardens or in attractive containers or raised beds with other cactus and succulent plants. It can also be used as a xeriscape planting in combination with other desert plantings or around pools or ponds as an accent. Use it against a tall wall for a vertical or architectural effect. It is native to Sonora, Mexico and the Baja peninsula of Mexico, where it grows on desert hillsides and in valleys.

Pachypodium lamerei

Madagascar Palm

Pachypodium lamerei
Madagascar Palm

This exquisite, fast-growing succulent reaches three to twelve feet with either a single or multiple thick, shiny, gray trunks that are covered in thorns. The trunk is spindle shaped with a whorl of glossy green, long leaves at the top, resembling a palm. When grown under optimum conditions, in mid to late spring, it produces wavy, white, fragrant flowers. The species usually does not produce flowers until later in maturity. All parts of this plant are highly poisonous if ingested. This succulent is actually not a true palm but related to the plumeria. It will grow in full sun but prefers partial to open shade conditions in the southwest desert. Do not plant it where it will receive reflected heat. It tolerates periods of drought but needs weekly irrigation during the hot, summer season or if planted in a container. Water the Madagascar palm less often during the winter and keep it on the drier side. This succulent should be planted in rich, well-draining soil. It is hardy into the low thirties Fahrenheit and needs protection from winter frosts. Provide occasional fertilizer applications for maximum growth and to induce blooms. Plant this exquisite succulent in entryways and raised planter beds. Use it for tropical effects or as a specimen in colorful containers. This plant looks good in combination with other bold foliated succulent type plantings. It is native to the islands of Southern Madagascar in Africa.

Pedilanthus bracteatus

Tall Lady Slipper

This interesting succulent grows four to six feet and can reach heights of nine feet tall in its native habitat. The plant has long cylindrical stems with medium sized oval leaves. All parts of this plant are hairy. During the warm seasons the plant produces reddish-pink bracts near the ends of its stems that represent a shoe. It will also produce a small leaf. Tall Slipper plant will grow in full sun to light shade but will not produce any flower color in deep shade. This succulent like well draining soils and does not like to be overwatered since it is extremely drought tolerant. It is hardy to twenty five degrees Fahrenheit and needs to be protected from winter frosts. If frosted back

Pedilanthus bracteatus
Tall Lady Slipper

*Pedilanthus macrocarpus

Lady Slipper

The attractive, slow-growing succulent is recognized by its bright red flowers that resemble an elegant shoe or slipper. The plant grows six feet tall and wide in a clumping, upright growth habit, with small pencil-like stems. A milky sap is emitted when the stem is broken or pruned. It has tiny, gray leaves that appear on new growth, but they fall quickly when the plant is moisture-stressed. The blooms appear in late spring or early summer and attract hummingbirds. It

during a cold winter, it is slow to recover in the spring. This plant contains a sap that could cause a allergic reaction, so where protective clothing and gloves when pruning or working around it. The succulent can be found natively in Mexico from the state of Sonora down into the state of Guerrero in southwestern Mexico where it grows in dry, deciduous woodlands. Use the tall Slipper plant in containers, in protected locations as an accent plant, around boulders or as a specimen in the landscape. It genus name Pedilanthus comes from the Greek word 'pedil' which means "shoe" and 'anthos' meaning "flower". Many members of this genus also have shoe-shaped flower structures that represent this genus.

Pedilanthus macrocarpus
Lady Slipper

is hardy to about thirty degrees Fahrenheit, but mature plants can handle lower temperatures before showing signs of frost damage. This plant is also drought-tolerant, but requires occasional irrigation during hot, dry spells. If planted in containers, water it weekly during the summer. The slipper plant likes well-draining soil. It also prefers to be planted in full sun or light shade and can tolerate reflected heat. Use it in containers or against low walls or as an understory plant, under trees. Plant the slipper plant with desert plants and cactus for its strong vertical effects. Use it in large containers mixed in with other striking cactus and succulent plants. The slipper plant is native to the Baja peninsula and northwestern Sonora, Mexico, where it grows on hillsides and in desert plains.

Portulacaria afra
Elephant's Food

Portulacaria afra

Elephant's Food

The attractive, evergreen succulent can grow to eight feet or more in its natural enviornment. It has small, circular, fleshy, bright green foliage on reddish brown stems. The leaves of these plants are edible and have a tart flavor. In its native habitat, the plant is heavily browsed and eaten by elephants, wild game, and tortoises. Elephants eat parts of the plant and spit out the leaves and seeds, which help to propagate the plant. It produces pink, star-shaped flowers in late winter to early spring but rarely blooms the southwest desert. The flowers are a good source of nectar for birds and insects. This plant likes full sun or light shade, and it is very drought resistant. It also prefers occasional water, especially during the hot, dry summer. Do not overwater this plant as it will immediately defoliate. It is hardy to thirty degrees Fahrenheit. There is a variegated variety with a mixture of cream and green foliage. Use this plant in containers, entryways, or patios. Combine it with other interesting low-water-use plants, or train it as a bonsai. It is native to rocky slopes and dry river valleys of the Eastern Cape of South Africa, and north into KwaZulu-Natal, Swaziland, Mpumalanga, and the Limpopo Province. This plant grows quickly to form a large thicket of growth in its native habitat.

Sansevieria cylindrica

Spear Sansevieria

Sansevieria cylindrica
Spear Sansevieria

This tropical succulent reaches two to four feet tall with a two to three-foot spread and has striking, greenish gray banded, smooth, upright leaves. The cylindrical-looking plant develops a fan shape with stiff, sharply pointed leaves that grow from a basal rosette. It grows from underground rhizomes. The spear sansevieria produces small, greenish white tubular blossoms that have a nice fragrance. It is drought resistant and only needs occasional irrigation. Water more frequently during the warmer season and allow the soil to thoroughly dry out between irrigation cycles. Do not overwater it. It is hardy into the low thirties Fahrenheit and will freeze during long periods of cold weather. Plant the spear sansevieria in partial to filtered shade and in well-draining soil. This succulent is very easy to grow and prefers yearly fertilizer applications. Use it in protected shade locations on porches, on patios, and in atriums. Plant the spear sansevieria in large or raised planters or

where water is not readily available. Use this exotic, tropical as a specimen or indoor plant where it will add interest and drama. This unusual succulent is native to Southwestern Africa.

Stenocereus montanus

Mountain Organ Pipe, Pitaya Colorada

Stenocereus montanus
Mountain Organ Pipe, Pitaya Colorada

This magnificent, candelabra-like, branching cactus grows to twenty-five feet tall and ten feet wide with prominent ribs and six to eight columnar stems. It is grayish green and has dark, central spines along its thick trunk. In late spring, it produces large, showy, nocturnal, bell-shaped flowers. The blooms appear toward the top of the plant and are white on the inside and rose on the outside. In late summer to early fall, greenish orange spiny fruit with edible seeds emerge. The seeds are eaten by animals. This slow-growing plant likes full sun and reflected heat. It is hardy to about twenty-eight degrees Fahrenheit. Plant this cactus where it can be protected from frosty conditions on the coldest nights. It is drought resistant and needs minimal water to survive. The mountain organ pipe also prefers well-draining soil. Use this specimen cactus in a protected area in cactus and succulent gardens or mix it with other tall, columnar species for its visual and sculptural effects. It is native to the Pacific coasts, valleys, canyons, and tropical deciduous forests of Southeastern Sonora and the Southwestern Chihuahua region of Mexico.

Stenocereus stellatus
Pitaya, Baja Organ Pipe Cactus

Stenocereus stellatus

Pitaya, Baja Organ Pipe Cactus

The slow-growing, columnar cactus reaches ten feet or more with a spread of five feet. It has a branching, treelike habit with short, bluish green trunks that develop at the base of the plant. Its stems are green with grayish white central spines with one pointing downward and the other pointing upward. In winter, the tips of this plant turn a brilliant red color. In summer, it produces a showy, night-blooming, pale pink, bell-shaped flower that is about two inches long. The flow-

ers appear toward the top of the plant. After the flower dies, a large, edible, slightly acidic, dark purple fruit emerges. The easy-to-grow species is cultivated for its fruit, which can be found in specialty markets throughout Mexico. The fruit is harvested when it is overripe and can be dried and made into jellies. The cactus is drought resistant and needs minimal water to survive. It likes well-draining, sandy soil, full sun, and reflected heat. This cactus is not tolerant of frost conditions and is only hardy to thirty degrees. It will develop mild tip burn if left uncovered in a frost. Use this attractive plant in cactus gardens, rock gardens, and low-water-use xeriscape situations. It can be also used in low planters along walls for its vertical height and silhouette. Mix it into large containers with other cacti and succulents for its interesting beauty and appearance. This plant has also been used as a living fence to provide a similar effect as the ocotillo offers. The Baja organ pipe is very easy to grow and maintain. It is native to Morelos, Puebla, and Oaxaca, Mexico, where it grows in tropical areas, deciduous, scrubby forests and rocky, limestone soils.

Stenocereus thurberi

Organ Pipe Cactus

Stenocereus thurberi
Organ Pipe Cactus

This distinctive night-blooming cactus grows in a columnar, treelike form to twenty feet tall or more, producing multiple stems that form clumps. Mature plants will reach twelve to fifteen feet wide with many branches. It produces erect, olive green stems with distinctive ribs. This cactus has closely spaced spines that are long and black, turning gray with age. It blooms only at night, producing three-inch, funnel-shaped flowers that are pinkish red with a whitish edge. The flowers open after sunset and close during the day. After flowering, the plant develops large, round, edible fruit that eventually loses its spines as it ripens. The seeds are dark brown and covered in a sweet, bright red pulp. Historically, the fruits have been harvested for food and the stems of this plant have been used for various medicinal purposes. The ribs were also used for construction materials by local inhabitants. The plant is hardy to twenty-five degrees Fahrenheit, and the tips of this cactus should be protected on cold nights. Covering them during periods of frost with a Styrofoam cup will help. Plant it in full sun with reflected heat and rich, well-draining soil. Give the plant plenty of room to grow. It needs minimal water to survive. Irrigate it once or twice during the hot, dry weather. Use it as an accent in containers, a foundation plant, or with other cactus for its structural beauty. The species is protected under Arizona's Native Plant Law and grows in abundance in Organ Pipe National Monument near the Mexican border. It is also native to Baja California, Sonora, and Sinaloa, Mexico, growing in rocky soil, on hillsides and along desert plains at 3,000 feet in elevation.

Stetsonia coryne

Argentine Toothpick Cactus, Toothpick Cactus

The distinctive, night-blooming cactus grows thirty feet tall and ten to fifteen feet wide. Its columnar, grayish green stems are approximately four inches in diameter with toothpicklike, grayish white spines, protruding from the plant. Its stems develop eight or nine rounded ribs with shallow grooves. The cactus grows at a moderate rate and produces many arms at maturity. In late spring to early summer, showy, white blossoms with gray edges open at night and close

Stetsonia coryne
Argentine Toothpick Cactus,
Toothpick Cactus

during the day. In late winter, the cactus develops a tangy, lemon-flavored fruit with black seeds. The white pulp and seeds are not very sweet, but the entire fruit can be eaten if it is cooked. The Argentine toothpick is hardy to eighteen degrees Fahrenheit. It likes full sun, reflected heat and sandy, well-draining soil. The cactus is drought resistant but prefers occasional irrigation during the hot, dry summer. The Argentine toothpick cactus is considered to be a mono-typic taxon. This means it is the only species in the genus Stetsonia. This is a great accent plant to use in cactus and succulent gardens and as a focal point. Use this specimen cactus in raised planters, among boulders, and in attractive containers. It also looks good up against a tall white or light-colored wall with its interesting growth habit and bold silhouette. It is native to the low, Southwesterndeserts of Argentina and Bolivia.

10

Installing Landscape Plants

in Rocky Point, Mexico

Sunset on the Sea of Cortez, Mexico

Rocky Point, Mexico is located on the northeastern shore of the Sea of Cortez. The name Rocky Point is an American name for the town of Puerto Penasco in the state of Sonora, Mexico. The drive time by automobile from Tucson, Phoenix or Yuma is approximately four hours. On the drive, you pass though a beautiful section of the Sonoran Desert. Halfway through the trip, you enter Organ Pipe National Monument, passing hundreds of organ pipe cactus, statuesque saguaro cactus and other species of native desert plants. As the sun begins to set, majestic colors of purples, oranges and yellows cast their colors over the desert landscape. You continue your excursion through the Arizona border town of Lukeville, and then on through Sonoyta, at the Mexican border. The town of Rocky Point is just over an hour drive from the border.

About thirty miles past the Mexican border, the road passes through Pinacate National Park, an ecological reserve comprised of mountains, volcanoes, dunes, washes and vegetation that survives on barely any water. There is a great abundance of plant species at Pinacate preserve as well as along the road leading into Rocky Point. Various types of wildflowers, ocotillo, creosote, saguaro, palo verde, mesquite, ironwood, acacia, brittlebush, burr sage and other plant species line the roadsides. Rainfall is scarce and unpredictable. Dust storms blow sand across the roadway and billowing dust clouds line up along the horizon, but little rain falls on the ground. When occasional rainstorms are present, the water rushes across the roads and landscape like a strong, gushing river.

As you drive toward the town of Rocky Point, majestic volcanic mountains jut and grow out of the ground. As the road flattens, you pass abundant species of organ pipe, cholla, saltbush, burr sage and other vegetation. Dust devils may blow across the highway scattering debris. After forty-five minutes or so on this highway, the road home turns east onto Caborca Highway bypassing the central part of town. This takes you toward the beach communities of Playa Encanto, Playa Dorado, and North Beach, toward the Mayan Palace Resort. As the drive continues eastward, you notice that both sides of the roadway are surrounded by abundant cholla cactus.

After crossing the railroad tracks and heading back toward town, about one-quarter of a mile, you turn left toward Playa Encanto Beach. That is the place I call home. The six-mile road that

Playa Encanto beach, Mexico

leads me to my "enchanted beach house" has been wet down and graded recently. As I look at my speedometer, my car is hovering at sixty miles per hour. My heart begins to race because I know the drive is almost over.

Playa Encanto beach is an amazing location where my husband and I decided to build our second home. It is also where the Sea of Cortez meets the Sonoran Desert. The most beautiful sunrises and sunsets appear on the horizon daily. While sitting on our patio facing the sea, we sometimes notice a pod of dolphin swimming along the surf's edge. The tide changes are extreme; they come in and go out every six hours each day, especially during the full and new moon. The tide pools created at low tide expose many different plants and sea life. Unfortunately, sometimes a whale, dolphin, sea lion or other aquatic creature may end up beached or dead on shore. Other times, families of sea turtles that have been hibernating all season suddenly hatch and find their way toward the sea. Life on the seashore is spectacular and full of all kinds of life.

Rocky Point averages about two inches of rain a year. The weather is perfect during the spring and fall, ranging in the mid-seventies to eighty degrees Fahrenheit. The evenings cool off to sixty degrees, or lower. The summer conditions are hot and humid. July, August and September temperatures can reach the mid-nineties with high humidity. Summer days can be uncomfortably hot as the humid air and heat combine for a sweltering climate. The rainy season produces heavy, but short rains. In the wintertime, the rains tend to be longer, lighter and widespread across the desert. Daytime temperatures in the winter are similar to Phoenix weather. The temperature is cold at night, usually without major freezes. However, a hard freeze hit Rocky Point in the winter of 2007 and again in 2011.

The weather and soil in Rocky Point make it a challenging place for landscapes. We have tried various plant species in our courtyard garden and along the beach side of our home. After almost 15 years of planting and replanting, I have succeeded in growing beautiful, healthy plants.

The first step is to have a good soil mix brought into your garden. The local soil is too sandy and needs to be heavily amended. There are several reputable plant nurseries in town that will deliver and install excellent soil. Having a good

drip irrigation system installed with a battery or automatic timer is a must. Sometimes, the beach communities may experience power outages from time to time. It makes sense to use battery timers that will not be affected by these outages. Our water system has a gate valve that separates the water supply from our house with our irrigation water. When we leave our Rocky Point house, we turn the gate valve off to the house. That protects the house from any potential water leaks when we are gone. The water source for the drip system remains on. We set our irrigation timer to water the plants according to the season. In the winter months, we water once per week. During the summer, we water plants two or three times per week.

We have an underground cistern in our garage that holds approximately one thousand gallons of water. Our water is delivered from town by a water truck, and the water tank is filled as needed. When needed, we apply small amounts of chorine tablets to treat the water. We have installed a separate filter system that treats the water going into the house. Since there is a great deal of salt in the local water as well as humidity in the air from the sea water, plants need to adapt to the salty environment.

Some of our plants suffer damage from time to time from the sea salt and wind. However, we discovered a cosmetic solution: we prune off the damaged tips of the plants. Some plants suffer more salt damage than others, and when planted

on the ocean-facing side of the house, we use species that are less sensitive to salt damage. Through our trials over the past fifteen years, I have provided a list of plants that will thrive in Rocky Point landscapes.

All perform best when planted in well-draining, amended soil. Additionally, these plants require supplemental irrigation in order to thrive. Their water needs increase dramatically during July, August and September when the temperatures soar to ninety degrees Fahrenheit and above.

Most of the plant species listed here are available in local Rocky Point plant nurseries. It takes hard

work and perseverance to maintain a seaside garden, but the results are well worth it. Have fun experimenting with your plants. Add garden art pieces and colorful pottery to make your Mexico outdoor living spaces creative, magical and whimsical.

-**Agave americana and Agave americana var. marginata**, *Century Plant and Variegated Century Plant* grow very large plant at maturity. These graceful accent plants produce many pups that are easily transplantable. Century plant has bluish grey leaves that grow in a downward curve. The variegated variety has broad leaves that arch and curl with a green, central band, and yellow to white stripes along its leaf margins. These two agaves grow with little water and full sun and are excellent choices for open spaces. The ends of the leaves may suffer salt burn from time to time. Prune back blackened tips as needed.

-**Agave decipiens**, *False Sisal* is a bright green, medium-sized plant that forms a tight symmetrical rosette of growth. It is a great plant for shade or filtered shade situations. This attractive plant produces many pups for reproduction, thrives in hot, humid locations and needs a well-draining soil. Use for its exotic, tropical effect.

-**Agave desmettiana**, *Smooth Agave* is one of the most popular agaves species in Rocky Point. It is readily available in most plant nurseries in town. The smooth, upright, medium-sized plant has long, bluish green leaves. It grows quickly and produces many pups for reproduction. There is also a variegated form.

-**Agave colorata**, *Blue Ice Agave* is a striking accent plant growing four feet high and two to four feet wide. It has short, broad, powder blue-gray leaves that have an impression on both sides. At maturity, it produces a ten feet tall, yellow flower stalk in late spring. As with all agaves,

A garden on Los Conchos beach

the flowering stalk signals the end of the plant's life cycle. Fortunately, the mother plant usually sends out smaller agave pups allowing for reproduction of the plant.

-**Agave geminiflora**, *Twin-flowered Agave* tolerates a range of exposure from full sun to shade. Its long, thin leaves add to the appeal of this striking plant. The leaves form a dense, compact ball. It grows fast and makes a nice accent plant in a short time. The plant flowers once in its lifetime, then dies but produces pups for reproduction.

-**Agave parryi var. huachucensis**, *Parry's Agave* forms a dense rosette of blue-gray leaves with toothed margins. At maturity, it produces ten to fifteen feet tall blooms that attract hummingbirds. This is a nice specimen plant for smaller, confined spaces. It likes full sun and needs minimal irrigation once established. The plant is hardy to cold. It does well in containers and smaller spaces.

-**Agave victoriae-reginae**, *Queen Victoria Century Plant* is an exquisite plant that looks like an artichoke carved out of a green stone. It has a dense, small, compact growth habit with white markings on both sides of its leaves. This plant grows to about eighteen inches wide and works well in small spaces or containers. The plant is drought resistant and slow growing. It likes full sun and well draining soil.

-**Agave weberi**, *Weber Agave* is a graceful plant that produces medium to large rosettes of fleshy, gray-green leaves with finely-toothed margins. It grows to heights of five feet with a six to ten feet spread. This agave likes to be planted in full to filtered shade in well-draining soil. It makes a beautiful accent against a wall and need space to grow and mature. It is one of my favorite Agaves.

-**Aloe ferox**, *Cape Aloe,* is a tall, single-stem aloe with leaves arranged in a rosette and is indigenous to South Africa. Its elegant shape produces leaf tips that grow in a downward shape. The spines along the leaf edge produce a reddish color. In spring, it develops candelabra-like flower spikes in yellow to red. This palmlike succulent is a beautiful specimen for any garden and a personal favorite plant of mine.

-Aptenia cordifolia, *Hearts and Flowers* is a perennial groundcover that spreads as it grows. It stays low to the ground and produces dark green, heart-shaped foliage. The flowers are reddish pink to purple and open in the sun. It makes a great container plant and is both salt and drought tolerant. This trailing perennial can be grown in full sun to light shade.

-Araucaria heterophylla, *Norfolk Island Pine or Monkey Puzzle Tree* is an excellent choice for height in your coastal garden. The interesting evergreen grows straight with vertical trunks and symmetrical branches. It has a distinct appearance with its widely spaced branches and triangular growth habit. This plant grows well in sandy soil as long as it receives water. It is highly tolerant to salt, heat and wind.

Playa Encanto beach

-Asparagus densiflorus 'Sprengeri', *Asparagus Fern* is a slightly woody plant with upright or trailing branches. Its long arching stems are covered with dark green needlelike leaves. This plant makes an excellent groundcover in shade or full sun. It produces inconspicuous white blooms in the summer followed by red berries. Asparagus fern is tolerant to salty conditions, drought, and will benefit from supplemental irrigation. It should be heavily pruned in early spring and again in the fall to look its best.

Los Conchas beach garden

-Beaucarnea recurvata, *Ponytail Palm* is native to Southeastern Mexico. It is a palmlike succulent with a rosette of long, green leaves that arch and droop. This plant grows six to eight feet tall or larger, with dense, flat foliage. It likes full sun and tolerates drought conditions. Use this showy accent in containers or with other succulents and cactus. It needs some maintenance to look good. Prune off the dry, salted tips of the leaves as needed to keep this plant looking healthy.

-Bougainvillea hybrids, *Bougainvillea* 'Barbara Karst' is a beautiful, low care and drought resistant tropical plant. It can be grown as a vine or shrub and produces brilliant color in the garden throughout the year. It is sensitive to frost and

Sunset on the sea of Cortez,
Playa Encanto beach, Mexico

wind but recovers quickly in the spring. The flowers produce a magnificent array of papery bracts in numerous colors, but the hot pink variety grows best along the Sea of Cortez. Bougainvillea is a must for your beach landscape. It makes a statement against a light-colored wall in any courtyard and can also be planted in containers as a bush type plant.

-Carissa macrocarpa, *Natal Plum* is an evergreen shrub with a loose, mounding appearance. The stems are thorny with forked spines and support dark, shiny green leaves. It tolerates drought and salty conditions but prefers to be planted in sandy, well-draining soil. In the spring, it creates an abundance of fragrant, white, star-shaped flowers. This shrub also produces a red fruit that can be eaten when ripe. The variety *Bonsai* has a compacted growth habit. *Prostrata, Boxwood Beauty* and *Horizontalis* are low-growing varieties suitable for groundcovers.

-Carpobrotus chilensis, *Common Ice Plant* is a succulent evergreen plant that produces small, asterlike flowers in shades of red, pink, purple or magenta, depending on the variety. The blossoms are extremely showy from early summer into the fall. Common ice plant grows six inches to one foot, spreading three feet through an aggressive rooting system. It is an excellent choice for

beachfront landscapes since it tolerates salty conditions and is very drought tolerant.

-Cephalocereus senilis, *Old Man Cactus* is a tall, columnar cactus native to Eastern Mexico. The most striking feature of this plant is the long, white hairs it produces to protect it from the sun. It likes well-draining soil and lots of sun to encourage the growth of hairs. Use this accent plant against a wall for vertical effects and accent. It grows well along the beach side of your landscape.

My beautiful enchanted,
Mexico garden

-Cereus repandus, Cereus repandus f. monsrose, Peruvian Apple *Night Blooming Cereus, Queen of the Night* is a columnar cactus that branches from the base up to thirty feet tall. It produces many pups that can grow as high. This cactus is recognized by its large, white blooms that open at night. Water the cereus monthly during the hot summer months. The plant is easy to propagate from cuttings. It can be used in containers and for vertical height in your seaside garden.

-Chamaerops humilis, *Mediterranean Fan Palm* offers beauty and versatility in seaside landscapes. It has triangular, fan-shaped leaves ranging from blue-green to gray-green. The plant produces multiple trunks that surround the main trunk. When the leaves are trimmed up to expose the trunk, it makes a beautiful specimen. Sometimes, it suffers from light salt burn on the ends of its leaves. Prune off damaged foliage as needed, for cosmetic purposes.

-Cleistocactus strausii, *Silver Torch Cactus* produces a group of slender, silvery blue columns up to six feet tall. It prefers some irrigation during the hot, summer months and grows great along the seaside, of the property. Silver torch likes the humidity, tolerates the salty air, is a vigorous grower and is easy to care for. This cactus produces burgundy-red flowers in the spring.

-Cycas revoluta, *Sago Palm* is not a real palm but is actually a cycad. It has an erect, sturdy trunk with dark green leaves that grow to three or four feet long. New growth emerges as a rosette of leaves coming from the stem near the ground. It prefers light or filtered shade in coastal gardens.

-Dasylirion quadrangulatum, *Spineless Green Desert Spoon* is a great accent plant that is easy to grow. It is native to Northeastern Mexico and produces long, green, stiff leaves. The plant sends up tall stalks of beautiful white flowers in the summer. Use this plant in full sun or light shade. It is drought tolerant and needs well-draining soil. Sometimes, the ends of its erect leaves will suffer some salt burn. Prune back as needed.

-Delosperma cooperi, *Trailing or Cooper's Ice Plant* is a hardy evergreen groundcover. This succulent plant has a prostate habit with small, glistening, medium to dark green leaves. It is fast-growing, heat tolerant and requires minimal irrigation to keep it looking lush. Small, purple flowers cover the plant in the spring and again in the fall. It likes full sun, well-draining soil and can be easily propagated from cuttings. This is a great choice to add color and accent in seaside gardens.

-Echinocactus grusonii, *Golden Barrel Cactus* is native to Mexico and is a signature plant of

A crisp fall day at North Beach, Puerto Penasco, Mexico

the Southwest. It produces large, sharp, yellow spines that are slightly curved. This fast growing cactus is very tolerant of drought conditions and salty air. Use as a container plant or specimen. The golden barrel adds color, texture and interest to any garden.

-Echinopsis peruviana, *Peruvian Torch Cactus* is a fast-growing columnar cactus that is native to the western slopes of Peru. The plant is bluish green in color with six to eight broad, rounded ribs on its stems. It produces large, white flowers. This plant can also be propagated easily from cuttings. Use up against a wall for its vertical appearance.

-Echinopsis spachiana, *Golden Torch Cactus* grows to heights of three to four feet and produces golden yellow spines. Over time, the cactus produces multiple columns. The night-blooming cactus offers exquisite, white, springtime flowers. It is drought and salt tolerant but likes supplemental irrigation during the hot summer. This plant does great along the coastal side of your property.

-Euphorbia tirucalli, Euphorbia tirucalli 'Sticks of Fire'; *Pencil tree Euphorbia* is an exotic plant that forms a mass of green, pencil-sized stems. It develops single or multiple trunks and cylindrical branches. This succulent can be grown easily from cuttings during the warm weather. It produces a milky-white substance when the stem is cut and is sometimes referred to as "milk bush" for this reason. The substance is toxic and may cause a reaction in sensitive skin. Plant this attractive succulent in full sun and hot locations where it makes a dramatic presentation. It is one of the most reliable plants for hot, salty beach climates.

-**Ferocactus pilosus**, *Mexican Fire Barrel Cactus* is native to central Mexico. It produces long, fishhook, red spines. In the spring, it develops red to yellow flowers. This reliable cactus is salt and drought tolerant and serves as a wonderful accent plant. The pleated shape of this cactus allows it to expand when it rains and store moisture in its tissues.

-**Ficus benjamina**, *Weeping Fig, Benjamin's Fig* is another excellent choice for height in your seaside garden. This tree has graceful, drooping branches and glossy, green leaves. It grows best in shade or partial shade. Avoid planting it in full sun. This plant is sensitive to cold and requires deep, infrequent irrigations. When planting, protect in a courtyard away from the sea air. It can burn from the salt air if exposed to heavy winds. It may drop some leaves during high winds and in cold weather but perks up quickly with new growth. Use for vertical height and greenery in your garden.

-**Ficus elastica**, *Rubber Tree Plant* is native to India and Malaysia. It is one of the oldest species grown as a houseplant and is recognized for its broad, tear-shaped, dark-green, glossy leaves. In coastal landscapes, use as a specimen in the ground or in a large container in a protected area close to the house, or entryway. It prefers filtered sun to shade and well-draining soil. The leaves and stems of the plant will bleed a white, sticky sap when broken or damaged.

-**Hesperaloe funifera**, *Giant Hesperaloe* produces stiff, green leaves up to six feet long with white fibers along its edge. In late spring, it sends up flower spikes that range from twelve to fifteen feet tall. It is drought and salt tolerant; however,

Norfolk Island Pines standing tall in a landscape on Los Conchas beach, Puerto Penasco, Mexico

it may suffer some salt burn along the edges of its leaves. Use as an accent in larger, open spaces of your garden.

-**Hesperaloe parviflora**, *Red Yucca* develops tall, upright, coral-pink flower stalks that sit on top of slender, graceful stems. The blooms of this Texas native attract butterflies and hummingbirds. The plant tolerates drought, sea spray and salty soils. Mix in the yellow flowering variety of this species for interest.

-**Hibiscus rosa-sinensis**, *Hibiscus* is an evergreen, flowering shrub. The plant is frost tender but does well in sunny, protected areas of seaside gardens. The blooms are large and come in a wide variety of colors including, yellow, orange, red and pink. The plant likes full sun and well-draining soil. Provide periodic irrigation and occasional fertilizer applications. Use in containers, raised beds or as an accent plant for color.

-**Leucophyllum laevigatum**, *Chihuahuan Sage* is an evergreen shrub with fragrant, grayish green foliage. It grows four to five feet tall and four to six feet wide. This plant needs full sun, moderate water and well-draining soil. It produces small, fragrant, showy flowers in spring and again in the fall. Chihuahuan sage is native to Southwestern Texas and Mexico.

-**Nerium Oleander**, *Dwarf Oleander var. Petite Pink* is a compact evergreen shrub that grows to four feet. It bears clusters of light pink blooms from April through the fall. It is an excellent choice for coastal gardens because of its tolerance to heat, salt and drought. This plant does not like direct exposure to salt spray; however, it is a versatile choice for sunny and hot locations.

-**Pedilanthus macrocarpus**, *Lady Slippers* produces succulent light-green stems that grow upright. The plant reaches four feet with a three feet spread. It is drought tolerant and requires minimal water. The lady slipper is a favorite and can be planted in containers or along the foundation of the house. New growth is tender to frost. This exotic plant grows fast with additional irrigation and is a great accent for coastal gardens.

-**Pelargonium species**, *Geranium* is a reliable choice to brighten up your seaside garden with immediate color from winter through spring, or until temperatures reach into the nineties. The compact plant is easy to grow. It has distinctive decorative markings on the foliage and produces prolific blooms in white and all shades of red and pink, depending upon the variety. There are many hybrids that also produce bicolored flowers. This colorful plant grows best in protected areas of the landscape away from the salty sea air but is tolerant of sea breezes. Plant in well-draining soil, with added soil amendments, and fertilize regularly to promote blooms. This plant is somewhat drought resistant, water once or twice per week for best results.

-**Schefflera arboricola,** *Dwarf Shefflera, Dwarf Umbrella Plant* is great for containers or in a bed protected from full sun or sea spray. The plant

A Norfolk Island pine on Los Conchas beach, Mexico

offers glossy, green leaves on brackets, in an umbrella shape and has a compact growth habit. It works well in larger containers. The variegated varieties have green and yellow foliage or green and creamy-white foliage. Provide supplemental water but allow the plant to completely dry out between irrigations. Install the umbrella plant in partial sun or full shade to avoid sunburn. Try the varieties *Trinette* and *Gold Capella* for their variegated forms.

-**Stenocereus thurberi**, *Organ Pipe Cactus* is native to the Southwest desert and is found in prolific numbers in the Organ Pipe National Monument near Lukeville, Arizona. This cactus likes heat, dull sun and needs minimal water to survive. The species has several narrow stems that grow upright from a single trunk. It blooms in late May through July producing lavender-white flowers. The blooms close up when temperatures begin to heat up during the daytime. Bats pollinate the flowers and feed on the nectar. Use as an accent plant or in a large container. Avoid overwatering.

-**Yucca aloifolia**, *Spanish bayonet* produces sharp, dark-green, bayonet leaves that stand erect from the center of the plant. It is native to coastal regions, grows quickly and tolerates salty sea air and soils. At maturity, this plant reaches five to fifteen feet and makes a nice accent in beds or as a background, behind smaller vegetation. In the spring, it develops large, creamy-white flowers.

-**Yucca baccata**, *Banana Yucca* has a stout growth habit and thick, fleshy leaves with sharp edges. This plant makes a nice accent against a tall, light-colored wall. In the spring, it produces beautiful, white flowers. Following the bloom cycle, the plant develops fleshy fruits resembling a banana. Use in containers or as an accent in coastal gardens.

-**Yucca elata**, *Soap tree Yucca* produces a single trunk with attractive, armlike branches and long, slender leaves with white threads along the margins. The older leaves dry up and bend downward to produce a thick thatch along the trunk of the plant. Striking, white flowers emerge in the spring. This is a great accent plant along a large wall in a courtyard near the beach.

-**Washingtonia filifera**, *California Fan Palm* is a fast-growing species that reaches fifteen feet at maturity. It has fan-shaped leaves that spread out to form an open crown. This palm is popular along the coast because of its drought resistance and salt tolerance. Use in groupings or in a large, open area that can accommodate the large head of palm fronds.

-**Washingtonia robusta**, *Mexican Fan Palm* is majestic palm with a solitary trunk topped with a crown of large, fan-shaped evergreen fronds. It is a spectacular palm for large landscapes, tolerating heat and salt. It is native to the riparian washes of Northern Mexico, Baja and Southern California.

Playa Encanto Beach,
Puerto Penasco, Mexico

Bibliography

AridZoneTrees.com. "Plant Species Information." http://www.aridzonetrees.com (accessed April–July 2008).

Bower, Janice E., Tony L. Burgess, and Raymond M. Turner. *Sonoran Desert Plants, An Ecological Atlas*. Tucson, Arizona: University of Arizona Press, 2005.

Brookbank, George. *Desert Gardening the Complete Guide.* Tucson, Arizona: Fisher Books, 1998.

CactusGuide.com. "Plant Species Information." http://www.cactusguide.com/cactus/genus (accessed November 2011).

Cactuspedia.info. "Plant Species Information." http://www.cactuspedia.info (accessed 2009–2011).

Dave'sGarden.com. "Plant Species Information." http://davesgarden.com/guides (accessed March 2008–January 2009).

Duffield, Mary Rose, and Warren Jones. *Plants for Dry Climates: How to Select, Grow and Enjoy*. Cambridge, Massachusetts: Perseus Publishing, 2001.

Faucon, Philippe. "Plant Species Information." Desert-Tropicals.com, 1998–1999. http://www.desert-tropicals.com/Plants (accessed 2008–2011).

Floridata.com. "Plant Species Information." Tallahassee, Florida. http://www.floridata.com (accessed 2008–2011).

Gentry, Howard Scott. *Agaves of Continental North America*. Tucson, Arizona: University of Arizona Press, 1998.

Irish, Mary. *Trees and Shrubs for the Southwest*. Portland, Oregon: Timber Press, 2008.

Irish, Mary. *Arizona Gardener's Guide*. Nashville, Tennessee: Cool Springs Press, 2003.

Irish, Mary, and Gary Irish. *Agaves, Yuccas and Related Plants, A Gardener's Guide*. Portland, Oregon: Timber Press, 2000.

Jones, Warren, and Charles Sacamano. *Landscape Plants for Dry Regions*. Tucson, Arizona: Fisher Books, 2000.

Mielke, Judy. *Native Plants for Southwestern Landscapes*. Austin, Texas: University of Texas Press, 1993.

Mountain States Wholesale Nursery. "Plant Species Information." Glendale, Arizona. http://www.mswn.com/index2.htm (accessed 2011).

Plantzafrica.com. "Plant Species." S A National Biodiversity Institute. http://www.plantzafrica.com/frames/plantsfram.htm (accessed 2011).

San Marcos Growers Nursery. "Plant Species Information." Santa Barbara, California. http://www.smgrowers.com (accessed 2011).

Shuler, Carol. *Low Water Use Plants for California and the Southwest*. Cambridge, Mass.: Perseus Publishing, 1993.

Starr, Greg. *Cool Plants for Hot Gardens*. Tucson, Arizona: Rio Nuevo Press, 2009.

Tellman, Barbara. *Invasive Exotic Species of the Sonoran Desert Region*. Tucson, Arizona: University of Arizona Press, 2002.

United States Department of Agriculture Database. "Plant Material Information." Natural Resources Conservation Service. http://www.plants.usda.gov (accessed 2011).

Plant Index

Q

R

S

X

Y

Z

About the Author

Meet the Author, Dawn Fried

Dawn Fried has been a lifelong plant enthusiast, landscape designer and a resident of Tucson, Arizona for more than thirty years. She graduated with high honors receiving a bachelor's degree in plant sciences from the University of Arizona and also worked toward her master's degree in landscape architecture at the University of Arizona.

Inspired by the diverse ecosystem of plant materials ranging from the saguaro cactus covered deserts in Southern Arizona to the rugged rock chasms carved by the Colorado River to some of the densest Ponderosa pine forests in Flagstaff, Dawn knew her calling was to design and create magnificent landscapes for others to enjoy.

With her husband David Morris, also a horticulturist, certified arborist and plant designer, the couple opened Horticulture Unlimited after graduating from college in 1979. The business is a thriving residential and commercial landscape design and maintenance company located in the heart of Tucson.

In addition to running the day to day operations of Horticulture Unlimited, Dawn, an identical twin, enjoys gardening, decorating and hiking several times a week on challenging, rugged trails throughout the mountains of Southern Arizona as well as annual backpacking treks to Havasupai or Bright Angel Trail in the Grand Canyon.

Another one of her favorite passions is chasing the tides along stretches of soft, sandy beaches on the Sea of Cortez in Puerto Penasco, Mexico, where she and her husband built and exquisitely landscaped a second home sixteen years ago.

Together, Dawn and her husband have raised three successful sons—Andrew, who manages their company; Bill, a bio chemist; and Jake, a mechanical engineer. The couple presently reside in their Tucson foothills home with their two dogs—Kira, a six-year-old Rhodesian Ridgeback mix, and Ollie, a three-year-old, black Labrador retriever.

CPSIA information can be obtained
at www.ICGtesting.com
Printed in the USA
BVHW012348170223
658792BV00020B/1463